TEMPLE CARE
WORKBOOK

A 10-WEEK HOLISTIC PROGRAM ADDRESSING ONE'S
SPIRITUAL, PSYCHOLOGICAL AND NUTRITIONAL NEEDS
FOR WEIGHT LOSS, WEIGHT MAINTENANCE AND
NUTRITIONAL HEALTH

FOR INDIVIDUALS OR GROUPS

DR. SONJA CHISOLM

AuthorHouse™
1663 Liberty Drive
Bloomington, IN 47403
www.authorhouse.com
Phone: 1-800-839-8640

First published by AuthorHouse   8/25/2010

ISBN: 978-1-4520-6349-2 (e)
ISBN: 978-1-4520-6348-5 (sc)

Printed in the United States of America

This book is printed on acid-free paper.

Table of Contents

Acknowledgments

I must give God *ALL* the praise, honor, and glory for this workbook. Through His Word (the Bible), prayer, tremendously supportive people and fasting, He has led me through the development and completion of this work. I thank God for providing me educational opportunities that have allowed me to acquire an A.S. Degree in Nutrition/Dietetics and a Ph.D. in Counseling Psychology. Also, God has led my path to various individuals throughout my life, who have helped me directly and/or indirectly with the formation of this book.

I deeply thank my husband, Troy, who is my spiritual partner, sent from God. Troy, our relationship has protected, provided and taught me so much, and I look forward to what God does with us next! You and our incredible son, Lance Armond, are truly my abundant blessings (Ephesians 3:20, 21)!

I thank John and Otha Barcus for the spiritual upbringing they have committed to giving me. Dad and Mom, I wouldn't have achieved what I have up to this point without you. I thank my father for providing stability in my life and spiritual teaching since I've been a small child. I also thank him for how he listened to the passions of my heart and years ago encouraged me to not being afraid to pursue a career in Psychology. I thank my mother for her never ceasing love and support. I also thank her for teaching me about the connection of the "mind, body, and spirit" beginning when I was just in junior high school and her help in writing this book! Both of my parents have significantly contributed to the development of this program that addresses the spiritual, psychological and nutritional needs of individuals.

I also thank my sister, Dorissa, who is so precious to me. I thank you Dorissa for how you have helped me see some things about the program that have improved it greatly. You continue to be a true friend and support and you are such a wonderful Aunt to Lance!

I thank all of the wonderful preachers, throughout the brotherhood, who contributed to the spiritual knowledge my father and mother provided me as a child. Literally, more than over a hundred ministers/preachers/evangelists have influenced my love for the Bible and for the study and understanding of it.

I also want to thank all of my friends who have read this book and given me invaluable feedback.

I give thanks to Dr. Donald Nicholas (my doctoral chairman) for exposing me (during the late 80's and early 90"s) to the scientific side of the mind, body, spirit connection. And thank you Dr. Tony Roach for your biblical teaching on the spirit, soul and body. I thank Bro. Jimmy Hurd for his support, solid biblical teaching and Jacqui, his wife, who is a wonderful friend. Also, I thank the Oakland Church of Christ, Kings Crossing Church of Christ and Carver Road Church of Christ members for empowering, loving and supporting me, my family and the development of this program. Also I owe tremendous thanks to Mr. Zachary Watson for his help with editing this workbook!

ALL GLORY AND HONOR BE TO GOD, THE FATHER, MY MASTER;
GOD, THE SON, MY SAVIOR;
AND GOD, THE HOLY SPIRIT, MY COMFORTER!

Preface

The word <u>diet</u> means "food normally eaten or selection of food for purposes of health" (Webster, 1995). Yet, I believe that what most people mean and feel when they say "Diet," is "Die it!" It's as if we are really struggling with an "it." Most of us, in this information society pretty much know <u>what</u> to eat (you know it's best to eat vegetables on a regular basis rather than pizza on a regular basis) but for some reason "it" gets in the way. We scream "Die it!" to something within us that has a never-ending appetite. "It" relentlessly hounds us until we give in to salty, fried or sugary sweet temptations. It's as if this "it" has a mind of its own! We've all experienced something similar to what Paul talked about in **Romans 7:15-25**, likewise, when we want to choose good, healthy food to eat, unhealthy, tempting foods are always present. Also, when we don't want to make unhealthy, destructive, acid reflux churning choices, we often end up making those very unhealthy choices!

Throughout this workbook we will address some spiritual tools and principles that will better equip us to deal with the "it" that is the true issue regarding our societal obsession and struggle with weight loss. The "it" that many of us want to die is simply what the Bible calls the "flesh," (carnal nature) which we all battle in various ways <u>every single day</u>. As God's children we know that the flesh and spirit are against one another and that we want to live after the spirit and not the flesh (Romans 8:1-15). Therefore, throughout this program, we will address this real and pervasive spiritual issue in accordance to God's Word/Bible to truly care for our temples/bodies.

I must at this point establish the fact that this workbook is not about "rules" but about gaining a spiritual understanding that can help you overcome the lure of having an unhealthy, destructive style of eating. Also, please know that I am in no way equating obesity with sin. What I do believe is that there are spiritual principles that directly and indirectly address our tendency to give way to our unhealthy, fleshly desires. **II Peter 1:3** says, **"…seeing that His divine power has granted to us everything pertaining to life and godliness through the true knowledge of him…"** Basically, Peter here is saying that God has given us (his creation) everything we need for our natural, everyday lives and for our spiritual lives! I believe that our God is amazingly engaged in our lives and has truly given us some spiritual insight into <u>everything</u>; even how to care for the temple He's given us. We only need to seek Him through His Word! This workbook is simply about the deep investigation of God's Word and what it says that can give us a better understanding of "temple care", particularly in the area of food and eating.

In developing this workbook I started off by conducting a topical word search on biblical scriptures that addressed such things as "eating", "food", "meat" etc… Next, I studied various bible commentaries to better understand the context of all the scriptures I had found. Lastly, I recognized that certain scriptures seemed to fit together to form a particular theme. The 6 themes or "spiritual principles" can be found in the readings of week 3 through week 8. Later, God's Spirit more clearly guided me to include the 6 "spiritual tools" introduced in week 1. God, our Father, has never asked His children to do anything without providing us access to His Power to get it done! Therefore, the spiritual tools are used to help provoke God's empowerment within us to live, day to day, the spiritual principles found in His Word. As I stated earlier, God has already given us *everything* unto "life and godliness". Throughout this program, you will be touched and challenged by spiritual, psychological and nutritional information that I pray will be life enhancing and changing for you.

> *You are the salt of the earth; but if the salt has become tasteless, how will it be made salty again? It is good for nothing anymore, except to be thrown out and trampled under foot by men. You are the light of the world. A city set on a hill cannot be hidden. Nor do men light a lamp, and put it under the peck-measure, but on the lamp stand; and it gives light to all who are in the house. Let your light shine before men in such a way that they may see your good works, and glorify your Father who is in heaven. Matthew 5:13-16*

Does this scripture mean that as Christians we must be a light to the world in one facet of our lives (spiritually) or in multiple facets of our lives (emotionally, relationally, professionally and physically)? Many of us believe that we are intended to "be a light" and glorify God, our Father, in every way we can. With this in mind, how one cares for their body/temple (which reveals a character which does or does not glorify God) can be one of the many ways in which we show God's light to the world.

As with any weight loss program it is recommended to discuss this program with your doctor before beginning. Also it is best to wait after pregnancy and nursing is complete before engaging in this program.

Introduction to Temple Care

"Know ye not that you are the temple of God and the Spirit of God dwelleth in you?"
1 Corinthians 3:16
&
"Or do you not know your body is the temple of the Holy Spirit who is in you, whom you have from God, and you are not your own? For you were bought with a price; therefore glorify God in your body and in your spirit, which are God's."
1 Corinthians 6:19, 20

The *Matthew Henry Commentary* interprets these passages (1 Corinthians 3:16 and 1 Corinthians 6:12-20) as meaning <u>every Christian's body can be considered the temple of God</u> (individually and collectively). Furthermore, Paul wants to make sure that we know that <u>the Holy Spirit dwells in our bodies</u>. Since we are God's temple, He desires that we devote ourselves to His holy use. In 1 Corinthians 6:12-20 our temples are not to be used for fornication (pre-marital sex) or for the enslavement to food. Paul, in some translations uses the word "meat" rather than food. If we allow our flesh/lusts to rule our lives rather then God's Spirit then our bodies are not being used for God.

It is so good to know that the presence of the Holy Spirit in us (Acts 2:38) implies "that the Christian is under the influence of God; that he rejoices in his presence, and that he has the views, the feelings, the joys which God produces in a redeemed soul, and with which he is pleased" (Barnes' Notes). It is truly amazing to know that God's Spirit is already in us and wants to divinely influence how we come to understand ourselves, others, our future, the world around us and, most importantly, the Godhead (God the Father, God the Son and God the Holy Spirit). With this being the case, wouldn't we want to produce the best temple environment we can for God's Spirit to dwell? And even more importantly, wouldn't we want the Holy Spirit to divinely influence our minds, bodies and spirits so much so that our temples would become healthier due to our increased freedom from the bondage of the flesh? My answer is yes! It is encouraging to think that God's Holy Spirit (residing in and influencing us) can create in us the kind of temple best fit for God's residence and holy use!

There are many other scriptures that support the importance of making sure that what we do with our temples is holy. For instance, let's look at Romans 12:1, which says, *"Brothers, I call upon you, by the mercies of God, to present your bodies to him, a living, consecrated sacrifice, well-pleasing to God, for that is the only kind of worship which is truly spiritual."* Simply put, God wants our literal bodies, our temples, to be sacrificed to Him. Now this text does not say to do so only on Sundays but what it implies here is daily sacrifice. In our everyday lives, while engaging in everyday bodily activities, we must live as if we are presenting those activities to God. Therefore, I am truly developing, daily, my spiritual character through activities (whether "mundane", "trivial", or "important") that I engage in with my body. Basically, Paul is saying, that when you make love to your spouse (I knew that that would get your attention!), or relate to your friends, it should be as an "act of worship to God". Also, when you are at work, work as if unto God. Or when teaching your children, do it as if unto God. Every bodily deed falls under this category, so this also includes how and what we eat on a daily basis. You see, we are being asked to think about engaging in this daily activity (multiple times a day) as an act being presented to God. And the crux of the matter for me in this text is that such everyday, God-focused activity is considered worshipful and spiritual!

The first book of Corinthians 10:31 says, ***"Whether then you eat or drink or whatever you do, do all to the glory of God."*** suggests that any action, even one that is as routine and "insignificant" as eating, is to reflect the spiritual being within you that then reflects God's glory. Again, everything we do ultimately has spiritual implications, whether holy or unholy!

Throughout the Temple Care program I pray three things for you. First, my prayer is that you come to deeply understand that how you care for your body *is a spiritual issue*. To care for your body, the permanent residence of God's Spirit, goes beyond health/bodily and psychological issues. The ultimate truth is that it's intended to be a spiritual place, for holy use. Many biblical scriptures are dedicated to the explanation for the purpose of the body/temple and its development. Therefore, its care is a spiritual matter.

Second, because how you care for your body is a spiritual issue, I pray that you sincerely ***seek God's Spirit to empower your spirit*** to overcome the destructive desires of your flesh. In reality, seeking God's aide is the only true way to overcome the flesh. So instead of battling your flesh, focus on strengthening your spiritual nature. I believe that this will equip you to care for your body, the dwelling place of God's Spirit, in a spiritual rather than fleshly/carnal manner.

Finally, I pray that you come to understand that the ***battle between the spirit and the flesh*** has been waging since the beginning of time and that how you care for your body is just one of the many ways that this battle is manifested. Your spirit" is immortal and is related to worship and divine communion with God (The New Unger's Bible Dictionary). God's Spirit which was mentioned earlier engages in divine communion with your spirit to influence you in accordance with God's Will. Your "flesh" is the earthly nature of man which is unable to commune with the Divine (God) and therefore is prone to sin (The New Unger's Bible Dictionary). To focus only on disciplining your flesh is incredibly frustrating, deceives you

about where your true power comes from and is often temporary. Yet, true development of your spirit will bring about long lasting, often completely liberating change in your spirit, mind and body. Also note that the spiritual understanding of the "mind" falls under the concept of soul. Soul means one's "understanding, will and active power" and it like the spirit is also immortal (The New Unger's Bible Dictionary). I mentioned during "Week One-Day 1…God Will Renew You Mind through His Word" that Christians are to allow God's Spirit to develop and increase our spirit and its nature (and therefore our souls) rather than allow the flesh to control our souls and therefore ruin our lives! As we move toward the next section "Program Goal" take a bit of time to read some supporting scriptures from Romans 8:1-11 entitled "Deliverance from Bondage" in the New American Standard Bible.

> Therefore there is now no condemnation for those who are in Christ Jesus. For the law of the Spirit of life in Christ Jesus has set you free from the law of sin and of death. For what the Law could not do, weak as it was through the flesh, God did: sending His own Son in the likeness of sinful flesh and as an offering for sin, He condemned sin in the flesh, so that the requirement of the Law might be fulfilled in us, who do not walk according to the flesh but according to the Spirit. For

those who are according to the flesh set their minds on the things of the flesh, but those who are according to the Spirit, the things of the Spirit. For the mind set on the flesh is death, but the mind set on the Spirit is life and peace, because the mind set on the flesh is hostile toward God; for it does not subject itself to the law of God, for it is not even able to do so, and those who are in the flesh cannot please God.

However, you are not in the flesh but in the Spirit, if indeed the Spirit of God dwells in you. But if anyone does not have the Spirit of Christ, he does not belong to Him. If Christ is in you, though the body is dead because of sin, yet the spirit is alive because of righteousness. But if the Spirit of Him who raised Jesus from the dead dwells in you, He who raised Christ Jesus from the dead will also give life to your mortal bodies through His Spirit who dwells in you.

Program Goal

The overall goal of this program is to grow spiritually by increased dependency on God regarding the care of His temple (your body). Many in the world, and many Christians, are just barely controlling their flesh through their own will-power, and it is sheer torture! Yet, it needn't be so difficult for the individual who chooses to regularly tap into God's reservoir of power! God can and will strengthen your spirit increasingly so that you are better able to control your flesh. You will achieve the "Program Goal" by living out the following two objectives.

Objective #1

First, you will use God's given **spiritual tools** to aide in provoking more of God's power and presence in your spirit to help you overcome your flesh. The tools you will be using are: God's Word/Bible, faith, brother/sisterhood, prayer, repentance and fasting.

Objective #2

Second, you will learn certain **spiritual principles** (from the Bible) about how to better care for His Temple/your body. You will see what Scripture says about: God's Image-you, temptation, gluttony, temperance, God's created food source, God's purpose for food, God's perspective on His food and God's Word on thanksgiving. Studying what God's Word says on these issues will help you change from the world's view about bodily care to a God inspired spiritual view. This spiritual view is what's ultimately important about our lives, and it affects not only our life here on earth but also our lives after the earth and our temples are gone.

At this point, let's spend a bit of time talking about the importance of using **spiritual tools** throughout the program. Once I thought that the tools in this program directly brought about spiritual change in us. However, at this point I believe that using these tools are merely an expression of our dependency on God which then *provokes Him to work* and directly change our spirits, our circumstances…

We all know about the amazing story of King David. We know that he loved God and God loved him greatly. During David's reign he sought the Lord about whether or not he should engage in battle (as he often did) with the Philistines. He also inquired whether or not he would be victorious against them. Basically David was seeking God's help and was expressing his dependency on Him.   God told David to go forth and fight because He would give him success over the Philistines. Yet, the Lord instructed David and his army to attack only after they heard the sounds of "horses hooves" (Adam Clarke's Commentary) moving through the tree tops! God's spiritual army was going before David directly affecting the Philistines in such a way that David's army couldn't help but win! Well, I believe that it is the same with our spiritual growth. We express that we need God's help with various spiritual challenges by using the many tools He has given us. Yet, through using these tools we don't directly manipulate and change our spirits, God does. I believe that God only knows what lies within the very depths of our being and how to change our spirits to help us become the people He wants us to be.   Therefore, I say all this to encourage you to not be deceived into believing that using the various tools throughout this program is "a lot of work". It is not a lot of work because God is doing all of the real work! Use the spiritual tools I mentioned earlier believing that *God will work* in your spirit so powerfully that your flesh becomes humbled and more obedient to God's Spirit and your growing spirit.

At this point I'd like to address a question a few individuals have asked me. The question (usually by "emotional eaters") is "To lose weight, do I have to work through every traumatic situation I've experienced since early childhood?" Through looking at the Word of God I believe that through God's very Spirit we do not have to trudge through every temporal/worldly circumstance, disappointment and/or trauma for healing. The scriptures show that God, upon request, often freed, healed, and released His children who were barren, betrayed, abused, depressed, anxious, etc. One common thread among these individuals was how their belief in God led to them to use spiritual tools to overcome their "circumstance"! Look at the lives of Jesus, Mary, Daniel, David, Hezekiah, Esther, Joseph, Moses, Abraham, Paul, Hannah… These individuals skillfully used spiritual tools such as prayer, fasting, repentance, faith, adherence to God's Word and/or having spiritual accountability and God powerfully impacted their difficult situations! Many emotional issues/struggles can be dealt with on a spiritual level which can directly and/or indirectly develop and strengthen one spiritually, emotionally and physically. One of the spiritual realities of our lives is skillfully worded in Ephesians 6:10-13 which says.

"Finally, my brethren, be strong in the Lord, and in the power of his might.
Put on the whole armour of God, that ye may be able to stand against the
wiles of the devil. <u>For we wrestle not against flesh and blood, but against
principalities, against powers, against the rulers of the darkness of this world,
against spiritual wickedness in high places.</u> Wherefore take unto you the
whole armour of God, that ye may be able to withstand in the evil day, and
having done all, to stand."

Addressing every trauma story is not always necessary when we realize that the real battle behind our pain has nothing to do with "flesh and blood". Our circumstances, stressors and "difficult" people in our lives are just a cover for Satan and his devices to keep us from living the way God wants us to! If we get overly lost in the story, the people, the circumstance at the worldly, physical, emotional level then we haven't learned how to fight the "real" battle, the spiritual battle with God's spiritual armour (i.e. spiritual tools). Learning to overcome the spiritual battle can only occur through using God's spiritual tools! Basically, I'm continually led to acknowledge that God's Word/the Bible reveals the truth about what life is all about and how to best grow in accordance to His Will. With that being said, in this program we will primarily use spiritual tools on the food and related emotional issues of our lives, all to the glory of God!

Now let's spend some time looking at the importance of studying and living the spiritual principles in this program. The knowledge we often receive from our society is that we need to lose weight to be prettier and/or happier, for our kids, and/or combat various health problems. These problems include chest pains, heart palpitations, fatigue, high blood pressure, high cholesterol, obesity, back and joint pain and the list goes on and on. Addressing many of these reasons are honorable, yet they do not reflect what is ultimately important about our lives. What is ultimately important is that God wants us to allow His Spirit to guide us and develop our spiritual nature. In doing this our lives on earth will not be ruled by our fleshly/bodily appetites that often lead to unhealthy and unhappy lives. One spiritual principle we will address in this program is gluttony. Now, it doesn't matter if you are a fat glutton or a skinny glutton, excessively giving way to the fleshly nature is what God is concerned about. The world tells us that if we don't have a weight/health problem then we can eat anyway we want. That however, is not what God's Word says. We will also address issues of being "mastered" by food/drink, what God considers "good for food" and many, many more spiritual concerns about which we need to have our minds "transformed" so that we can reflect God's glory practically through our temple care. God's Word enlightens us at our very spiritual level about how to grow more spiritual here on earth. This guidance, in the long run, will positively affect all areas of our lives including our health. So basically, spiritual tools are used to increase our dependency on God Who will increasingly strengthen and change our spiritual nature so that we can actually practice the spiritual principles we read about in God's Word.

If we truly allow spiritual/biblical principles to correct our understanding and views, which are daily deluded by worldly views/values, and regularly use God's given tools, then our spirit, mind and body can't help but become healthier. Some of you may ask, "Is true, long lasting weight loss and weight maintenance actually possible?" Of course it is! In fact, Christians should be really good at changing and growing spiritually! Our life here on earth is *all* about changing to become more and more like the people God wants us to be. Because we are terribly imperfect, Jesus died for our imperfection (sin), which therefore inspires us to live a life of change to become more and more like Him. God so much expects us to be creatures of change that He's provided us aid to do so, such as the Holy Spirit (God's Spirit), God's Word (the Bible), prayer, fasting… He even sacrificed His Son, Jesus Christ, so that even when we mess up, as we are changing, we can always confess our sin, repent, and get back on the right track. With this being the reality of our lives as God's children, believe that we can all change! So, know that throughout this program you will be encouraged to change regarding your spiritual understanding and character, not for a month or two, but for a lifetime!

The bottom line is that any one can become more disciplined and lose weight or become healthier. Many people lose weight all the time and some even keep it off for a lifetime. Yet, they miss the spiritual knowledge/lesson and spiritual character development (through dependency on God) that God desires us to experience through *every* single life occurrence! Let me rephrase this important statement. Every life experience (whether grand or trivial) can be used as an opportunity for continued spiritual growth/dependency on God.

Now, upon reading scriptures included in this workbook, many people immediately become convicted to care for their temple in a way that is reflected in God's Word. Yet, I'm finding two very different Christian responses in my support groups after being convicted by the power of the Word. Some Christians try to "*do* more changing for God" rather than first focus on "*be* more dependent on God". The Christian who starts off primarily doing (work oriented) will eventually run out of steam. They'll run out of steam either during the program or after completing the program because they are depending on their own will-power. Very few will maintain the bible based changes for a lifetime based on their own will-power. Question: When you think of the power God has placed within you, through His Spirit, why would you choose to struggle with your own will power rather than depend on God and His Power? Truly, I am finding that the Christians who focus first on being more dependent on God through the regular usage of spiritual tools (i.e. prayer, fasting, brother/sister support, repentance and studying His Word) tend to accomplish their goals more so than the Christians who try to care for their temples in a way reflected in the bible by their own will-power, motivation and excitement.

Your Temple Needs A Loving Foundation!

And we have known and believed the love that God has for us. God is love; and he that dwelleth in love dwelleth in God, and God in him.
1 John 4:16

If you do not start this program deeply knowing and believing in God's love for you, then God, who is Love, is not able to fully live in you (1 John 4:16). Therefore, I believe that whatever intentions or thoughts you have and actions you take in this program can be distorted by Satan. Now many of us *know* that God loves us but we don't truly *believe* it, and therefore our lives are never really changed and made great by it! I believe that God wants us to come to love ourselves based on how He loves us (and it's not self-generated nor does it come from others). For example, I was hanging out with some girlfriends the other day and a couple of them began to honestly share how they felt about their bodies. They made statements like "I need to lose more weight", or "I find myself comparing my body to certain people", or "I don't like how big my thighs are" or "I'm never fully at peace with my body". Neither of them were overweight (they had normal Body Mass Index scores), yet they were trying to reach some expected body image that they considered beautiful. The sad part is that they will never truly reach peace and satisfaction as long as they look to the world's standard of beauty. In fact, I believe that the foundation of our standard of beauty in this society is actually based on the premise that it is unattainable. You lose 10 pounds, and then decide you must lose 5 more, and then you lose 5 more pounds but your hips and buttocks **still** "look too big"- and you haven't even gotten to your facial features yet where your eyes are too big, your nose is crooked, and you have dark circles under your eyes. Do you get my point? At some very basic level, in our society, it's believed that physical beauty isn't really beauty if everyone could attain it!

As I stated earlier, our thoughts and actions toward health can easily become distorted when we do not deeply possess the knowledge of and belief in God's love for us. For instance, have you been preoccupied with food, fearing, hating and then loving it uncontrollably? Have you brow beaten yourself for eating "wrong"? Have you severely deprived yourself of food or engaged in unhealthy dieting to lose weight? Do you say negative things about your ability to change your way of eating? Do you say negative things about various parts of your body? Do you often compare your body to others and take pride in that you think you look better then some one else? Do you often compare your body to others and wish at some level you had what they have? Honestly, I could go on and on and on because I've heard others and myself at various times share some of these thoughts and statements. Have you heard yourself thinking any of the statements above? If so, then please recognize that *nothing* stated above reflects that you know of and truly believe in God's love for you-*nothing*.

In Mark 12:30, Jesus proclaims that first of all, we should love God with all of our heart, soul, mind and strength. And then secondly, He says in verse 31, ***"You shall love your neighbor as yourself"***. Therefore, many people agree that we should love God, others and ourselves. God's Word even tells us how to love Him. For instance, 1 John 5:3 says, ***"For this is the love of God, that we keep his commandments: and his commandments are not grievous.*** The Word also tells us how to love others. Jesus says in John 13:34, ***"A new commandment I give to you, that you love one another, even as I***

have loved you, that you also love one another." Likewise, when it comes to loving ourselves, God's Word suggests that we love ourselves based on the love God has for us (1 John 4:16).

We must come to realize that the world tells us that we can receive love for ourselves through others and/or through generating love for ourselves. Yet, whatever love can be experienced by self generation or others is fleeting and can *always* be taken away. For instance, say you are a people pleaser in hope that the people you please will love you. Consequently, you believe that you'll *feel* love *from others* and, therefore, love yourself more. Unfortunately, this experience is never enough because you can never please everyone or anyone all of the time. Next, let's say that you have been taught to *generate love for yourself* by recognizing all of your wonderful, beautiful, giving attributes. Let's say that attributes such as being a good student or a good, caring mother causes you to reap good things which make you feel love for yourself. Although those attributes are honorable and God is pleased whenever we use the grace/gift(s) He has given us, such abilities aren't always permanent, or consistent. Just think about the good student who now hates herself/himself or has even physically hurt himself/herself or others because they've failed a class or exam. Or what about the good, caring mother who considered herself a good mother until her child went to prison. Afterwards, she may live with self-hate and guilt because she now believes that if she had been a better mother then her child would not be in prison. Believe me, positive affirmations and self-generated love, although superficially effective, don't come close to the love God intended us to know and believe in ourselves. I believe that starting a health program without this love God intends for us sets us up to be vain, obsessed with worldly values and keeps us from using this experience as an opportunity for spiritual growth.

> ***"For God so loved the world that He gave His only begotten Son, that whosoever believeth in Him shall not perish but have everlasting life."***
> ***John 3:16***

I find that even today, with the teaching I've experienced regarding this scripture, I *still* struggle to grasp the depth of God's sacrifice. Then translating it into an understanding of what it means about the type and degree of love He has for me becomes even more difficult! And then, to top that off, embedding that information deep into my heart so that it impacts how I feel about myself and others everyday seems near impossible! It brings tears to my eyes to know that a full understanding of what God did for such an unworthy people is limited by our very humanity. *Yet*, through continued study and practice of God's Word, we can come to know and believe His Love for us more and more deeply! And this understanding will translate into us developing the kind of love for ourselves that God intends for us to have.

Reality is that we can learn to love ourselves through self-esteem or God-esteem. In building your self-esteem, you may primarily focus on challenging your negative thoughts you have and think more positively and/or change from irrational thinking to more rational thinking. Or you can primarily focus on changing your thoughts to the words of love God has for and about you and believe them…for you are His created child. I continue to strive to know and believe God's words such as; I am fearfully and wonderfully made and just plain marvelous (Psalms 139:13), I am crowned with honor and glory (Psalms 8:5), and that my name is written on the palm of His hand (Isaiah 49:16). And there are so many, many more spiritual truths about who you and I are and how loved we are by the most powerful, wise and always present Being in the universe! Let's let God's Words of truth give us the type of esteem that He desires us to have!

Read the following exercises and decide if they are something you'd like to engage in for the next few minutes. **Participation in every workbook exercise is not expected, so choose the one(s) that seem to be interesting to you or touch a cord in you.**

<u>Love Exercise #1</u>

Write about how the impact of God's sacrifice of His Son, Jesus, affects you.

What do you feel regarding God's love for you?

How can His love for you affect how you love yourself and the temple He has given you?

<u>Love Exercise #2</u>

Relax God Already Loves You!

Find a quiet place in your home and sit or lie down. If sitting, make sure that your back is supported, that your hands are resting in your lap or to your sides and that both feet are on the floor. Take 10 deep breaths, and with each breath imagine sinking more deeply into a peaceful, state of relaxation. Next, think about one part of your body you have been dissatisfied with. Continue to breathe deeply and slowly. Spend a few moments reflecting on the abusive beliefs, abusive statements, abusive acts and negative mental pictures you have tortured yourself with regarding this part of your body/temple. Now, imagine yourself letting go of the psychic pain you have held onto regarding that part of your body. Just relax and breathe, and let go of the pain. Lastly, if you feel comfortable, apologize to that part of your body/temple and repent to God (if you are ready to make a change) for committing such unloving thoughts, words and behaviors against His temple-you!

Next, when you are ready, think of another part of your body that you have been dissatisfied with and engage in the exercise explained above. Continue with different body parts until you feel comfortable to stop, and then write about your experience with the exercise.

Preparatory words before beginning the next section "Accessing Spiritual Tools"

For the first week of the program I believe that it is very important that you begin to understand and practice some of the spiritual tools that we will be using as we learn various spiritual principles (again from God's Word). If you can begin the program (which starts in the next section entitled "Accessing Spiritual Tools") at the beginning of the week, Sunday, then that would be great. I also recommend that you spend 5-10 minutes every morning with the reading for the day to get you started in the right direction. If you cannot complete the written exercises in the morning, then try to do it sometime throughout the day. Don't feel pressured to do *every* exercise in this workbook, yet do the ones that you connect with the most. At the end of each day I recommend that you complete a F.I.R.E form (Food Intake Recognition Evaluation form) and also answer "yes" or "no" regarding if you used the spiritual tools (ST) and spiritual principles (SP). At this time, please see Appendix A which gives a completed example of the F.I.R.E. form.

Through *daily* seeing, reading, thinking about, praying about and writing in this workbook, over a period of time, you will change in spiritual ways that will deeply change your lifestyle. A similar method was used when God instructed the children of Israel to remember certain sentences from the law that He considered most important for them (Exodus 13:2-10, Exodus 13:11-16, Deuteronomy 6:4-9 and Deuteronomy 11:13-21). God had them write these important, life-guiding concepts on hardened calf skin and place them on their foreheads, or write them on their hands, and on the door posts of their homes and gates for the sole purpose to read daily, learn, remember and live. So, think of this workbook as a similar physical reminder of spiritual guidance regarding how to have a healthier, God-centered lifestyle. Feel free to write your responses all throughout the book. I've left empty spaces on pages along with lined areas to write all throughout the workbook so feel free to journal throughout the program! Also, almost everyday you will see the following:

EVERDAY QUESTIONS:

How did the Holy Spirit try to influence your temple care today?_____

How did your flesh want to respond?_____

How did you respond?_____

You see, being that God's Spirit resides in us, to guide, influence and comfort us, it is important to learn to hear Him! As you go throughout this program, God's Spirit will try to guide you in caring for your body in accordance to His Word. Learn to be more respectful by listening to and responding to His Voice. You know, if your spouse and/or loved one ignored you whenever you spoke to them you would probably feel very hurt and disrespected. Try to remember this example as God's Spirit speaks to you. Now you may hear God's voice tell you that that brownie is not "good for food" and you may eat it anyway. But then at least acknowledge that God was speaking to you. For instance, you may say, "Lord God, I heard you and I'm still struggling with being "mastered" by my flesh that wants foods that are harmful to me. I want to eat more of the food you created which is truly "good" and learn to not always give in to my bodily cravings. Strengthen my spirit God so that I'm ruled less and less by my flesh/body!" Again, learn to respond to God in honesty, in love, and in dependency so that His Voice may never become inaudible and leave you to your own destruction.

SECTION ONE

SPIRITUAL TOOLS (ST)
Week One

"...do you not know your body is the temple of the Holy Spirit who is in you..."
1 Corinthians 6:19

Week One-Day 1-Sunday
<u>God Will Renew Your Mind Through His Word</u>
"And be not conformed to this world, but be ye transformed by the <u>renewing of your mind</u>, that you may prove what is that good, and acceptable, and perfect, will of God."
Romans 12:2

Spiritual Tool #1= Changing your thoughts from worldliness to Godliness
You may be saying, "What part does the mind (which is just a portion of the soul) play in the spirit-flesh battle which we are addressing?" Well, how I understand it is that God has created the mind, it is absolutely amazing and very beneficial for this life on earth yet it is simultaneously limited. The mind can not fully function in the realm of the immortal spirit. Consequently, man, through the power of his mind, can not truly direct his own footsteps (Proverbs 14:12 and Proverbs 16:2 & 3), and we are encouraged to not depend on our own understanding/mind but God's (Proverbs 3:6). For instance, your mind may consistently tell you that you can not make this truly, long-lasting, healthy life-style change. Yet, again, the mind is limited! The mind can not understand the ways in which God's Spirit will work in your spirit, mind (and the rest of your soul) and body for your health and lifestyle change! Consequently, the mind either serves/supports the fleshly nature or the spiritual nature. Therefore, it is best for us to use our minds to serve our spiritual development more so then our fleshly desires. For an in-depth study of the spirit, soul and body I recommend reading "God's Love Bank" by Dr. Anthony Roach.

To no longer conform to this world, regarding the issue of health, means to let go of how we buy into the world's standard of beauty, how we compare our bodies to the bodies of other individuals, how we are preoccupied with food, how we accept what the world says is good or bad food, how we accept the food portion size we are often given at restaurants (and at home!), and how we engage in verbal and/or physical abuse toward ourselves to motivate ourselves to lose or gain weight. We must transform our minds and renew them with God's Word to be able to truly manifest what He has intended for our lives. We can gain knowledge about nutrition and make behavioral changes yet miss the opportunity to use our issue of health as a God-led, spirit growing event! Again, many say that every life experience is an opportunity for true growth, which is spiritual growth, yet may not know how to *apply* this concept to everyday experiences like their thoughts and behaviors regarding their bodies and food. Every life experience, whether routine or unusual, can provide an opportunity for spiritual growth. One spiritual tool we will use is God's Word renewing our minds. This renewal is not about changing worldly concepts to healthier worldly concepts but to God-given concepts from the Bible. That will be accomplished by studying the biblical concepts from this workbook. As I pointed out in the introduction, ***II Peter 1:3*** says, ***"...seeing that His divine power has granted to us everything pertaining to life and godliness through the true knowledge of him...",*** meaning that God has given us (his creation) everything we need for our natural, everyday life and for our spiritual life through His knowledge.

Another powerful scripture is from ***John 17:17, "Sanctify me with thy truth, thy word is truth".*** The Wycliffe Commentary interprets this scripture as meaning that we can be set apart for God and His Will if we learn what He wants us to do and how He wants us to do it. In this study we will be learning some of the spiritual truths from God's Word that will teach us what he wants us to do regarding our health. *We will be sanctified in the area of health and weight loss by God's teaching.* Then as you renew your mind (becoming more sanctified) you must daily, diligently practice **Proverb 4:23, "Guard your heart (mind) with all diligence, for from it flows the issues of life."** Now, I don't know if it's because I'm a psychologist or not but this is one of my favorite scriptures. Basically, Bible commentaries interpret this scripture as saying that it is very important for us to actively protect and guard our minds/thoughts because whatever is in our minds (positive or negative, good or evil) will become the issues/realities of our lives. The *Matthew Henry Commentary* states that "Our lives will be regular or irregular, comfortable or uncomfortable, according as our minds are kept or neglected." With this being the case, I ask if one of your issues in life is being overweight, obese, bulimic, anorexic, having high cholesterol or high blood pressure (due to style of eating)? If so, then what could be in your mind (or way of thinking) that manifests into one of your "issues"?

Let's begin by assessing what your thoughts (and some behaviors) are regarding care for your temple. The Temple Care Questionnaire is designed to assess the degree of similarity between your eating behavior and a more scripturally based concept of eating.

KEY: ST=Spiritual Tool and SP=Spiritual Principle

ST-I engaged in spiritual mind renewal
(Read scriptures and daily reading on Temple Care) _____

How did the Holy Spirit try to influence your temple care today?_____
How did your flesh want to respond?_____
How did you respond?_____

GOD DESIRES A PEOPLE WHOSE CHARACTER REVEALS A SPIRITUAL MINDSET RATHER THAN A WORLDLY MINDSET, REGARDING ALL LIFE ISSUES.

Temple Care Questionnaire

Instructions: Answer each question to your best ability, and circle the number that fits your experience most accurately.

<u>Circle your answer</u>

1. **I take care of my body as God's temple when it comes to eating nutritionally?**
   1-hardly ever   2-sometimes   3-most of the time   4-almost all of the time

2. **In my kitchen, I have more fresh or frozen God-created food than boxed, bagged or canned processed foods.**
   1-hardly ever   2-sometimes   3-most of the time   4-almost all of the time

3. **I experience the spiritual fruit of temperance (Holy Spirit aided self-control) when it comes to eating right on a daily basis.**
   1-hardly ever   2-sometimes   3-most of the time   4-almost all of the time

4. **Yesterday, at least _____ percent of the food I ate was uncooked or steamed vegetables.**
   1-zero   2-twenty-five   3-fifty   4-seventy-five

5. **Yesterday, at least_____percent of the food I ate was fresh fruit.**
   1-zero   2-twenty-five   3-fifty percent   4-seventy-five

6. **Yesterday, I ate only when I was hungry.**
   1-not at all   2-some of the day   3-most of the day   4-all day long

7. **I have people in my life who are good examples as to how to eat in a way that is in accordance to God's will.**
   1-no   4-yes

8. **There is someone I have (or can have) regular contact with that is a good example of the nutritional/health changes I want to make.**
   1-no   4-yes

9. **I can have direct or indirect contact with the person stated above.**
   1-almost never   2-once a week   3-twice a week   4-three or more times a week

10. **I have a role model whose life in general inspires me to change my nutritional habits. I can be exposed to him or her.**
    1-once a week 2-twice a week 3-three times a week 4-four or more times a week

11. **I tend to eat to temporarily soothe my emotions ("I just *feel* like eating...", or stress, boredom, depression...).**
    1- almost all of the time 2- most of the time   3-sometimes   4-hardly ever

12. I want better health, so I take action daily toward living a healthy lifestyle.
   1-hardly ever   2-sometimes   3-most of the time   4-almost all of the time

13. I tend to be preoccupied with my weight, my eating habits, or feelings of guilt regarding my eating habits.
   1- almost all of the time   2- most of the time   3-sometimes   4-hardly ever

14. I understand how God wants me to view myself and my temple/body.
   1-hardly ever   2-sometimes   3-most of the time   4-almost all of the time

15. I understand how God wants me to view the food He has created.
   1-hardly ever   2-sometimes   3-most of the time   4-almost all of the time

16. I live in an environment where me changing my style of eating is supported or at least attainable.
   1-not at all   2-sometimes   3-most of the time   4-almost all the time

17. I have a good body image based on God's Word.
   1-hardly ever   2-sometimes   3-most of the time   4-almost all of the time

18. In general, I eat only when I'm hungry.
   1-hardly ever   2-sometimes   3-most of the time   4-almost all of the time

19. I try to lose weight through diets that sometimes concern me regarding whether or not they are healthy for my temple/body.
   1- almost all of the time   2- most of the time   3-sometimes   4-hardly ever

20. Even if I'm no longer hungry, I eat until my plate is clean.
   1- almost all of the time 2- most of the time   3-sometimes   4-hardly ever

21. I have purposefully fasted.
   1-no   4-yes

22. I fast for spiritual reasons.
   1-never   2-sometimes   3-often   4-fair frequently

23. Within the past month, I've had a stomachache and have eaten anyway.
   1-almost all of the time 2- most of the time   3-sometimes   4-hardly ever

24. I have a health-related issue that is primarily caused by my style of eating.
   1-yes   4-no

25. I have a health-related issue that is not caused by my style of eating but is worsened by my style of eating.
   1-yes   4-no

26. I compare my body shape, size and/or weight to others.
    1- almost all of the time 2- most of the time   3-sometimes   4-hardly ever

27. Through God, I feel as if I can truly lose weight and can keep it off throughout my lifetime.
    1-hardly ever   2-sometimes 3-most of the time   4-almost all of the time

28. I tend to feel helpless regarding eating certain foods/drinks and/or to eating too much food.
    1- almost all of the time 2- most of the time   3-sometimes   4-hardly ever

29. In rating how often I am obsessed/preoccupied with weight and/or food, it is
    1- almost all of the time 2- most of the time   3-sometimes   4-hardly ever

30. I plan to work hard to be healthier.
    1-hardly ever   2-sometimes 3-most of the time   4-almost all of the time

31. As a religious person, I feel that eating is one of the few pleasures I can engage in.
    1- almost all of the time 2- most of the time   3-sometimes   4-hardly ever

32. I ask God to bless my food so that it will nourish and cleanse my body in the way in which He intended it too.
    1-hardly ever   2-sometimes 3-most of the time   4-almost all of the time

33. I see many of the vegetables that God created as being the perfect fuel for my body and tasting good.
    1-hardly ever   2-sometimes 3-most of the time   4-almost all of the time

34. I see many of the fruit that God created as being the perfect fuel for my body and tasting good.
    1-hardly ever   2-sometimes 3-most of the time   4-almost all of the time

35. I see the meat that God created as being the perfect fuel for my body and tasting good.
    1-hardly ever   2-sometimes 3-most of the time   4-almost all of the time

36. I eat to provide my body health and strength and not to satisfy emotional/spiritual deficits.
    1-hardly ever   2-sometimes 3-most of the time   4-almost all of the time

37. I understand the difference between my own hunger drive versus my appetite.
    1-hardly ever   2-sometimes 3-most of the time   4-almost all of the time

38. I understand what <u>God's created food</u> means.
    1-hardly ever   2-sometimes 3-most of the time   4-almost all of the time

39. I intentionally contact/ask others to help and support me with my weight loss/health goals.
1-hardly ever   2-sometimes 3-most of the time   4-almost all of the time

40. I see overly processed food in a desirable, positive way (i.e. soda, brownies, chips…)
1- almost all of the time 2- most of the time   3-sometimes   4-hardly ever

41. Within this past month, even when my body has needed food, I have <u>severely</u> deprived myself of eating in an attempt to lose weight or in fear of gaining weight.
1- most of the month   2- often   3- a little bit   4- not at all

42. Within this past month, I have vomited, used laxatives and/or diuretics in an attempt to lose weight or in fear of gaining weight.
1- most of the month   2- often   3- a little bit   4- not at all

43. I have a bowel movement at least every day.
1-hardly ever   2-sometimes 3-most of the time   4-almost all of the time

44. I glorify God through how I care for the temple/body He has given me, particularly regarding how I eat.
1-hardly ever   2-sometimes 3-most of the time   4-almost all of the time

45. According to the Bible, I truly understand what caring for my temple means.
1-not really   2-a little bit   3-for the most part   4-yes, I do

46. I have a biblical understanding of what temptation means.
1-not really   2-a little bit   3-for the most part   4-yes, I do

47. I have an understanding of how temptation can influence my temple care.
1-not really   2-a little bit   3-for the most part   4-yes, I do

48. I understand the good that can come from my temptations.
1-not really   2-a little bit   3-for the most part   4-yes, I do

Calculate your total score for all 48 questions.

Total Score = _____

This pre-program assessment score will be compared to your post-program assessment score to help determine your progress.

Body Mass Index

Body Mass Index or BMI is a tool for indicating weight status for adults over 20 years old.
This information is a modification of the BMI chart on the National Heart Lung and Blood Institute website.

Height in inches	Normal Weight Range BMI Range 18.5-24.9	Overweight Range BMI Range 25-29.9	Obese Obese 30+
58	91-118	119-142	143+
59	94-123	124-147	148+
60 (5 feet)	97-127	128-152	153+
61	100-131	132-157	158+
62	104-135	136-163	164+
63	107-140	141-168	169+
64	110-144	145-173	174+
65	114-149	150-179	180+
66	118-154	155-185	186+
67	121-158	159-190	191+
68	125-163	164-196	197+
69	128-168	169-202	203+
70	132-173	174-206	207+
71	136-178	179-214	215+
72 (6 feet)	140-183	184-220	221+
73	144-188	189-226	227+
74	148-193	194-232	233+
75	152-199	200-239	240+
76	156-204	205-245	246+

What BMI weight range are you in? _____

What are your thoughts *and* feelings about your results?

_____

Pre-Program Information/Commitment Form

Please answer the questions that apply to you.

The Temple Care program is going to primarily help you accomplish what goal?
Circle: Spiritually Focused Weight loss & Nutritional Health or Spiritually Focused Weight Maintenance & Nutritional Health)
 Why have you chosen this goal?
_____

Complete questions and if your goal is weight loss/nutritional health answer **
questions and for weight maintenance/nutritional health answer ++ questions.
**++ My weight today is_____

**++What is your typical weight range?_____

**What is the weight range you would be satisfied to achieve within the next 70 days?
_____

** Why have you chosen your particular weight range as a goal?
_____

**++Being that outside of our Heavenly Father, you know yourself the best, so what would you say is the #1 reason for any of the following; you weighing more or less then is healthy for you; you having health problems related to food and/or you taking poor care of your health in general?
_____
_____

 **++ What is the #2 reason?
_____
_____

**++ What would it take for you to accomplish your goal and why?
_____
_____

**++ List any medication/drug you are currently taking that may negatively affect your health.
_____
_____
_____
Do you exercise? Yes___ No___
If so, what do you do and how often?_____

Sign if you commit to completing the program to your best ability.

_____   _____
            Name   Date

"...do you not know your body is the temple of the Holy Spirit who is in you..."
1 Corinthians 6:19

Week One-Day 2-Monday
God Will Work Through Your Faith
"For as the body without the spirit is dead, so <u>faith</u> without <u>works</u> is dead also."
(James 2:26)

Spiritual Tool #2 = Works/Actions

There are well over 300 biblical references about the concept of faith, and I'd like to focus on an aspect of faith that helped me when I began to use my health as an opportunity for increased spiritual growth. *Vine's Expository Dictionary* states that faith is a "firm persuasion", "trust" and "...stands in contrast to belief in its purely natural exercise, which consists of an opinion held in good 'faith' without necessary reference to its proof." This is the faith that I've prayed about and have asked God to strengthen within me for years. Hebrews 11:1 expresses this concept very well; "Now faith is the substance of things hoped for, the evidence of things not seen." Yet, like looking only at one side of a coin, I've spent more time looking at one side of faith.

Looking at the other side of faith is what has helped me and many other people actually change our styles of eating. James expresses this point so well when he says, ***"For as the body without the spirit is dead, so faith without works is dead also" (James 2:26).*** I have come to realize that in many areas of my life I've had faith but a dead faith! This is the kind of faith that says, "I know that God wants me to excel academically to glorify Him", <u>yet</u> infrequently *reads* or completes homework assignments (this comment is to inspire a few of my students!). Or what about choosing to marry, knowing God desires that I marry a spiritual, "man of God" <u>yet</u> I *date* men who are not interested in God. Or, bringing it home to health/nutrition, "I know that God wants me to take good care of this body He's given me so that I can reflect His glory and work on earth" <u>yet,</u> *eat* unhealthy foods that cause bodily problems and, for some, premature death! So, we must remember that faith is about showing some healthy behaviors, actions, or works to prove that it is really alive! God wants a type of people who have the type of character that will exhibit their faith in Him and His power in their lives by *working their faith* and He will do the rest!

Below is an opportunity to "work" your faith by completing the next 2 exercises called "Favorite Foods Created by God" and "F.I.R.E." I named the last exercise F.I.R.E. because monitoring and documenting what one actually eats daily will often light a fire beneath people to do better.

FAVORITE FOODS CREATED BY GOD

I'd like for you to spend a few minutes making a list of all of the food that has been directly created by God that you enjoy eating. Before you complete your list see Appendix C and D with a list of "UNIVERSAL FOODS" and an example of my own favorite foods created by God.

Also, *if* you are blessed to be able to purchase all organic foods (particularly meat) this is wonderful because, unfortunately, we have sprayed and injected various foods with chemicals (i.e. hormones, steroids and antibodies) that may be harmful to our bodies over an extended period of time. Otherwise, do the best with what you have and can purchase.

_____'s Favorite Food Created by God List

(Individual's Name)

OR

The _____Family's Favorite Food Created by God List

(Family Name)

FRUITS

VEGETABLES (and Oils)

MEAT (and Oils)

FISH/SEAFOOD

<u>NUTS/SEEDS (and Oils)</u>

<u>BEANS</u>

<u>GRAINS (and Oils)</u>

<u>FAVORITE SEASONINGS (spices, herbs…)</u>

<u>FRESH (NONPASTEURIZED) JUICES</u>

Now, empty your cabinets and refrigerator of the unhealthy food, and go out and buy some of the healthy food from your list! This is the faith (action) part of your temple care. Don't rationalize with yourself about why you need to keep the unhealthy food in the house! The bottom line is that if you keep them in the house, then you will eventually eat it. Basically, it means that deep down you eventually plan on eating that particular item. So breathe deeply and let it go, knowing that God will strengthen you to do so.

I often buy God's created foods that have specials/price cuts on them.   So when blueberries are on sale, then I'll buy them (also this provides some variety in what I eat). I find that there are certain items I buy no matter what the cost, like items on my "Favorite Foods" list. Also, buying healthy foods in bulk and/or frozen foods is a smart way to go. For instance, at Sam's Club (one of my favorite stores) I can purchase 4-5 pounds of frozen vegetables for just 2-5 dollars! Whether you go fresh or frozen, make sure you protect against having a refrigerator full of fresh food that will quickly go bad! I buy most of my favorite foods frozen to protect from spoilage. For instance, I buy large bags of corn, green beans, peas, broccoli, salmon (from Sam's Club again) and greens (collard, mustard…) and some frozen beans (although dry ones will not spoil, frozen beans cook more quickly). Yet, I never buy frozen spinach because I like the taste of fresh spinach (for salads) better. Also, I prefer the taste of fresh, rather than frozen fruit, and make sure that I don't purchase a month's worth of fresh fruit that will go bad within a week. I know some people who enjoy visiting the market everyday after work to pick up the evening's dinner items. This habit does help eliminate the issue of food going bad, and if it works for you, then this is great.

Again, I do recommend that you clean your refrigerator and cabinets out and only have the God given food which you like the best in your home. For those of you with family members, complete the Favorite Food list all together. Be open to trying this lifestyle change for at least the duration of the program and revise your favorite list as you go along.

While developing this book, I asked my sister about her thoughts and feedback. One of the first things she said to me was "Sonja, you are going to have to explain what types of food we can eat, how much we can eat, what is processed versus natural…". Now at first, I thought, yes, of course I have to do that because I know that this is what the majority of weight loss programs do. For example, usually diet and/or nutritional plans give examples of sample meals. Yet, later I thought, "How odd". We have evolved to the point of human genome mapping and animal cloning yet don't know HOW to eat! Obviously, something is fundamentally wrong here! Yet, for the sake of honoring not only her request but many, many other individuals I've talked to, I've provided a format of a food plan which shows examples of my own food intake included in **Appendix D**.

F.I.R.E

FRESH FRUIT   * NATURAL OILS/FATS
****
                                                       *
                                                       *
****
FRESH VEGETABLES (CAN BE STEAMED)   *NATURAL SWEETNERS
                                                       *
                                                       *
****
GRAINS   * MEAT/SEAFOOD/BEANS/NUTS
                                                       *
                                                       *
****
COOKED FRUIT   *COOKED VEGETABLES
                                                       *
                                                       *
****
PROCESSED FOODS   *PROCESSED LIQUIDS
                                                       *
                                                       *
****

KEY: ST=Spiritual Tool and SP=Spiritual Principle

ST- I engaged in spiritual mind renewal (Read scriptures and daily reading on Temple Care) _____ **ST- I used the tool of faith** _____

How did the Holy Spirit try to influence your temple care today?_____

How did your flesh want to respond?_____

How did you respond?_____

GOD DESIRES A PEOPLE WHOSE CHARACTER REFLECTS A SPIRIT OF SUCH DEEP BELIEF IN HIS UNSEEN WORLD THAT THEY WORK TOWARD THAT WHICH IS PRESENTLY UNSEEN.

"...do you not know your body is the temple of the Holy Spirit who is in you..."
1 Corinthians 6:19

Week One-Day 3-Tuesday
<u>God Will Work Through Your Brother/Sisterhood</u>
"Therefore <u>comfort each other and edify</u> one another, just as you also are doing."
1Thessalonians 5:11

***Spiritual Tool #3* = Support**

I remember watching a morning news show back in 2006 or 2007 that said obesity is becoming the #1 lifestyle choice that prematurely kills individuals in the U.S., replacing cigarette smoking. The statement that actually impacted me, though, during the show was when it announced that our government was going to take an initiative to promote health (exercise and eating right) to combat this apparent social issue. Now, I believe that it is honorable that our government sees fit to help us out, yet it struck me as odd, and I asked, "Do we really need our government to keep us from killing ourselves due to how we eat?"

. Our environment is definitely one factor that greatly influences our eating style. Larger portions served in restaurants have influenced us to eat more because, of course, we have to get our money's worth. Also on our streets are gigantic billboards with hot savory, juicy, tender, buttery, spicy, creamy and milk chocolaty foods that are constantly stimulating our senses, even when we are not hungry. In fact, some of us are more affected than others. Research is showing that obese people are more prone to be influenced to eat due to cues (internal and external) than non-obese individuals (Butcher, Mineka and Hooley, 2004). Further more, there are television commercials around the clock that tempt all of us toward eating in an unhealthy way. So, everywhere in our society, our style of eating is overtly and covertly being influenced by environmental influences.

One spiritual technique to help combat negative societal influences is having a strong support system. The principle of helping, encouraging and supporting one another is spoken of all throughout the Bible. In fact, God did not intend for the Christian walk to be endured alone. So, as a community of believers, we are encouraged to help one another throughout life. Paul, in *I Thessalonians 5:11,* says that the Christians must *"encourage one another, and build up one another, just as you also are doing."* Also, in *Acts 20:35*, Luke reminds the Christians to "help the weak". I believe that for many of us to reject the constant, unhealthy style of eating and to maintain healthy styles of eating we need an encouraging support system. We will develop a support system as we work through the program.

Accountability/Support partner #1 is God and His Word. God's inspired word says in Isaiah 41:10 and 13, *"Fear thou not, for I am with thee: be not dismayed; for I am thy God: I will strengthen thee; yea, I will help thee; yea, I will uphold thee with the right hand of my righteousness...For I the Lord thy God will hold thy right hand, saying unto thee, Fear not; I will help thee."* This is the God I serve! One who lets His people know that He will be with us, supporting us and helping us through difficult times! I also love knowing that God even provides the Holy Spirit to help us when we don't even know how to articulate our pain to Him! As stated in *Romans, "And in the same way the Spirit also helps our weakness; for we do not know how to pray as we should, but the Spirit Himself intercedes for us with groanings too deep for words..."* My Lord, God is so good to us all! I pray that throughout this program, you come to know and truly understand that which David exclaimed in *Psalms 28:7, "The Lord is my strength and my shield; my heart trusted in Him, and I am helped: therefore my heart greatly rejoices; and with my song will I praise Him."* There are many, many scriptures that show that God, our Father, is always in support of us, yet we must strive to do what is right, good and pleasing in His sight.

My greatest change from having a "sweet tooth" began to sincerely happen when I began to listen and respond to God's Spirit within me. God led me to honestly respond to Him when I would uncontrollably lust for and usually overindulge in sweets. You see God revealed to me that His attempt to influence me (as I discussed in the introduction) would be in every area of my life. He desires only good for us and that includes good health. Therefore, when I'm tempted to ingest various toxins into my temple because it tastes good, His Spirit begins to trouble me a bit! I've chosen to no longer ignore His guidance for my best and try to follow His lead and at the very least respond to His guidance. Think about it, how would you feel if someone you loved kept ignoring you when you were trying to communicate to them? Now of course, they have a right to do or not do what they want yet their dismissal of me even saying anything is what would hurt me. That is why you will frequently answer a question about whether or not God speaks to you about your health and how are you responding. I've come to respond in obedience more than not over the years. Praise God! Yet, there are still times when I have to respond in repentance, thank Him for His concern and ask for more of His strength so that I can do more of what He wants me to do.

Accountability/support partner # 2 is you! Yes, you! You must learn to support yourself through knowing that you are walking with God through the study of His Word! One of my biggest life/spiritual challenge has been that my behavior was often determined by what others thought was right. Praise God, I've come to truly feel and know that although relating with others is important, those relationships should not replace my relationship with myself. You must honestly answer to God and yourself before you can honestly answer to someone else.

Accountability/support partner #3 is a friend, a family member, a co-worker or an accountability group. I prefer a group support system more so than you experiencing the program alone. An accountability group is often more reliable and consistent than an individual due to the structure of having regular meetings, sharing and holding one another accountable. Group also provides numerous examples of people who are making the same significant spiritual advances in the program as you.

Below, write a couple of beginning thoughts about whom you'd like to and/or could possibly ask to be a part of your support system. Or, if you want to begin a group, then think and write about the setting where you'd like the group to meet and what people you would like to have in the group. For instance, would you like to meet with people at church, work, or your apartment building/clubhouse? Also would you like to meet with your family members (i.e. sisters, brothers, aunts…) or church members? More than likely, you have a significant number of people around you who want to lose weight and/or become healthier from a spiritual perspective. Many people are interested in having support as they become healthier to better glorify God in their temples. Also think about how long you and the group would like to meet. For instance, maybe you want to meet once a week, one hour for the 8 weeks of the program and then once a month for the rest of the year. Also decide what date you'd like to begin (I recommend within the next week or two), and set a concrete date with the individuals you talk to.

Plans for developing a social support system

How did the Holy Spirit try to influence your temple care today?_____

How did your flesh want to respond?_____

How did you respond?_____

F.I.R.E

FRESH FRUIT   * NATURAL OILS/FATS

****

                                              *

                                              *

****

FRESH VEGETABLES (CAN BE STEAMED)   *NATURAL SWEETNERS

                                              *

                                              *

****

GRAINS   * MEAT/SEAFOOD/BEANS/NUTS

                                              *

                                              *

****

COOKED FRUIT   *COOKED VEGETABLES

                                              *

                                              *

****

PROCESSED FOODS   *PROCESSED LIQUIDS

                                              *

                                              *

****

ST-I used the tool of spiritual mind renewal (Read scriptures and daily reading on Temple Care) _____**ST**-I used the tool of faith_____ **ST-I used the tool of support** _____

GOD DESIRES A PEOPLE WHOSE CHARACTER REVEALS A SPIRIT THAT HELPS OTHERS AND HUMBLY ACCEPTS HELP FROM OTHERS WHEN IN NEED.

"...do you not know your body is the temple of the Holy Spirit who is in you..."
1 Corinthians 6:19

Week One-Day 4-Wednesday
God Will Work Through Your Prayer Life
"Now in the morning as he returned into the city, he hungered. And when he saw a fig tree in the way, he came to it, and found nothing thereon, but leaves only, and said unto it, Let no fruit grow on thee henceforward for ever. And presently the fig tree withered away. And when the disciples saw it, they marveled, saying, How soon is the fig tree withered away! Jesus answered and said unto them, Verily I say unto you, If ye have faith, and doubt not, ye shall not only do this which is done to the fig tree, but also if ye shall say unto this mountain, Be thou removed, and be thou cast into the sea; it shall be done. And all things, whatsoever ye shall ask in __prayer__, believing, ye shall receive."
Matt 21:18-22

Spiritual Tool #4=Prayer
"Prayer is the expression of man's dependence upon God for all things".   This quotation simply says so much about how prayer plays a part in our lives! If you are not praying to God about everything, then you probably are not depending on God regarding everything in your life. The intimacy we share with God must continually grow to be the most intimate relationship in our lives because he is the only Being that can be everything to us.

Another one of my favorite scriptures is in *Philippians 4:6, "Be careful for nothing, but in everything by prayer and supplication with thanksgiving let your requests be made known unto God."* The part of this scripture that touches me the most at this time in my life is "let your request be made known unto God". God wants me to express to Him all of my requests, although, He already knows them. So, throughout this program I challenge you to use the tool of prayer, in *detail*, *clarity* and *consistency*. Many of my clients, who have been prayer warriors, have expressed surprise at their realization that although they've struggled with weight issues they've never consistently and deeply expressed their need for God's help for these issues through prayer. Therefore, I recommend that throughout this program you pray before each meal about the theme of the week that you are on in the program and/or other struggles and temptations you are having regarding your temple care.

Other individuals I've worked with have not experienced the power of prayer because they have really tried to deny aspects of their weight/health problems or they've minimized them. When that happens, one is unable to access the power of this spiritual tool because he or she isn't honest enough about their issues to make their request clearly known to God. We must challenge ourselves to engage in the honest, intimate prayer life that God desires of us and address the easy and the difficult.

Why seek someone else's assessment about yourself and your health without first seeking it from God?   I'd like for you to start the program off in prayer requesting some assessment feedback from God.   I encourage you in prayer to ask God a question along the lines of the following: *"Lord, why am I overweight (or struggle with high blood pressure, or high cholesterol, or continue eating foods that I'm allergic to or that are harmful to me...)?"* You probably already know what doctors, magazines, television, nutritionists, psychologists, your spouse, family and friends tell you about your struggle. Also, I recognize that God may have been speaking to you through some of the people I just mentioned. We know through His Word that He loves us so much that He will use any means to send us the messages we so desperately need (i.e. even a donkey as shown in Numbers 22:20-35!). Yet, this exercise (and the overriding message of this book) is about you and God developing a more intimate relationship and you increasingly become the person He wants you to be. You may find, through directly asking God questions, that other people's answers are similar to His, or you may find that He has wanted to reveal a deeper, different, spiritual message to YOU personally. Show Him that you value and seek His personal guidance in every area of your life and will deepen your intimacy with Him by making your request more clearly known. You may also say something to the effect of, *"Lord I now ask, after receiving everyone else's opinion, what is YOUR truth about why my weight/health is the way that it is?"*

Then after you pray, be still, relax and continue your life believing that He will answer you. If you hear God's answer, or have heard it for a while now, write it down below. Be detailed and honest, holding nothing back from yourself, fully allowing God to reveal what He desires you to know.

_____

_____

_____

If you don't hear any thing yet then that's okay. Just have faith that the God you and I serve is not a God of riddles and that He's given us His Word, His Son, the Holy Spirit, His love, His mercy, and His grace, and He will give you His answer.

"For everyone who asks receives, and he who seeks finds, and to him who knocks it shall be opened." Matthew 7:7

Trust that as you continue throughout the program, God will answer your question. When He does, return to this section and write the answer in the space provided above. Also, I recommend that you pray daily (perhaps before each meal) about the different topics we will cover weekly and how they relate to you.

How did the Holy Spirit try to influence your temple care today?_____

How did your flesh want to respond?_____

How did you respond?_____

F.I.R.E

FRESH FRUIT   * NATURAL OILS/FATS

****
*
*
****

FRESH VEGETABLES (CAN BE STEAMED)   *NATURAL SWEETNERS
*
*
****

GRAINS   * MEAT/SEAFOOD/BEANS/NUTS
*
*
****

COOKED FRUIT   *COOKED VEGETABLES
*
*
****

PROCESSED FOODS   *PROCESSED LIQUIDS
*
*
****

ST-I used the tool of spiritual mind renewal (Read scriptures and daily reading on Temple Care) _____**ST**-I used the tool of faith_____**ST**-I used the tool of support_____
ST-I used the tool of prayer _____

GOD DESIRES A PEOPLE WHOSE CHARACTER REVEALS A SPIRIT OF ACTIVE, INTIMATE COMMUNICATION WITH HIM REGARDING EVERYTHING.

"...do you not know your body is the temple of the Holy Spirit who is in you..."
1 Corinthians 6:19

Week One-Day 5-Thursday
God Will Work Through Your Repentant Heart
"Now I rejoice, not that you were made sorry, but that your sorrow led to repentance.
For you were made sorry in a godly manner, that you might suffer loss from us in
nothing. For godly sorrow produces repentance leading to salvation, not to be regretted;
but the sorrow of the world produces death."
11 Corinthians 7:9-10
Spiritual Tool #5=Repentance

Repentance means, "Godly sorrow" or "a turning away from sin and back toward God."
Many of us have heard of this biblical concept, yet I'm not sure if many of us really use
this powerful tool for change to its fullest, most liberating sense!   Repentance is not about
consuming guilt and/or remorse which can lead one through a vicious cycle of feelings of
failure, powerlessness and hopelessness. This cycle is what most individuals feel when
they live a life of poor health due to their unhealthy lifestyles. They feel guilty about how
they treat their bodies (temple of God), and feel like they can never really change their
behavior. This often leads to feelings of powerlessness over their own behavior and
hopelessness about ever being able to change. Consequently, they continue their unhealthy
lifestyle and/or an unhealthy, preoccupation with their body (and sometimes the bodies of
others too!) Sound familiar to you?

God's Word reveals a much better understanding of repentance. The true power of this
biblical concept of repentance is not really about me feeling guilty about doing, thinking,
or saying something that doesn't glorify God but is one of the greatest God-given tools to
help me transform more and more into the spiritual being He desires me to be. Some
people feel that if they are repenting all of the time, then they are going to feel worse about
themselves because of the constant realization of sin which then leads many to guilt. Yet,
praise God, repentance should liberate us through knowing that as I honestly use this God-
given, spiritual tool, I am becoming increasingly transformed in heart and mind into the
spiritual being God wants me to be! Use this tool! Use it in all sincerity regularly
throughout this program and you'll find your heart and therefore your actions slowly
changing!!

Also, positive fruits and consequences of true repentance need to become manifested in
our lives. *Matthew 3:8 says, "Bring forth therefore fruits meet for repentance."* So,
when our hearts/minds are really changing, then our actions will become changed too,
consequently changing our entire lives! When there is repentance, something has got to
change; some type of fruit needs to be brought forth! My father used to say, "If you steal a
horse and repent for stealing the horse there is still something else you must do. You must
give the horse back otherwise your repentance bears no fruit." Please entertain this thought
with me. If you are overweight, and were gluttonous last month and gained 5 pounds
(which means you ate 17,500 more calories than usual), do you just repent? Well, I would
recommend bearing some fruit also! One manifestation of fruit would be you decreasing
the amount of food/calories you normally take in. When we sincerely repent, we must
gradually and consistently work on changing our behavior. So, the before mentioned
individual may find that he or she may start this program off repenting everyday and being

led by the Spirit to produce fruit on a daily basis. When we allow God's Spirit to guide us in producing fruit of repentance, we can move on in the Spirit-led direction, free from worldly guilt. Sometimes I think people "still feel guilty" (after repenting) because they never gave the horse back!

*Important
Begin reading Day 6 before Saturday to prepare your mind for how you will use the spiritual tool of fasting.

God wants a people who honestly admits their weaknesses to Him and honestly strives toward manifesting different fruit/results.

How did the Holy Spirit try to influence your temple care today?_____
How did your flesh want to respond?_____
How did you respond?_____

F.I.R.E

FRESH FRUIT   * NATURAL OILS/FATS
****
               *
               *
****
FRESH VEGETABLES (CAN BE STEAMED) *NATURAL SWEETNERS
               *
               *
****
GRAINS   * MEAT/SEAFOOD/BEANS/NUTS
               *
               *
****
COOKED FRUIT   *COOKED VEGETABLES
               *
               *
****
PROCESSED FOODS   *PROCESSED LIQUIDS
               *
               *
****

ST&SP-I used the tool of spiritual mind renewal (Read scriptures and daily reading on Temple Care) _____ **ST**-I used the tool of faith___ **ST**-I used the tool of support_____
ST-I used the tool of prayer_____ **ST-I used the tool of repentance** _____

"...do you not know your body is the temple of the Holy Spirit who is in you..."
1 Corinthians 6:19

Week One-Day 6-Friday
God Will Work Through Your Preparation For Your Spiritual Fast

Fasting can be and is used in many ways for various purposes. Today, the concept of fasting has primary taken on a different meaning than when Jesus and the early New Testament Christians spoke of and/or practiced it. Today, some individuals use fasting as a compensatory tool. For example, one may overeat one day or week and then impulsively and/or fearfully try to relieve their guilt through fasting afterwards. Such thinking and behavior can promote an unhealthy eating pattern. I believe that fasting out of fear and guilt can set one up for unhealthy eating patterns such as binging and/or purging behavior or, for others, overly restrictive food intake (not eating enough food).

Others use fasting as a health tool. Correct fasting can encourage the body to rid itself of toxins. These toxins can come from various sources, such as devitalized, refined food; environmental pollution; certain water sources; soap; lotions and many more chemicals.

We will primarily use fasts for spiritual development and secondarily for physical health. Let's see what God's word reveals to us about the use of fasting for spiritual development.

The New Unger's Bible Dictionary defines the concept of fasting as:

> The expression used in the law...'humble your souls', implying the sacrifice of the personal will, which gives fasting all it's value. The very essence of fasting is about grief and sorrow, following along the lines of when someone is extremely sad one often foregoes eating. This essence was long ago applied to the religious world because the soul, when oppressed and burdened by a sense of sin, is so filled with grief that the body refuses food. It is, therefore, appropriate to scenes of penitence, of godly sorrow, of suffering, and to those facts connected with religion which are suited to produce grief, as the prevalence of iniquity, or some dark impending calamity, or storm, or tempest, pestilence, plague, or famine. It is also useful to humble us, to bring us to reflection, to direct the thoughts away from the allurements of this world to the bliss of a better.

As similarly stated above, **throughout the Old and New Testament people fasted when they were distressed or experiencing a trying circumstance (i.e. barren Hannah), or an outward showing of inward sorrow (i.e. David grieving the death of Jonathan and Saul).**

Question: Have your thoughts regarding your weight, food or state of health brought about feelings of sorrow and distress? If so, explain.

Response
#1_____

Pray about this concern throughout your day of fasting.

The Matthew Henry Commentary states that Matthew 6:1-18 speaks of alms, prayer and fasting. It is suggested that fasting be addressed last because it is not really considered a duty or requirement for us today. Yet (this is big!), it can be used as a "means to dispose us for other duties". I thought this comment was profound, in that **we can use the flesh-**

denying, spiritual tool of fasting to motivate or make us willing to engage in the duties which God does ask of us (i.e. to be temperate and not gluttonous!).

Question: Do you need motivation to eat and care for your body/temple in a way that reflects Godly character and which therefore glorifies God? If so, explain.
Response # 2

Pray about this concern throughout your day of fasting.
USE THIS SPIRITUAL TOOL, AND THE OTHER TOOLS THROUGHOUT THE PROGRAM WHEN YOU FIND YOUR MOTIVATION WANING!

I recommend that whenever you feel hunger throughout your day of fasting to find a quiet place to get on your knees (if you can't physically get on your knees, then do it mentally). Lay your hunger, distress and/or lack of motivation on the altar of sacrifice to God, and take time out at that moment to pray.

Another reason for fasting has been to strengthen ones petition (request) to the Lord (i.e. when David pleaded for the life of his and Bathsheba's son). It has also been used to endow one with extraordinary power and focus (i.e. Jesus Christ fasted in preparation for his direct temptation from Satan). There were even public fasts (i.e. the Day of Atonement), and on a national scale, it was used to seek God's intervention during war (i.e. the sons of Israel defeating the sons of Benjamin).

Tomorrow's fast will be used to help you channel your energy and attention away from food for the day and focus on evoking God's presence with you throughout this program. Pray all throughout the day (reflecting on your concerns you wrote about under Responses 1 & 2 and others you may have). For those of you, who must cook for others, try to arrange it so that you will not have to cook or even clean the dishes at all tomorrow. This fast will help you jump-start a different type of relationship with food through God's power.

Do not be afraid of fasting. The early Christians typically fasted two times a week. Although I am not recommending this frequency, please know that spiritual fasts were a normal part of the life of Christ and the early Christian life and I hope you use this powerful spiritual tool throughout this program.

Lastly, remember *Matthew 6:16-18:*

"And whenever you fast, do not put on a gloomy face as the hypocrites do, for they neglect their appearance in order to be seen fasting by men. Truly I say to you, they have their reward in full. But you, when you fast, anoint your head and wash your face so that you may not be seen fasting by men, but by your Father who is in secret; and your Father who sees in secret will repay you."

This passage simply reminds us to remain focused on how fasting is a form of communication with God. We must not seek sympathy or praise from others for our fasting experience; otherwise it is done in vain. Of course, others such as loved ones will know that you are fasting because you will not be eating with or around them, yet make sure that you are not intentionally seeking recognition through your fast. Remember that your fast is about you and God, no one else. Wycliffe states, "...the pain and inconvenience which we may endure by the most rigid fasting are not meritorious in the sight of God. They are not that at which he aims by the appointment of fasting. He aims at justice, truth, benevolence, holiness (Isaiah 58:6-7); and he esteems the act of fasting to be of value only as it will be the means of leading us to reflect on our faults, and to amend our lives." (Wycliffe, 1962)

Practicalities for your Fast

First thing in the morning drink one full glass of prune juice with one glass of water behind it (you should notice results any where from ½ to 3 hours later (this is to help cleanse your colon). Some people warm their juice like tea or coffee before drinking yet for others; if you feel it best, use something milder. You can use this technique 1-2x a month. During the other times of fasting intake 3 tablespoons of olive oil and drink about 16 ounces of very warm water afterwards.

Throughout the day, I tend to drink lots of water and 1 homemade power packed fruit smoothie (10-12 strawberries, handful of blueberries, 1Tbsp raw, non-pasteurized honey, and soymilk or rice drink). Try to intake only liquids so that your digestive system can better rest during this time. I also recommend that you consciously keep peaceful and relaxed knowing that you CAN complete the fast through Christ! Sing your favorite spiritual songs (keep a song on your lips rather than food!) to God, your Father throughout the day especially if you become tempted to falter! Also, keep one of your most encouraging, favorite scriptures, writing on an index card, with you throughout the day to help keep you focused. Also, I do not recommend that you exercise on your day of fasting (I know that many of you are so disappointed about this!).

Now as you can tell, this fast does incorporate some liquids yet it is different then the other type of fast you will begin during week 2 of the program. **The fast for this first week focuses on starting this program off evoking God's aid to experience completing the Temple Care program successfully.** I see it as a **spiritually focused fast**. Also this fast is more limited in the liquid options because its focus is more about turning from the flesh toward the spirit whenever we feel hunger.

The other type of fast which you will experience, once a week (beginning at week 2), will more clearly focus on using healthy, beneficial juices for our temples and is recommended primarily if you want to lose weight. If you are interested in nutritional health and not weight loss then know that if you still want to use this fast for its resting/cleansing purpose then you will more than likely lose weight also. I see this fast as a **health focused fast**, yet please know that I encourage you to feel free to use this time (as any time) to deepen your relationship with God, so you can make this day very spiritually focused also. We will use God's created food on a weekly basis to cleanse our temples and allow it to rest from the hard work of digestion. **See Appendix F**, for your juicing options during weeks 2-10 of the program or until you reach your weight loss goal. At this point, I challenge you to choose a day of the week that you can commit to having your juice fast. **Circle the day which will work best for you** (i.e. Tuesdays seem to work best for me and just in case I'm unable to have or complete my fast that day then I still have an opportunity to make it up on another day of the week before the week ends).

My Day for a Juice Fast
(see Appendix F for other options)
Sunday   Monday   Tuesday   Wednesday   Thursday   Friday   Saturday

Almost everything and everyone in the world at some point needs to be intentionally cleansed and receive extra rest and so we will do this for our temple and its digestive system. Again, you'll experience having at least one fast a week (i.e. juice fast which is health focused) and if you find that you are really struggling to complete the program successfully then re-read Day 6 and evoke God's aid by making your regular health fast more focused on receiving God's help.

I must share with you that after a few weeks of juice fasting, God's Spirit has led me to focus more intently on my relationship with Him. On the day of my juice fast I pray and meditate a lot on issues that loved ones have brought to my attention. I also use that day to allow greater intimacy between me and God through me learning how to better "be still" and listen to what He has to say to me about various issues in my personal life. Pray intensely on this day for the "chronic stressors" in your life, like if you are struggling with being single, or being married, or with a child, or with your health… The weekly juice fast day has become such a pure, special time for me that I look forward to it! I also take a nice hot bath at the end of the day (drink a lot of water) and just thank God for the opportunity to focus a bit more intently on Him, His Greatness and the joy I feel being able to surrender to and depend on Him more.

For those who have a goal of weight loss, when you get to your goal (See "Maintenance Plan" page 173), I recommend that you still use your fast day as a cleansing day and eat only whole fruit, vegetables, light soups and salads. I reached my goal by taking myself through the book 3 consecutive times (24 weeks) and lost 20 pounds. Now I maintain my weight loss by exercising moderately 3x a week and by eating only fresh, whole, uncooked fruit and vegetables and salads one day a week (sometimes I'll throw in a baked potato or sweet potato). So, walk yourself (preferably with a brother/sister for support) through the program as much as you need. You'll find that you get better at letting God's Spirit truly change and strengthen your spirit the more you go through the workbook!

"Why Fast?"

Some have asked this question and I encourage fasting for 4 reasons; *yet* if you feel that God's Spirit is saying otherwise to you, then please heed it.

Reason #1 is to give a clear message to your flesh! Fasting tells your fleshly appetite "You and your impulses are no longer in control of me!" Yes, we need food for health, life and "strength" (addressed in Section 6 "God's Purpose for Food") yet we have allowed our flesh to use food outside of its God-given purpose…to our great misery and premature destruction.

Reason #2 is to give a clear message to your mind! Our minds often tell us "I *have* to have that donut, or soda pop or fried onion rings!" or "Even though I'm full, I *have* to keep eating this food because *it tastes so good!*" or "I'm stressed so I *need* some chocolate!" Fasting tells your mind, I am no longer giving way to your impulses, lusts/cravings and inappropriate ways of coping with emotional/psychological discomfort.

Reason #3 is to say to your spiritual self "I value your development and will humble my flesh and mind and focus on feeding you today, my spirit". My spirit always gets excited when I commit to its care through prayer, fasting, reading God's Word! My flesh almost always struggles with my spiritual development/commitments! And my mind gives my spirit a fight off and on, yet, once it is clear that my intent is focused on my spiritual growth then my mind usually "gets with the program".

Reason #4 is basically given on the entire first page of this day's reading (don't hesitate, you can read it again!). Fasting is used to evoke greater power from God's Spirit that resides in you! Or possibly better said, fasting helps increase in you greater submission to God's Powerful Spirit that resides in you! Fasting is one spiritual tool that tells God's Spirit, "I need help though Your power and not my own! I need You God and my mind, body and spirit surrenders to Your guidance, will and correction!" What wonderful tools God's has given us for our growth in Him!

Now, in preparing for our spiritual fast tomorrow, spend some time in prayer today to gear your body, mind and spirit for the challenge. I have had so many people (especially women) tell me how they were surprised that this experience was not as intimidating as they thought and some even felt empowered afterwards! Why empowered? Well, they for the first time in their lives evoked submission of their bodies/temples to their spirit and they knew that food would never torment them the same as before. Praise God! What are some of the things you'd like to pray to God about as you prepare for this fast? Also, remember to look at your two responses (Response #1and 2) above.

_____
_____
_____

How did the Holy Spirit try to influence your temple care today?_____
How did your flesh want to respond?_____
How did you respond?_____
GOD DESIRES A PEOPLE WHOSE CHARACTER REVEALS A SPIRIT THAT IS NOT CONTROLLED BY THE FLESH THROUGH CALLING FORTH GOD'S AID IN TIMES OF STRUGGLE.

F.I.R.E

FRESH FRUIT   * NATURAL OILS/FATS

****
                                               *

                                               *

****

FRESH VEGETABLES (CAN BE STEAMED)   *NATURAL SWEETNERS
                                               *
                                               *

****

GRAINS   * MEAT/SEAFOOD/BEANS/NUTS
                                               *
                                               *

****

COOKED FRUIT   *COOKED VEGETABLES
                                               *
                                               *

****

PROCESSED FOODS   *PROCESSED LIQUIDS
                                               *
                                               *

****

ST-I used the tool of spiritual mind renewal (Read scriptures and daily reading on Temple Care) _____ **ST**-I used the tool of faith____ **ST**-I used the tool of support_____
ST-I used the tool of prayer____ **ST**-I used the tool of repentance _____
ST-I prepared to use the tool of spiritual fasting – yes/no

"...do you not know your body is the temple of the Holy Spirit who is in you..."
1 Corinthians 6:19
Week One-Day 7-Saturday
__God Will Work Through Your Fasting__

Good Morning! I pray that you (along with God's help) are still preparing for this day of spiritual focus and fasting. ***Morning Exercise***-What is your prayer to God right now as your day is beginning?

___

Night Exercise

What was the day of fasting like for you?

___

Did you at anytime during the day feel God aiding you? Spend some time witnessing to the power of God during this day by writing about it.

___

What did you like the most about your fasting experience?

___

Did anything become a "stumbling block" for you and if so, what and why?

___

In preparation for breaking your fast tomorrow (also your weekly juice fasts) make sure that you have your favorite fruit, vegetables, salads, homemade soups (with homemade meat stock yet without meat, beans, nuts or grains) and lots of water around for the day. See in Appendix F, "Juice Fast Alternative" for homemade soup suggestions. Also, I recommend reading "Breaking the vicious cycle" by Elaine Gottschall and/or "Gut and Psychology Syndrome" by Dr. Natasha Campbell-McBride for the benefits of homemade meat stock and other natural ways to improve the health of your digestion system.

Make sure you eat lightly after your fast day. With both the spiritual and health focused fasts it is important to eat light, easy to digest foods. Please remember that in using this workbook you can always re-read and re-answer various sections that touch your heart and help you as you go through the process of improving your knowledge and character to be more reflective of God.

F.I.R.E

FRESH FRUIT   * NATURAL OILS/FATS
****
                                               *
                                               *
****
FRESH VEGETABLES (CAN BE STEAMED)   *NATURAL SWEETNERS
                                               *
                                               *
****
GRAINS   * MEAT/SEAFOOD/BEANS/NUTS
                                               *
                                               *
****
COOKED FRUIT   *COOKED VEGETABLES
                                               *
                                               *
****
PROCESSED FOODS   *PROCESSED LIQUIDS
                                               *
                                               *
****

ST -I used the tool of spiritual mind renewal (Read scriptures and daily reading on Temple Care) _____ **ST**-I used the tool of faith_____ **ST**-I used the tool of support_____
ST-I used the tool of prayer_____ **ST**-I used the tool of repentance _____
ST-I used the tool of spiritual fasting – yes/no
GOD DESIRES A PEOPLE WHOSE CHARACTER REVEALS A SPIRIT THAT IS NOT CONTROLLED BY THE FLESH THROUGH CALLING FORTH GOD'S AID IN TIMES OF STRUGGLE.

SECTION TWO

SPIRITUAL PRINCIPLES (SP)
Weeks 2-10

God's Created Image--You!
Week 2

"...do you not know your body is the temple of the Holy Spirit who is in you..."
1 Corinthians 6:19

Week 2-Day 8-Sunday
God's Created Image--You!
"And <u>God created man</u> <u>in His own image</u>, in the image of God He created him; <u>male</u> <u>and female</u> He created them."
Genesis 1:27

Congratulations! For many of you yesterday was the first day in which you've intentionally fasted, and for others, it was the first time you fasted for spiritual reasons, so congratulations to you! Also don't forget the day you committed for your juice fast this week. I hope that you begin today using the spiritual tool of prayer because we must sincerely desire and call forth God's guidance and strength as we go toe to toe with our flesh.

Now that we've addressed the spiritual tools (i.e. spiritual mind renewal/the Word, faith, prayer, brother/sister support, repentance and fasting) you are encouraged to use throughout the program, we will begin the section on spiritual principles today. I prefer that people start this part of the program on a Sunday. Not only because it is the first day of the week, but also because it is often a day of contradiction for many individuals. About 90% of the U.S. population believes that there is a sovereign God, and many of these people acknowledge that Sunday is the Lord's Day and attend some type of religious worship service. The contradiction is that many who recognize the Lord's Day, and even worship on this day, will after Sunday morning services participate in "communal gluttony" (we'll look at what the bible says about gluttony)! You know, you gather at a potluck/fellowship dinner, with friends and/or family in a spirit of love and unity and eat until you can barely stand up straight or bend over! I know that I have done it before! I challenge you to begin this day in a spirit of honestly seeking God's truth regarding how He wants you to eat. Why? Because He created you and, similar to any good parent, has provided life principles for *every* area of human life! Don't forget the scripture I discussed earlier! ***II Peter 1:3*** says, ***"...seeing that His divine power has granted to us everything pertaining to life and godliness through the true knowledge of him."*** Therefore, I recommend that you begin each day's assignment in prayer and be open to what God's Word, through His Holy Scripture, is revealing to you regarding your temple care.

As we move from spiritual tools to spiritual principles/truths it only seems right for us to start at the beginning of the Bible. Let's spend some time looking at the fact that God created us. Many individuals begin weight loss programs over-identifying with one facet of their beings--their bodies (I'm fat, therefore I'm unattractive) and/or under-identify with the beauty of their total being (mind, body and spirit) through being God's creation. I believe to lose weight in a healthy, spiritual way we must focus on the totality of our being. God's Word gives us true clarity about how we can better understand how to spiritually address the issue of weight loss and health. This week we will address the spiritual truth of God's Created Image--You!

There are so many beautiful interpretations regarding our scripture for the day yet I feel compelled to start with this particular fact about creation. The Matthew Henry Commentary states, "...that man was made last of all the creatures, that it might not be suspected that he had been, in any way, a helper to God in the creation of the world..."

(Matthew Henry Commentary). This workbook is written based on the truth that *God, being the creator of man and the world, is the best source to turn to when we need clarity about man and the world.* It can be truly humbling to know that we have had absolutely nothing to do with our existence and that to understand our existence, we must turn to God. Hence, in even addressing the issue of existing in a healthy way, we will continually look at what God's Word (the bible) has to say. Being that God has created all things with the highest form and most precious being YOU, what areas of your life have you forgotten about or never really thought about seeking His guidance?

_____

_____

What does it feel like to seek God's guidance in the area of caring for your temple?

_____

_____

God's Created Image?

The following reading is a direct quote from The New Unger's Bible Dictionary, 1988.

IMAGE OF GOD

"Man's nature has generally suffered loss from sin, but even in those respects in which the loss has been greatest, "in righteousness and holiness," the loss is not such as to render him incapable of divine renewal. With these preliminaries in view, the chief significance of the idea or the contents of the divine image, may be summarized as follows: (1) Spirituality. Man's likeness to God is not, as some of the early Latin Fathers fancied, a bodily likeness. God is Spirit, and the first great point of resemblance between man and his Creator is found in man's spiritual nature. His life is inbreathed from God-a distinguishing fact in his creation (see Gen 2:7; Job 32:8). With this stands connected the fact of man's immortal nature and destiny, for God is the Eternal Spirit. The general teaching of Scripture is that this feature survives. (2) Personality. God is a person; He is conscious of His own existence. He is the Supreme Intelligence. He is free. Man is also self-conscious; he is endowed with intelligence, rationality, and freedom. And at this point, despite sin, there still may be discerned in man wonderful vestiges of his inherent greatness and likeness to the divine. (3) Holiness. God is the Holy One. Man was created pure, with no inherent tendency to sin; with such qualities in his nature that he was after the image and likeness of the righteous and holy God. (4) love. God is love. The cardinal virtue, or moral excellence, proclaimed for man in the Scriptures is love. Man originally bore, and again may bear, the divine likeness in this respect. But here, as elsewhere, we see the necessity for restoration. (5) Dominion. God is sovereign. He created man to rule (see Gen 1:26; Ps 8:6; etc.). Whether the place assigned to man in the creation is to be considered a feature of his likeness to the divine or in the consequence of that likeness, is a question that has been much discussed. The latter is the more exact view, as reference here is to his position rather than to his nature. And yet man's royalty in the natural world is still so great that it must suggest his original complete fitness for it."

Journal your response about what it means to be created in the image of God.

_____

_____

_____

_____

_____

How did the Holy Spirit try to influence your temple care today?_____

How did your flesh want to respond?_____

How did you respond?_____

F.I.R.E

FRESH FRUIT   * NATURAL OILS/FATS
****
                                                  *
                                                  *
****
FRESH VEGETABLES (CAN BE STEAMED)   *NATURAL SWEETNERS
                                                  *
                                                  *
****
GRAINS   * MEAT/SEAFOOD/BEANS/NUTS
                                                  *
                                                  *
****
COOKED FRUIT   *COOKED VEGETABLES
                                                  *
                                                  *
****
PROCESSED FOODS   *PROCESSED LIQUIDS
                                                  *
                                                  *
****

ST-I used the tool of spiritual mind renewal (Read scriptures and daily reading on Temple Care) _____ **ST**-I used the tool of faith____ **ST**-I used the tool of support_____
ST-I used the tool of prayer____ **ST**-I used the tool of repentance _____
ST-I used the tool of spiritual fasting – yes/no; juice fast – yes/no

GOD DESIRES A PEOPLE WHOSE CHARACTER REVEALS A SPIRIT THAT HONORS HIS TRUTH REGARDING ALL THINGS BECAUSE HE CREATED EVERYTHING KNOWN AND UNKNOWN.

"...do you not know your body is the temple of the Holy Spirit who is in you..."
1 Corinthians 6:19

Week 2-Day 9-Monday
God's Created Image--You!
"Then the Lord <u>God formed man</u> of dust from the ground, and breathed into his nostrils the breath of life; and man became a living being."
Genesis 2:7

God created and made the animals yet *formed* you and me, which reflects something special and different. Granted, we must with all humility recognize that the material God chose to make us was from humble, don't know what else it is used for, dust. Yet, the care He took to form us and give us His very breath is what miraculously transformed us into the magnificent beings we are. Our God and what He performed is absolutely breathtaking and the following passage very powerfully conveys this reality.

> "What it was that was thus blown into the unconscious frame we do not know. Life in all its forms and degrees is a mysterious principle, which for centuries has baffled the earnest enquiries of physiologists and, notwithstanding the great advances of science in the present day, is as inscrutable as ever. We know something of life by its manifestations and enjoyments, as well as by its opposite, death. But what is that subtle invisible element, which, when infused into an organized body like that of man, not only imparts health, sensation, and capacity of action, but gives to each organ and tissue the elective power of absorbing from the air, and from other foreign substances whatever is suited for its own assimilation and nourishment, science cannot tell us, and revelation has not made known. We see the effects which life produces; but we must be content, perhaps forever, to remain ignorant of both its nature and the mode of its operation."

(Jamieson, Fausset, and Brown Commentary, 1997)

Mind Matters Exercise

How do you typically *think* about yourself on a daily basis?

1. ---
----
2. ---
----
3. ---

In what ways could your typical thoughts (stated above) influence your *behaviors* that cause your weight problems? Make sure that your individually numbered behaviors correspond to the above individually numbered thoughts.

1. ---
----
2. ---
----
3. ---

Now recognizing the truth that you are created in God's image, what *thoughts* about yourself come to mind?

1. ---
----
2. ---
----
3. ---

In truly thinking of yourself as being created in God's image how would you envision your *behavior* changing when it comes to eating (be specific)?

1. ---
----
2. ---
----
3. ---

How did the Holy Spirit try to influence your temple care today?_____

How did your flesh want to respond?_____

How did you respond?_____

<u>**F.I.R.E**</u>

FRESH FRUIT   * NATURAL OILS/FATS
****
                                               *
                                               *
****
FRESH VEGETABLES (CAN BE STEAMED)   *NATURAL SWEETNERS
                                               *
                                               *
****
GRAINS   * MEAT/SEAFOOD/BEANS/NUTS
                                               *
                                               *
****
*****
COOKED FRUIT   *COOKED VEGETABLES
                                               *
                                               *
****
PROCESSED FOODS   *PROCESSED LIQUIDS
                                               *
                                               *
****

<u>**ST-I used the tool of spiritual mind renewal**</u> (Read scriptures and daily reading on Temple Care) _____ **ST**-I used the tool of faith_____ **ST**-I used the tool of support_____
ST-I used the tool of prayer_____ **ST**-I used the tool of repentance _____
ST-I used the tool of spiritual fasting – yes/no; juice fast – yes/no

GOD DESIRES A PEOPLE WHOSE CHARACTER REVEALS A SPIRIT THAT HONORS HIS TRUTH REGARDING ALL THINGS BECAUSE HE CREATED EVERYTHING KNOWN AND UNKNOWN

"...do you not know your body is the temple of the Holy Spirit who is in you..."
1 Corinthians 6:19

Week 2-Day 10-Tuesday
God's Created Image--You!

"For Thou didst form my inward parts; Thou didst weave me in my mother's womb. I will give thanks to Thee, for I am fearfully and wonderfully made; Wonderful are Thy works, And my soul knows it very well. My frame was not hidden from Thee, When I was made in secret, And skillfully wrought in the depths of the earth. Thine eyes have seen my unformed substance; And in Thy book they were all written, The days that were ordained for me, When as yet there was not one of them."
Psalms 139:13-16

What personal message do you receive from this spiritual truth from God's Word?

_____
_____
_____
_____
_____
_____
_____
_____
_____
_____

   All throughout this day, I'd like to encourage you to repeat what the Psalmist exclaimed, ***"I will give thanks to Thee, for I am fearfully and wonderfully made; Wonderful are Thy works, And my soul knows it very well"!*** Just as you are TODAY, exclaim this truth in silent reverence and/or in loudly proclaimed joy! Give thanks for the created wonder of you, which is separate and apart from whether you are fat, skinny, nutritionally healthy or have unhealthy high blood pressure or high cholesterol. Give thanks for the fact that you have been fearfully and wonderfully made by God and that God actually weaved you in your mother's womb.

Write what it felt like to exclaim the above stated truth throughout the day (Evening Exercise).

_____
_____
_____
_____
_____
_____
_____
_____
_____
_____

How did the Holy Spirit try to influence your temple care today?_____
How did your flesh want to respond?_____
How did you respond?_____

F.I.R.E

FRESH FRUIT	* NATURAL OILS/FATS

****

*
*

****

FRESH VEGETABLES (CAN BE STEAMED)   *NATURAL SWEETNERS
*
*

****

GRAINS   * MEAT/SEAFOOD/BEANS/NUTS
*
*

****

COOKED FRUIT   *COOKED VEGETABLES
*
*

****

PROCESSED FOODS   *PROCESSED LIQUIDS
*
*

****

ST-I used the tool of spiritual mind renewal (Read scriptures and daily reading on Temple Care) _____ **ST**-I used the tool of faith____ **ST**-I used the tool of support_____ **ST**-I used the tool of prayer____ **ST**-I used the tool of repentance _____ **ST**-I used the tool of spiritual fasting – yes/no; juice fast-yes/no

GOD DESIRES A PEOPLE WHOSE CHARACTER REVEALS A SPIRIT THAT HONORS HIS TRUTH REGARDING ALL THINGS BECAUSE HE CREATED EVERYTHING KNOWN AND UNKNOWN.

"...do you not know your body is the temple of the Holy Spirit who is in you..."
1 Corinthians 6:19
Week 2-Day 11-Wednesday
God's Created Image—You!
"This is the book of the generations of Adam. In the day that <u>God created man, in the likeness of God</u> made he him; <u>male and female</u> created he them; and blessed them, and called their name Adam, in the day when they were created."
Genesis 5: 1, 2

As we are beginning this journey toward a more God led way of caring for our bodies/God's temple, I believe there's a burning issue that must be addressed. As we continue to recognize how "fearfully and wonderfully" we are made, we must look at how this truth fits with the specific goal of weight loss. At this very moment, I believe we should all slowly walk to our bathrooms, or at least in our minds imagine walking. And, as we are slowly walking, we should pray a sincere prayer to God to speak to us. When we get in front of the bathroom mirror, we should, with head held high, God's Spirit in our very being, and biblical knowledge of our uniquely created state, exclaim, "I am not Halley Berry!" To my male readers, instead of Halley's name, you can insert "The Rock", or any other glamorous individual you may secretly desire to have a body like. Truly *relax* (breath deeply) and accept that you weren't created to have _____'s (fill in the blank) legs, or muscles, or breasts, or hips…! You get the point!

Such a mental exercise may be funny, yet, to honestly look on the serious side of this message, listen to a startling fact. Researchers have conducted multiple studies that assess a woman's level of self-esteem in relation to her exposure to materials that show extremely thin, very beautiful women. It's been found that shortly after viewing a top name fashion magazine; many women experience a significant drop in their self-image (Butcher, Mineka and Hooley, 2004)! This is only after a few minutes! Although many variables can contribute to such an outcome, I do believe that understanding our true identity would help protect us from feeling bad about ourselves when we are momentarily exposed to beautiful, glamorous people. In truly addressing your weight concerns in a healthy, spiritual way, you must recognize and believe that *<u>you</u> were created in <u>God</u>'s own image, that <u>God</u> weaved <u>you</u> in your mother's womb and that <u>God</u>'s very breath flows through <u>you</u>, currently shielding you from death!* Question: Do you see that your self image is all about <u>you</u> and <u>God,</u> being that <u>you</u> are in <u>His</u> likeness?

So, as individuals seeking God's truth, we need not equate our desire for weight loss/health to wanting to look like a movie star or someone else. Sure, others can be inspiring to us, yet we must not try to aspire to be them! Also, we need not get in shape so that we can barely wear clothing to attract the opposite sex in hopes that our self-image will be increased! Remember, your self-image and need to lose weight is about <u>you</u> and <u>God,</u> not anyone else (boyfriend, girlfriend, husband, or wife). Love that God has created <u>you,</u> and focus on the spiritual growth He desires for you and many of your weight/health issues will improve! And as this growth continually occurs you will glorify God more and more as His very creation in His very likeness. **"For you have been bought with a price: therefore glorify God in your <u>body,</u> and in your <u>spirit</u>, which are God's."**
I Corinthians 6:20

In contrast, it disturbs me to see someone who loses sight of her/his spiritual challenge and obsessively tries to lose weight (for whatever reason) when he or she doesn't need to lose weight. As a general guideline, check out the Body Mass Index in the "Spiritual Tools" section to see if you really need to lose weight. Often one is struggling with spiritual/emotional issues if they are trying to lose weight needlessly. If you don't need to lose weight, I encourage you to focus on the spiritual tools and principles that we cover in this program to improve your temple care rather than losing weight (i.e. through weekly spiritual fasts). Just studying God's Word about caring for your body/God's temple will change your understanding of yourself and will help you develop a more spiritual mindset which will help you let go of your unhealthy tendencies.

How did the Holy Spirit try to influence your temple care today?_____

How did your flesh want to respond?_____

How did you respond?_____

<u>**F.I.R.E**</u>

FRESH FRUIT	* NATURAL OILS/FATS

****
*
*
****

FRESH VEGETABLES (CAN BE STEAMED)   *NATURAL SWEETNERS
*
*
****

GRAINS   * MEAT/SEAFOOD/BEANS/NUTS
*
*
****

COOKED FRUIT   *COOKED VEGETABLES
*
*
****

PROCESSED FOODS   *PROCESSED LIQUIDS
*
*
****

<u>**ST-I used the tool of spiritual mind renewal**</u> (Read scriptures and daily reading on Temple Care) _____**ST**-I used the tool of faith_____ **ST**-I used the tool of support_____
ST-I used the tool of prayer_____ **ST**-I used the tool of repentance _____
ST-I used the tool of spiritual fasting – yes/no; juice fast-yes/no

GOD DESIRES A PEOPLE WHOSE CHARACTER REVEALS A SPIRIT THAT HONORS HIS TRUTH REGARDING ALL THINGS BECAUSE HE CREATED EVERYTHING KNOWN AND UNKNOWN.

"...do you not know your body is the temple of the Holy Spirit who is in you..."
1 Corinthians 6:19

Week 2-Day 12-Thursday
God's Created Image--You!
"Know ye that the Lord He is <u>God</u>: it is <u>He that hath made us, and not we ourselves;</u>
we are His people, and the sheep of His pasture."
Psalms 100:3

I hope *and pray* that you are still on the road that you have started on! Well, the issue of self esteem and weight loss was so good to me yesterday that I feel led to continue that theme today. An interesting survey was conducted by *Psychology Today* regarding the body image of its readers. Data was analyzed from the years 1972, 1985 and 1996, and although there were many findings, one truly struck me hard. It was reported that 15% of women and 11 % of the men surveyed said that they would sacrifice more than 5 years of their God-given lives to be at the weight they want! Twenty-four percent of women and 17% of men said they would give up more than 3 years of their God-given lives to be at the weight that they want! (Butcher, Mineka and Hooley, 2004). I believe that these statistics may shed some light on the degree to which one believes weight affects their quality of life and self esteem.

This workbook is for the believers in God's Word who want to enhance their spiritual life in such a way that they glorify God in their very bodies. I consider this kind of practical, daily growth in our Lord as giving us a better quality of life! I wonder how long the above mentioned people spent focusing on and being distracted by their weight! God did not intend for you or me, His highest creation, to become fixated/obsessed with food and weight. Let's seek God's wise instruction about <u>how</u> He wants us to live, <u>what</u> He wants us to know, think and feel about temple care; <u>change</u> our ways; and <u>move on</u> to the greater things He has in store for us!

1. How much mental energy do you spend thinking about what to eat, when to eat, or how not to eat? Explain what this is like for you. Rate on 1 (not much) to 10 (too much) scale and discuss.

    _____
    _____
    _____

2. How much mental energy do you spend on trying to cover/camouflage body fat or on feeling guilty about   the weight you've already gained? How much time and/or energy do you spend feeling bad/not good enough about your weight/body, guilty about what you ate, and/or fearful about the weight you could gain? Rate and discuss.

    _____
    _____
    _____

3. How much time/energy do you spend trying to deny/ignore how your lifestyle contributes to your weight/health problems? Also, do you end up spending time, money and/or discomfort in dealing with indigestion, constipation, high blood pressure, high cholesterol, medication, extra doctor/hospital visits, or surgery due to your negative style of eating?

_____

_____

_____

As God's very creation, let's conquer this satanic tactic of obsession and/or death, through God's Word and guidance.   Then, let's give all that extra time, mental energy and money to more productive work in God's Kingdom!

How did the Holy Spirit try to influence your temple care today?_____
How did your flesh want to respond?_____
How did you respond?_____

<u>F.I.R.E</u>

FRESH FRUIT   * NATURAL OILS/FATS
****
                                                 *
                                                 *
****
FRESH VEGETABLES (CAN BE STEAMED)   *NATURAL SWEETNERS
                                                 *
                                                 *
****
GRAINS   * MEAT/SEAFOOD/BEANS/NUTS
                                                 *
                                                 *
****
COOKED FRUIT   *COOKED VEGETABLES
                                                 *
                                                 *
****
PROCESSED FOODS   *PROCESSED LIQUIDS
                                                 *
                                                 *
****

<u>ST-I used the tool of spiritual mind renewal</u> (Read scriptures and daily reading on
 Temple Care) _____   **ST**-I used the tool of faith_____   **ST**-I used the tool of support_____
ST-I used the tool of prayer_____   **ST**-I used the tool of repentance _____
ST-I used the tool of spiritual fasting – yes/no; juice fast-yes/no

**GOD DESIRES A PEOPLE WHOSE CHARACTER REVEALS A SPIRIT THAT
HONORS HIS TRUTH REGARDING ALL THINGS BECAUSE HE CREATED
EVERYTHING KNOWN AND UNKNOWN.**

"...do you not know your body is the temple of the Holy Spirit who is in you..."
1 Corinthians 6:19
Week 2-Day 13-Friday
<u>God's Created Image--You!</u>
"What is man, that Thou art mindful of him? and the son of man, that Thou visitest him? <u>For Thou hast made him a little lower than the angels, and hast crowned him with glory and honor!</u> Thou made him to have dominion over the works of Thy hands; Thou hast put all things under his feet, All sheep and oxen, yea and the beasts of the field, The fowl of the air, and the fish of the sea, and whatever passes through the paths of the seas. O Lord, our Lord, How excellent is Thy name in all the earth!"
Psalms 8:4-9
Why *Me* Lord?

David asks a thought-provoking question. Why, Lord, do you pay attention to me (and mankind)? Lord, why do you care for me? Not only does our Lord actually think about us and care for us, but, also He placed mankind in the control seat over the rest of His creation! What amazing love that God would prepare this world for our dominion and comfort for His glorification! Why me Lord?

As I'm baffled by the thought of what God has lovingly created for and in mankind, I can only conclude that He truly loves me for who I am. As the spiritual being He's created me…I am loved by Him. Even with or without money, with or without educational degrees, with or without prestige, with or without beauty…God loves me. Yet, in the midst of His love for me, it's not about me; but Him, the Great I Am, *in* me--the likeness in which I am created! *Please humble me more and more Lord, purge me of what I believe (what the world tells me) is great in me. Lord, please give me more of the only true greatness I can ever possess—You!*

"O Lord, our Lord, How majestic is THY NAME in all the earth!"
King David

It is often difficult to change the understanding of who we are (and therefore embrace and utilize the Power in us), yet I believe to successfully go through this program, you must more deeply understand spiritual principles and regularly use God's spiritual tools. Many of us don't quite see ourselves as being created in God's image and learn to manifest it more in our lives. Many of us have bought into defining ourselves by our weight or body image and have many problems changing this notion due to deeper fears. For instance, some people fear that they'll lose love and support by others if they lose weight because at some level, they will be changing a part of themselves. Some fear attracting more sexual interest from the opposite sex. Others fear the pounds melting away because it may reveal their own sexual struggles, not trusting their own ability to spiritually handle the increased sexual attention. Some know that various individuals in their lives may become jealous or threatened by their weight loss. Others fear the ambiguity regarding how their lives may change as they see and interact with themselves, others and the world differently. Yes, people usually respond to the changes we make, whether physically, emotionally or spiritually but that's okay: don't be afraid. Relax, be still and believe that while you are changing, you and God will safely navigate the new experiences in your life as you come to understand the magnitude of being created and loved by God.

What do you fear could happen if you actually believed what God's word says about you as His creation? What's the truth about that fear? How does God's spiritual reality change that fear into something beautiful? Look back on the daily scriptures we've addressed so far, and think about what you want to write before you do so._____

How did the Holy Spirit try to influence your temple care today?_____
How did your flesh want to respond?_____
How did you respond?_____

<u>**F.I.R.E**</u>

FRESH FRUIT   * NATURAL OILS/FATS
****
                                                        *
                                                        *
****
FRESH VEGETABLES (CAN BE STEAMED)   *NATURAL SWEETNERS
                                                        *
                                                        *
****
GRAINS   * MEAT/SEAFOOD/BEANS/NUTS
                                                        *
                                                        *
****
COOKED FRUIT   *COOKED VEGETABLES
                                                        *
                                                        *
****
PROCESSED FOODS   *PROCESSED LIQUIDS
                                                        *
                                                        *
****

<u>**ST-I used the tool of spiritual mind renewal**</u> (Read scriptures and daily reading on Temple Care) _____   **ST**-I used the tool of faith_____   **ST**-I used the tool of support_____
ST-I used the tool of prayer_____   **ST**-I used the tool of repentance _____
ST-I used the tool of spiritual fasting – yes/no; juice fast-yes/no

GOD DESIRES A PEOPLE WHOSE CHARACTER REVEALS A SPIRIT THAT HONORS HIS TRUTH REGARDING ALL THINGS BECAUSE HE CREATED EVERYTHING KNOWN AND UNKNOWN

"...do you not know your body is the temple of the Holy Spirit who is in you..."
1 Corinthians 6:19
Week 2-Day 14-Saturday
Week One Summary
<u>God's Created Image--You!</u>

God knows us better than we know ourselves, because He created us, and He knows us like He knows Himself! God, knowing Himself, His omnipotence, His omnipresence, and His omniscience, created you and me in His Image. We inherently have the right ingredients, from God's very image/likeness to reflect who He is! Although we are tarnished by sin, if correctly cultivated, can live a life that reveals some of God's very Being here on earth! God understands us at our most basic material level (because He created us and understands our sinful nature) and shared His own life-activating agent with us by His breath. "By an act of Divine omnipotence man arose from the dust; and in the same moment in which the dust, by virtue of creative omnipotence, shaped itself into a human form, it was pervaded by the Divine breath of life, and created a living being..."(Matthew Henry Commentary, 1991).

In truly submitting to the reality that God created me, I open my understanding to accept that He has even seen my "unformed substance", therefore knowing the truth about me and *what is best for me*. Also, knowing the reality that God understands, better then I, the gravity of my sinful nature (that which falls away from His Image/Likeness), I strive to better understand His truth/word to be a better reflection of Him in my spirit, soul/mind and body.

How did the Holy Spirit try to influence your temple care today?_____
How did your flesh want to respond?_____
How did you respond?_____

F.I.R.E

FRESH FRUIT   * NATURAL OILS/FATS
****
                                                    *
                                                    *
****
FRESH VEGETABLES (CAN BE STEAMED)   *NATURAL SWEETNERS
                                                    *
                                                    *
****
GRAINS   * MEAT/SEAFOOD/BEANS/NUTS
                                                    *
                                                    *
****
COOKED FRUIT   *COOKED VEGETABLES
                                                    *
                                                    *
****
PROCESSED FOODS   *PROCESSED LIQUIDS
                                                    *
                                                    *
****

ST-I used the tool of spiritual mind renewal (Read scriptures and daily reading on
Temple Care) _____ **ST**-I used the tool of faith____ **ST**-I used the tool of support_____
ST-I used the tool of prayer____ **ST**-I used the tool of repentance _____
ST-I used the tool of spiritual fasting – yes/no; juice fast-yes/no

**GOD DESIRES A PEOPLE WHOSE CHARACTER REVEALS A SPIRIT THAT
HONORS HIS TRUTH REGARDING ALL THINGS BECAUSE HE CREATED
EVERYTHING KNOWN AND UNKNOWN**

Self Regulating Sheet

Looking back on this week's F.I.R.E. forms how did you do?

1. Spiritual mind renewal (reading what the bible says about Temple Care)
How did I rate this week with this spiritual tool? ____
1-10 (1=not well at all) (10= praise God really well!)

2. Faith (actions toward Godly Temple Care)
How did I rate this week with this spiritual tool? ____
1-10 (1=not well at all) (10= praise God really well!)

3. Support (contacting spiritual support partner/s and discuss Temple Care)
How did I rate this week with this spiritual tool? ____
1-10 (1=not well at all) (10= praise God really well!)

4. Prayer (praying to God about any and every issue regarding my Temple Care)
How did I rate this week with this spiritual tool? ____
1-10 (1=not well at all) (10= praise God really well!)

5. Repentance (expressing Godly sorrow and changing my ways through the Holy Spirit)
How did I rate this week with this spiritual tool? ____
1-10 (1=not well at all) (10= praise God really well!)

6. Fasting (not eating for 1 day or 3 dinners and replace with prayer, singing, reading God's Word...)
How did I rate this week with this spiritual tool? ____
1-10 (1=not well at all) (10= praise God really well!)

7. This week the following came easy for me regarding care of my temple?

_____

_____

8. This week the following was very difficult for me regarding caring for my temple?

_____

_____

After evaluating my ratings this week, these two spiritual tools (choose the lowest rated ones) are what I need to improve on next week regarding temple care?

_____

_____

Tip: Jot down some scriptures on patience and carry them to encourage you as you go through the program.

God's Word on Temptation
Week Three

"...do you not know your body is the temple of the Holy Spirit who is in you..."
1 Corinthians 6:19

Week Three-Day 15-Sunday
God's Word on Temptation

The word "temptation" in many biblical passages has to do with testing one's character, integrity or quality.

> "God is 'tempted' by Israel's distrust of Him, as if the people were actually challenging Him to show His perfections (Ex 17:2; Ps 78:18; Acts 15:10; Heb 3:9, and often); Abraham is 'tempted', being called upon to offer up Isaac (Gen 22:1); and Jesus is 'tempted' to a spectacular Messiahship (Matt 4 and parallel passages (see TEMPTATION OF CHRIST)). No evil is implied in the subject of these temptations. Temptation therefore in the Scripture sense has possibilities of holiness as well as of sin."(International Standard Bible Encyclopedia)

Today many scholars understand temptation in two very different ways. In one way it means that one has been "afflicted" in some way that causes suffering. This affliction is in no way the result of sin. You can say that such an individual is going along in life experiencing righteousness through Christ and is unjustifiably hit with faith testing difficulty. The other way in which temptation is understood is also through one who has experienced difficulty yet it is due to the desire of their fleshly nature. This individual is going along in life and due to weaknesses and sinful desires may fall for evil. (New Unger's Bible Dictionary and Nelson's Bible Dictionary)

GOD DESIRES A PEOPLE WHO DEPEND ON HIM TO HELP THEM HONESTLY ADMIT TO AND OVERCOME THEIR TEMPTATIONS.

How did the Holy Spirit try to influence your temple care today?_____

How did your flesh want to respond?_____

How did you respond?_____

F.I.R.E

FRESH FRUIT   * NATURAL OILS/FATS

****
*
*

****

FRESH VEGETABLES (CAN BE STEAMED)   *NATURAL SWEETNERS
*
*

****

GRAINS   * MEAT/SEAFOOD/BEANS/NUTS
*
*

****

COOKED FRUIT   *COOKED VEGETABLES
*
*

****

PROCESSED FOODS   *PROCESSED LIQUIDS
*
*

****

<u>ST-I used the tool of spiritual mind renewal</u> (Read scriptures and daily reading on Temple Care) _____ **ST**-I used the tool of faith____ **ST**-I used the tool of support_____ **ST**-I used the tool of prayer____ **ST**-I used the tool of repentance ___
ST-I used the tool of spiritual fasting – yes/no; juice fast - yes/no
<u>SP-I'm being honest about and coping with my food temptations</u> ____

"…do you not know your body is the temple of the Holy Spirit who is in you…"
1 Corinthians 6:19

Week Three–Day 16-Monday
God's Word on Temptation

"*Blessed is the man that endureth temptation:* for when he is tried, *he shall receive the crown of life,* which the Lord hath promised to them that love him. Let no man say when he is tempted, I am tempted of God: for *God cannot be tempted with evil, neither tempteth he any man…*"
James 1:12&13

Yesterday, we looked at the two differing meanings of temptation. In today's passage we see that the individual who patiently deals with afflictions due to no fault of their own is blessed. Why? Because such testing is an opportunity to strengthen ones spiritual character *through God's power*, not our own. And when our character is found to be of the highest worth through accessing God's power and grace, He then approves of us by promising a "crown of life". Regarding verse 13, the second verse in today's reading, the Matthew Henry Commentary states the following:

> "All moral evil is owing to some disorder in the being that is chargeable with it, to a want of wisdom, or of power, or of decorum and purity in the will. But who can impeach the holy God with the want of these, which are his very essence?"

In this verse, the meaning of temptation changes from verse 12 by pointing out that it is something that taps into one's fleshly desire that may bring about evil. We know that our God has no evil within Himself therefore He can not be tempted unto evil or tempt unto evil.

GOD DESIRES A PEOPLE WHO DEPEND ON HIM TO HELP THEM HONESTLY ADMIT TO AND OVERCOME THEIR TEMPTATIONS.

How did the Holy Spirit try to influence your temple care today?_____

How did your flesh want to respond?_____

How did you respond?_____

F.I.R.E

FRESH FRUIT   * NATURAL OILS/FATS

****

                                                               *

                                                               *

****

FRESH VEGETABLES (CAN BE STEAMED)   *NATURAL SWEETNERS

                                                               *

                                                               *

****

GRAINS   * MEAT/SEAFOOD/BEANS/NUTS

                                                               *

                                                               *

****

COOKED FRUIT   *COOKED VEGETABLES

                                                               *

                                                               *

****

PROCESSED FOODS   *PROCESSED LIQUIDS

                                                               *

                                                               *

****

<u>ST-I used the tool of spiritual mind renewal</u> (Read scriptures and daily reading on Temple Care) _____ **ST**-I used the tool of faith____ **ST**-I used the tool of support_____
ST-I used the tool of prayer____ **ST**-I used the tool of repentance ___
ST-I used the tool of spiritual fasting – yes/no; juice fast - yes/no
<u>SP-I'm being honest about and coping with my food temptations</u> ____

"...do you not know your body is the temple of the Holy Spirit who is in you..."
1 Corinthians 6:19

Week Three–Day 17-Tuesday
God's Word on Temptation
"But <u>every man is tempted</u>, when he is <u>drawn away of his own lust, and enticed</u>."
James 1:14

Tailor Made

You may be coming to understand through this week's readings so far, which understanding of temptation applies to how you eat and care for your temple. The scripture for today is addressing the meaning of temptation which is when ones fleshly desire provokes them toward evil. It is so important to know and understand that that which tempts you can be very different from that which tempts me. And even if we are tempted by the same external prompts the reason why it tempts each of us can still be very different.

Whatever appears to be the external cause of your temptation is NEVER the real issue! In fact, God's spiritual reality tells us that it is that which is *within you* that is the *real issue*. "The combustible matter is in us, though the flame may be blown up by some outward causes." (Matthew Henry Commentary) Many, many people spend so much time in denial and believe external circumstances and/or people are their problem. For instance, in my support groups I usually have at least one person who believes that their spouse is the reason why they do not take better care of themselves. They say things like, "Well, it's because he brings junk food into the house" or "she won't cook good food for me" or "He eats late at night when we are watching movies and always offers me something to eat…" The list truly goes on and on! The spiritual reality is that what ever tempts you reveals *your own* tailor-made fleshly weakness.

Honestly

I recommend that you spend some time in prayer before completing this next exercise by filling in the blanks.

Honestly, I overeat because _____
_____.

Honestly, I often blame my overeating on _____
_____.

because _____
_____.

Honestly, I do not eat healthier because _____
_____.

Honestly, I often blame eating unhealthy on _____
_____.

Honestly, some other things I have said to excuse the poor care of my temple has been
_____,
_____,

and _____.

I can honestly overcome, through the power of the Holy Spirit, these temptations by growing in the spiritual areas of

_____

_____.

(Write down biblical concepts from the bible)

GOD DESIRES A PEOPLE WHO DEPEND ON HIM TO HELP THEM HONESTLY ADMIT TO AND OVERCOME THEIR TEMPTATIONS.

How did the Holy Spirit try to influence your temple care today?_____

How did your flesh want to respond?_____

How did you respond?_____

FRESH FRUIT   * NATURAL OILS/FATS
****
                                                 *
                                                 *
****
FRESH VEGETABLES (CAN BE STEAMED)   *NATURAL SWEETNERS
                                                 *
                                                 *
****
GRAINS   * MEAT/SEAFOOD/BEANS/NUTS
                                                 *
                                                 *
****
COOKED FRUIT   *COOKED VEGETABLES
                                                 *
                                                 *
****
PROCESSED FOODS   *PROCESSED LIQUIDS
                                                 *
                                                 *
****

<u>ST-I used the tool of spiritual mind renewal</u> (Read scriptures and daily reading on Temple Care) _____ **ST**-I used the tool of faith____ **ST**-I used the tool of support_____
ST-I used the tool of prayer____ **ST**-I used the tool of repentance ___
ST-I used the tool of spiritual fasting – yes/no; juice fast - yes/no
<u>SP-I'm being honest about and coping with my food temptations</u> ____

"...do you not know your body is the temple of the Holy Spirit who is in you..."
1 Corinthians 6:19

Week Three–Day 18-Wednesday
God's Word on Temptation
" Then when lust hath conceived, it bringeth forth sin: and sin, when it is finished, bringeth forth death."
James 1:15

Temptation that occurs due to our fleshly desires has a two part "mode of operation". First, temptation draws one away from that which is good. I'm sure you understand this concept. Think about one healthy behavior you had in the past and when you were drawn away from continuing that healthy behavior. Second, temptation entices one to get close to and embrace that which is evil. So, as you were being drawn away from a good habit (i.e. eat fruit as dessert) you were also enticed to embrace an unhealthy habit (i.e. eat sugar-laden processed desserts). Now in today's scripture, one is enticed to "cleave" to or hold onto something that is no good for them for a long period of time. (Matthew Henry's Commentary)

What good temple care habits have you been drawn away from and what unhealthy habits have you been cleaving to?

Drawn away from _____   Cleaving to _____
Drawn away from _____   Cleaving to _____
Drawn away from _____   Cleaving to _____

"After sin is brought forth in actual commissions, the finishing of it is its being strengthened by frequent acts and settled into a habit. And, when the iniquities of men are thus filled up, death is brought forth. There is a death upon the soul, and death comes upon the body." (Matthew Henry Commentary)

The final result of habitual sin is death. Over a period of time, habitually giving in to temptations brings about death of the "soul" or mind/conscience. Ones spirit (the part of us that can commune with and worship God) becomes weaker as God's Spirit within us becomes grieved and is unable to influence one back toward godliness. Inevitably, the body follows the deadened mind/conscience by experiencing health problems and then literal premature death can occur. Are there health habits that you practice that can bring about your premature death? Discuss

_____

_____

GOD DESIRES A PEOPLE WHO DEPEND ON HIM TO HELP THEM HONESTLY ADMIT TO AND OVERCOME THEIR TEMPTATIONS.

How did the Holy Spirit try to influence your temple care today?_____
How did your flesh want to respond?_____
How did you respond?_____

F.I.R.E

FRESH FRUIT   * NATURAL OILS/FATS
****
                                               *
                                               *
****
FRESH VEGETABLES (CAN BE STEAMED)   *NATURAL SWEETNERS
                                               *
                                               *
****
GRAINS   * MEAT/SEAFOOD/BEANS/NUTS
                                               *
                                               *
****
COOKED FRUIT   *COOKED VEGETABLES
                                               *
                                               *
****
PROCESSED FOODS   *PROCESSED LIQUIDS
                                               *
                                               *
****

ST-I used the tool of spiritual mind renewal (Read scriptures and daily reading on Temple Care) _____ **ST**-I used the tool of faith_____ **ST**-I used the tool of support_____
ST-I used the tool of prayer_____ **ST**-I used the tool of repentance ____
ST-I used the tool of spiritual fasting – yes/no; juice fast - yes/no
SP-I'm being honest about and coping with my food temptations _____

"...do you not know your body is the temple of the Holy Spirit who is in you..."
1 Corinthians 6:19

Week Three–Day 19-Thursday
God's Word on Temptation
"There hath no temptation taken you but <u>such as is common to man.</u>"
1 Corinthians 10:13

"Common to man" can be translated as "small, short, moderate" (Adam's Clarke Commentary). When we address the temptations of the flesh regarding food, it is best to put the situation in its proper, spiritual perspective. Looking at the many temptations of God's people before you, in reality, your temptation regarding food (i.e. brownies, cookies, pizza...) is truly "small, short" and "moderate"! "Our temptations or trials have been but trifling in comparison of those endured by the Israelites..." (Adam's Clarke Commentary)

Another important point to remember is that the temptations we experience are normal and expected. *Many* people experience similar temptations as you and I in regards to food and caring for their bodies. Some have dealt with their temptations and triumphed. *Assuredly we will overcome even more so with the aid of God's very Spirit moving within and influencing us!*

GOD DESIRES A PEOPLE WHO DEPEND ON HIM TO HELP THEM HONESTLY ADMIT TO AND OVERCOME THEIR TEMPTATIONS.

How did the Holy Spirit try to influence your temple care today?_____

How did your flesh want to respond?_____

How did you respond?_____

F.I.R.E

FRESH FRUIT   * NATURAL OILS/FATS
****
                                               *
                                               *
****
*****
FRESH VEGETABLES (CAN BE STEAMED)   *NATURAL SWEETNERS
                                               *
                                               *
****
GRAINS   * MEAT/SEAFOOD/BEANS/NUTS
                                               *
                                               *
****
COOKED FRUIT   *COOKED VEGETABLES
                                               *
                                               *
****
PROCESSED FOODS   *PROCESSED LIQUIDS
                                               *
                                               *
****

<u>ST-I used the tool of spiritual mind renewal</u> (Read scriptures and daily reading on Temple Care) _____ **ST**-I used the tool of faith_____ **ST**-I used the tool of support_____
ST-I used the tool of prayer_____ **ST**-I used the tool of repentance ___
ST-I used the tool of spiritual fasting – yes/no; juice fast - yes/no
<u>SP-I'm being honest about and coping with my food temptations</u> ____

"...do you not know your body is the temple of the Holy Spirit who is in you..."
1 Corinthians 6:19

Week Three–Day 20-Friday
God's Word on Temptation

"...but <u>God is faithful</u>, who will <u>not suffer you to be tempted above that ye are able</u>; but will <u>with the temptation also make a way to escape, that ye may be able to bear it.</u>"
1 Corinthians 10:13

"This is a general promise, just as applicable to all Christians as it was to the Corinthians. It implies: That all the circumstances, causes, and agents that lead to temptation are under the control of God. Every man that tempts another; every fallen spirit that is engaged in this; every book, picture, place of amusement; every charm of music, and of song; every piece of indecent statuary; and every plan of business, of gain or ambition, are all under the control of God. He can check them; he can control them; he can paralyze their influence; he can destroy them." (Matthew Henry's Commentary)

Again, God does not *cause* one to experience temptation yet He may *allow or permit* it to come from elsewhere. Because God allows temptations to come (at times) we must see them as being allowed for some good reason. I believe that if we are honest about what tempts us then it can become a conscious invitation toward increased spiritual growth *or* increased carnal/fleshly growth (Barnes Notes). This is the crux of the Temple Care Workbook! We experience many temptations that due to our own desires/lusts can destroy our health, God-esteem... Yet, if we answer temptation's invitation to grow spiritually, we can, through seeking God's guidance and strength ("God is faithful"), successfully change what is within us so that we no longer succumb to such temptations!

Recognize

I now better recognize that my temptation of _____ (regarding food/drink) is from my own tailor-made, unique weakness which through God's help can increase my spiritual growth in the following way(s)_____
_____.

I now better recognize that another temptation of mine is _____ (regarding food/drink), and is from my own tailor-made, unique weakness which can through God's help increase my spiritual growth in the following way(s)_____
_____.

GOD DESIRES A PEOPLE WHO DEPEND ON HIM TO HELP THEM HONESTLY ADMIT TO AND OVERCOME THEIR TEMPTATIONS.

How did the Holy Spirit try to influence your temple care today?_____
How did your flesh want to respond?_____
How did you respond?_____

F.I.R.E

FRESH FRUIT   * NATURAL OILS/FATS
****
                                         *
                                         *
****
FRESH VEGETABLES (CAN BE STEAMED)   *NATURAL SWEETNERS
                                         *
                                         *
****
GRAINS   * MEAT/SEAFOOD/BEANS/NUTS
                                         *
                                         *
****
COOKED FRUIT   *COOKED VEGETABLES
                                         *
                                         *
****
PROCESSED FOODS   *PROCESSED LIQUIDS
                                         *
                                         *
****

<u>ST-I used the tool of spiritual mind renewal</u> (Read scriptures and daily reading on Temple Care) _____ **ST**-I used the tool of faith_____ **ST**-I used the tool of support_____
ST-I used the tool of prayer_____ **ST**-I used the tool of repentance ____
ST-I used the tool of spiritual fasting – yes/no; juice fast - yes/no
<u>SP-I'm being honest about and coping with my food temptations</u> _____

"…do you not know your body is the temple of the Holy Spirit who is in you…"
1 Corinthians 6:19

Week Three–Day 21-Saturday
God's Word on Temptation
"There hath no temptation taken you but such as is common to man: but God is faithful, who will not suffer you to be tempted above that ye are able; <u>but will with the temptation also make a way to escape, that ye may be able to bear it.</u>"
1 Corinthians 10:13

<u>Summary</u>

Many of us have believed temptations to be so negative that we try to deny or minimize the fact that we even have them! This coping style does not work in the physical world or spiritual realm! For instance, how can we safely navigate our car around town if we keep closing our eyes whenever we get to rough roads! Do not be afraid of or overwhelmed by the temptations that reveal your weaknesses. Humbly and graciously address temptation's invitation toward increased dependency on God to overcome it!

God's Escape Route

I hear some truly amazing stories from my support group members about how God REALLY does provide a way of escape from tempting situations! I've heard of everything from people receiving calls that freed them from a tempting situation to God putting the gracious words of "no thank you" into mouths before they could even think about saying no! Begin to start really looking for the ways of escape God provides for you regarding your temptation with food/drink. Also look for how God's Spirit tries to impart strength to you when you need it the most!

Discuss this topic with your accountability partner. Then make a list of the ways in which God has provided you both ways of escaping temptations this week.

_____
_____
_____
_____
_____
_____

GOD DESIRES A PEOPLE WHO DEPEND ON HIM TO HELP THEM HONESTLY ADMIT TO AND OVERCOME THEIR TEMPTATIONS.

How did the Holy Spirit try to influence your temple care today?_____
How did your flesh want to respond?_____
How did you respond?_____

F.I.R.E

FRESH FRUIT   * NATURAL OILS/FATS
****
                                         *
                                         *
****
FRESH VEGETABLES (CAN BE STEAMED)   *NATURAL SWEETNERS
                                         *
                                         *
****
GRAINS   * MEAT/SEAFOOD/BEANS/NUTS
                                         *
                                         *
****
COOKED FRUIT   *COOKED VEGETABLES
                                         *
                                         *
****
PROCESSED FOODS   *PROCESSED LIQUIDS
                                         *
                                         *
****

ST-I used the tool of spiritual mind renewal (Read scriptures and daily reading on Temple Care) _____ **ST**-I used the tool of faith____ **ST**-I used the tool of support_____
ST-I used the tool of prayer____ **ST**-I used the tool of repentance ___
ST-I used the tool of spiritual fasting – yes/no; juice fast - yes/no
SP-I'm being honest about and coping with my food temptations ____

Self Regulating Sheet

Looking back on this week's F.I.R.E. forms how did you do?

1. Spiritual mind renewal (reading what the bible says about Temple Care)
How did I rate this week with this spiritual tool? ____
1-10 (1=not well at all) (10= praise God really well!)

2. Faith (actions toward Godly Temple Care)
How did I rate this week with this spiritual tool? ____
1-10 (1=not well at all) (10= praise God really well!)

3. Support (contacting spiritual support partner/s and discuss Temple Care)
How did I rate this week with this spiritual tool? ____
1-10 (1=not well at all) (10= praise God really well!)

4. Prayer (praying to God about any and every issue regarding my Temple Care)
How did I rate this week with this spiritual tool? ____
1-10 (1=not well at all) (10= praise God really well!)

5. Repentance (expressing Godly sorrow and changing my ways through the Holy Spirit)
How did I rate this week with this spiritual tool? ____
1-10 (1=not well at all) (10= praise God really well!)

6. Fasting (not eating for 1 day or 3 dinners and replace with prayer, singing, reading God's Word...)
How did I rate this week with this spiritual tool? ____
1-10 (1=not well at all) (10= praise God really well!)

7.   This week the following came easy for me regarding care of my temple?

_____
_____

8.   This week the following was very difficult for me regarding caring for my temple?

_____

9.   After evaluating my ratings this week, these two spiritual tools (choose the lowest rated ones) are what I need to improve on next week regarding temple care?

_____
_____

God's Word on Gluttony
Week Four

"...do you not know your body is the temple of the Holy Spirit who is in you..."
1 Corinthians 6:19
Week Four-Day 22-Sunday
<u>**God's Word on Gluttony**</u>
"...And put a knife to your throat, If you are a man of <u>great appetite</u>."
Proverbs 23:2

What a powerful passage!   In this scripture we are being warned against the indulgence of the appetite. In fact, "put a knife to your throat" means that one needs to restrain themselves, "as it were with a sword hanging over thy head, from all excess." (Matthew Henry Commentary) In all reality, the majority of us do not get overweight without being gluttonous or excessive with the food we eat and/or drinks we drink. A part of the definition of gluttony is simply excessive eating/overeating.

> "A person who is debased and excessive in his eating habits. Gluttony is more than overeating. In its association with drunkenness (Proverbs 23:21; Deut 21:20), it describes a life given to excess. When Jesus was called a 'gluttonous man' (Matt 11:19), His critics were accusing Him of being loose and excessive by associating with tax collectors and sinners. (Nelson's Illustrated Bible Dictionary, 1986,)

So again, the majority of us have become overweight by eating excessively. A very, very small percentage of individuals in our society gain extra weight while eating moderately. Many of us don't even know when we are being gluttonous or minimize the reality that we are gluttonous. In addressing the biblical passage above, which in many bibles is in a section entitled "On Life and Conduct", we see that having a great appetite is ill advised. In fact, the Eastern figure of speech put a knife means to avoid the dangers of gluttony by restraining one's appetite. Why such a drastic metaphor? I believe that this passage suggests that an unchecked, excessive lifestyle in anyway will lead to serious consequences in the long run...so please check yourself!

Can we restrain our appetite to a healthy degree? Of course we can; otherwise the Bible wouldn't suggest it. Basically, the restraint that God places on one's appetite is to "Do thyself no harm". Can you believe that, sometimes, we are actually embarrassed or apologetic for saying "no" to unhealthy, *harmful* choices or for doing no harm to ourselves! I encourage you, this week, to be proud of your attempts, through the Holy Spirit, to be healthier and to no longer choose to do yourself harm. We'll discuss this in more detail in the section *"God's Purpose for Food"*.

Earlier, I came from emptying my trash at my apartment complex and saw a beautiful sight! I saw a young woman, who's quite obese, walking (in exercise) around the apartment complex with her head held high! Now maybe she just has excellent posture, but to me she projected that she felt good about herself and what she was doing. When you are at a fellowship gathering, proudly make the healthy choices (at least more often than not)! Many thin and not so thin people appear embarrassed to say "no" to unhealthy choices, particularly in public. Some people don't want to make "healthy statements" because they may have challenging days, give in to unhealthy choices (which are inevitable!) and may be called on the carpet about it. At that time just say, "I'm doing the best I can and today is a rough day. Yet, I'm already heading back on the right track through God's help!" Also, others don't want to "offend" the person who is offering them an unhealthy choice. For such individuals, I recommend that you pray to God for the courage to break away from "people pleasing" so that you can allow God's Spirit to guide you toward greater health. Again, become more conscious of doing no harm to your body, God's temple.

Now, some of you may be saying, "I never stuff myself or eat in excess. I usually stop eating when I feel satisfied and am no longer hungry." Yet, there are many other ways in which I believe we eat excessively. Do you snack and nibble on food throughout the day? You see snacking/nibbling often means you are not really hungry because you don't want to eat a full meal. Do you eat the currently prescribed six small meals a day even if you aren't hungry or diabetic? If you answered yes to either one of those questions, then you are eating excessively. In fact, you are actually conditioning yourself to eat when you are not hungry, which is excessive eating.

Some people say they eat six meals to keep their metabolism from slowing down and if you want to maintain a certain metabolic level, than this could be fine. However, rather than eating to change your metabolism, why not exert some energy to change your metabolism (and again eat only when you get hungry)! For instance, take a short, brisk walk. In fact, researchers say that exercising for just minutes everyday can help keep your metabolism from getting sluggish and reduce your risk of heart disease by 50% (10 minutes of walking 5 days a week) (National Heart, Blood and Lung Institute). After awhile everyone's body will experience a decreased metabolic rate (which means decrease weight loss) if they decrease their caloric intake over a long period of time. Therefore I encourage you to keep your metabolic rate from slowing down. Walk the stairs in your home for 10 minutes, but don't eat! You'll experience quite a bit of liberty if you eat when you need food rather than having to think about fitting six meals into your day. In fact, I believe that when we unnaturally have to think about food so much it can actually set one up to become preoccupied or obsessed with food and weight.

For individuals who have set as a goal, weight loss (and who are not currently exercising), I challenge you at this time to help keep up your metabolic rate by engaging in some form of exercise at least 10-15 minutes every day. As you begin to naturally feel the benefits of exercise (over time) then challenge yourself to do more. I strongly recommend that you find exercises you can do at home any time of the day. For instance, we have "Exercise on Demand" on our television so anytime of the day or night I can exercise. Or quickly walk in place while watching 10 minutes of your favorite television show. Or you can record exercise shows, or purchase a couple of inexpensive exercise DVD's… The key is to find something you can start off doing *at home. Why?* So the weather, gym fees, the time of day, and many other circumstances will not excuse you from exercising. Later, once you've established the habit or discipline of exercise then you'll be more successful if you'd like to venture out to gyms, outdoor tracks…. Currently, I enjoy various exercises on "Exercise on Demand" and Hot Bikram Yoga, which seems to meet the needs of my body and it feels really good. Find something that you like and your body responds well too. **For those who are already exercising, keep up the good work and don't change a thing!** For instance, if you are walking 30 minutes 3+ times a week then please continue doing so…you are already on the right track, praise God!

Lastly, make sure you use the spiritual tools to evoke God's power to discipline yourself to exercise regularly.

The Stop Short Exercise

Question: How is it that I or someone else, who may fix a plate of food for me, always knows *exactly* how much food will satisfy my hunger? Often, we eat everything on our plates, so how do we know the exact amount of food that would satisfy our hunger? I venture to say that often we clean our plates because that's what we've been conditioned to do rather than because we are still hungry. What I'd like for you to do for the rest of this week, with *every* meal you eat, is to stop eating before you clean your plate leaving *at least* 1 bite of each type of food on your plate. "Stop short" and see whether you are still hungry. You may recognize that your hunger will be satisfied before you finish cleaning your plate.

Feel free to journal about this experience.

_____
_____
_____
_____
_____
_____

GOD DESIRES A PEOPLE WHOSE CHARACTER REVEALS A SPIRIT FREE FROM THE BONDAGE OF GLUTTONY.

F.I.R.E

FRESH FRUIT   * NATURAL OILS/FATS
****
                                               *
                                               *
****
FRESH VEGETABLES (CAN BE STEAMED)   *NATURAL SWEETNERS
                                               *
                                               *
****
GRAINS   * MEAT/SEAFOOD/BEANS/NUTS
                                               *
                                               *
****
COOKED FRUIT   *COOKED VEGETABLES
                                               *
                                               *
****
PROCESSED FOODS   *PROCESSED LIQUIDS
                                               *
                                               *
****

ST-I used the tool of spiritual mind renewal (Read scriptures and daily reading on Temple Care) _____ **ST**-I used the tool of faith_____ **ST**-I used the tool of support_____
ST-I used the tool of prayer_____ **ST**-I used the tool of repentance ___
Exercise (10+ minutes) ___
ST-I used the tool of spiritual fasting – yes/no; juice fast-yes/no
SP-I'm being honest about and coping with my food temptations _____
SP-I ate more than what I needed _____

How did the Holy Spirit try to influence your temple care today?_____
How did your flesh want to respond?_____
How did you respond?_____

"...do you not know your body is the temple of the Holy Spirit who is in you..."
1 Corinthians 6:19

Week Four–Day 23-Monday
God's Word on Gluttony
Numbers 11

Kibroth-hattaavah

Long, long ago in a far away land walked a nomadic tribe. This tribe had all of its needs miraculously taken care of, food, clothing, shelter, yet they were not content. They cried to God that what He provided was not enough; they wanted more. More specifically, they wanted thick, juicy meat to eat rather than bread. They told God, who so lovingly provided for them daily, that just looking at the bread He had given them caused them to feel disgust. So, they all agreed to cry and whine in unison to get God's attention. God, with a terrifying calmness (which they didn't really notice because they were too busy being in tantrum mode), instructed the tribe to prepare themselves for a revelation from Him the next day. He told them that He would give them meat, so much meat that they could eat from it for a month. He also mentioned that that meat would start to come out of their noses, and that they would eventually hate it. Later, powerful winds pulled quail up from the sea and carried them to land, heaping them into stacks almost 36 inches above the ground! The tribe, in their greed flew upon the spoil with such an insatiable appetite that they spent an entire day collecting the quail for fear of losing. They wanted to make sure they had gathered a large amount for the future before they began eating, not once heeding to the warning from God about how they'd become extremely full of it and hate it. As soon as the people stopped collecting the quail and began to eat, God unleashed a plague on them due to their greed and ungratefulness.

The story's end is told in the book of Psalms 78:20-31, "We do not know anything as to who were smitten, or how many; the Psalmist tells us that they were 'the fattest' and 'the chosen' in Israel, and we may naturally suppose that those who had been foremost in the lusting and the murmuring were foremost in the ruin which followed" (The Pulpit Commentary). The Israelites were smitten with a plague or some bodily disease. Yet, it is unknown to what degree miraculous or natural was the consequence. Numbers 11:33 and 34 states, "And while the flesh was yet between their teeth, ere it was chewed, the wrath of the LORD was kindled against the people, and the LORD smote the people with a very great plague. And he called the name of that place Kibroth-hattaavah: because there they buried the people that lusted." (King James Bible) Other commentaries state that Kibroth-hattaavah means "the graves of lust"(The New Unger's Bible Dictionary, 1988.) or "graves of craving".

The New International Version of the Bible (Life Application Study Bible) addresses Numbers 11:34 and states the following:

"Craving or lusting is more than inappropriate sexual desire. It can be an unnatural or greedy desire for anything (sports, knowledge, possessions, influence over others). In this circumstance, God punished the Israelites for craving good food! Their desire was not wrong; the sin was in allowing that desire to turn into greed. They felt it was their right to have fine food, and they could think of nothing else. When you become preoccupied with something until it affects your perspective on everything else, you have moved from desire to lust."

What food(s) do you seem to not only desire but crave and often consume greedily? Discuss _____
_____
_____
_____
_____

How often do you eat more than what you need (eat excessively)? Discuss_____
_____
_____
_____

How have food/drink affected your perspective about your body, health, temple care?
_____
_____

"The Stop Short Exercise" (introduced yesterday)

I encourage you to continue practicing this exercise and journal your experience. Also, keep in mind to not nibble throughout the day.
_____
_____

In *Natural Health* (July, 2004), it's said that some studies suggests that about 25% of what we eat could be considered passive overeating! "In other words, three-quarters of the way through a big bowl of pasta, you may be perfectly satisfied. But if there's more in the bowl, you'll eat it." Let's work on lessening our tendency toward gluttony by stopping short, and learn to eat only what's needed. Remember that you can always come back to eat the rest of your meal when you become truly hungry again.

EVERDAY QUESTION:

How did the Holy Spirit try to influence your temple care today?_____

How did your flesh want to respond?_____

How did you respond?_____

FRESH FRUIT   *NATURAL OILS/FATS
****
                                               *
                                               *
****
FRESH VEGETABLES (CAN BE STEAMED)   *NATURAL SWEETNERS
                                               *
                                               *
****
GRAINS   * MEAT/SEAFOOD/BEANS/NUTS
                                               *
                                               *
****
COOKED FRUIT   *COOKED VEGETABLES
                                               *
                                               *
****
PROCESSED FOODS   *PROCESSED LIQUIDS
                                               *
                                               *
****

ST-I used the tool of spiritual mind renewal (Read scriptures and daily reading on Temple Care)_____ **ST**-I used the tool of faith____ **ST**-I used the tool of support_____

Exercise (10+ minutes) ___ **ST**-I used the tool of prayer____

ST-I used the tool of repentance _____

ST-I used the tool of spiritual fasting – yes/no; juice fast-yes/no

SP-I'm being honest about and coping with my food temptations _____

SP-I ate more than what I needed _____

GOD DESIRES A PEOPLE WHOSE CHARACTER REVEALS A SPIRIT FREE FROM THE BONDAGE OF GLUTTONY.

"...do you not know your body is the temple of the Holy Spirit who is in you..."
1 Corinthians 6:19

Week Four–Day 24-Tuesday
God's Word on Gluttony
"Woe to thee, O land, when thy king is a child, and thy <u>princes eat in the morning!</u>"
Ecclesiastes 10:16

This scripture, although brief also relays the concept of gluttony. Solomon talks about how a country can be negatively affected by its leaders.

> "Nor is it much better with a people when their princes eat in the morning, that is, make a god of their belly and make themselves slaves to their appetites. If the king himself be a child, yet if the princes and privy-counsellors are wise and faithful, and apply themselves to business, the land may do the better; but if they addict themselves to their pleasures, and prefer the gratifications of the flesh before the dispatch of the public business, which they disfit themselves for by eating and drinking in a morning, when judges are epicures, and do not eat to live, but live to eat, what good can a nation expect!"(Matthew Henry's Commentary)

Question: Do you ever feel as if you eat excessively and are a slave to your appetite? If so, how do you feel when you are in this situation? What state are your spirit and the Holy Spirit in at this time?

_____
_____
_____

How do you feel when your hunger is satisfied?

_____

How do you feel when your hunger has been satiated moderately beyond satisfaction?

_____

How do you feel when you hunger is extremely satiated beyond satisfaction?

_____
_____

0---5--10
Not Satisfied   Satisfied   Beyond Satisfaction

On a scale from 1-10 how would you like to rate your satisfaction level as an indicator in knowing when to stop eating? Write down number and practice stopping at this rating when eating. _____

Contact your accountability partner and discuss your thoughts and responses to the questions above. Then tell what the experience of talking about this to your support/accountability partner was like for you? (Remember to continue the "Stop Short" and stop nibbling exercises)_____

How did the Holy Spirit try to influence your temple care today?_____
How did your flesh want to respond?_____
How did you respond?_____

**GOD DESIRES A PEOPLE WHOSE CHARACTER REVEALS A SPIRIT FREE
FROM THE BONDAGE OF GLUTTONY.**

F.I.R.E

FRESH FRUIT   * NATURAL OILS/FATS
****
                                                    *
                                                    *
****
FRESH VEGETABLES (CAN BE STEAMED)   *NATURAL SWEETNERS
                                                    *
                                                    *
****
GRAINS   * MEAT/SEAFOOD/BEANS/NUTS
                                                    *
                                                    *
****
*****
COOKED FRUIT   *COOKED VEGETABLES
                                                    *
                                                    *
****
PROCESSED FOODS   *PROCESSED LIQUIDS
                                                    *
                                                    *
****

ST-I used the tool of spiritual mind renewal (Read scriptures and daily reading on
Temple Care) _____ **ST-**I used the tool of faith_____ **ST-**I used the tool of support_____
ST-I used the tool of prayer_____ **ST-**I used the tool of repentance ___
Exercise **(10+ minutes)** ___
ST-I used the tool of spiritual fasting – yes/no; juice fast-yes/no
SP-I'm being honest about and coping with my food temptations _____
SP-I ate more than what I needed _____

"…do you not know your body is the temple of the Holy Spirit who is in you…"
1 Corinthians 6:19
Week Four–Day 25-Wednesday
God's Word on Gluttony
"For many walk, of whom I often told you, and now tell you even weeping, that they are enemies of the cross of Christ, whose end is destruction, whose <u>god is their belly (appetite)</u>, and whose glory is in their shame, who set their minds on earthly things."
Philippians 3:18, 19

Paul reveals the character of those who are enemies of the cross of Christ and whose end is inevitably destruction. He says that the god of such individuals is their bellies. In essence, Paul is saying that we must guard against allowing our sensual appetites to be our god/idol; always seeking to please them and make provision for them. The Matthew Henry Commentary states that having our bellies be our gods is "…a scandal for any, but especially for Christians because we sacrifice the favor of our God, the peace of our conscience and our eternal happiness to it!"

The word sacrifice does often come to mind when we think of a "god" or idol. Sometimes, I wonder what one is willing to sacrifice to their god (belly). Think about what you have sacrificed to the "god", your belly, throughout these years? Is it your willingness to be led by the Holy Spirit regarding food/drink, how you feel about yourself, the health of your gallbladder, the health of your blood pressure, the well-being of your loved ones because they are always worried about you…?

1._____
2._____
3._____

GOD DESIRES A PEOPLE WHOSE CHARACTER REVEALS A SPIRIT FREE FROM THE BONDAGE OF GLUTTONY.

F.I.R.E

FRESH FRUIT   * NATURAL OILS/FATS
****
                                                 *
                                                 *
****

FRESH VEGETABLES (CAN BE STEAMED)   *NATURAL SWEETNERS
                                                 *
                                                 *
****

GRAINS   * MEAT/SEAFOOD/BEANS/NUTS
                                                 *
                                                 *
****

COOKED FRUIT   *COOKED VEGETABLES
                                                 *
                                                 *
****

PROCESSED FOODS   *PROCESSED LIQUIDS
                                                 *
                                                 *
****

ST-I used the tool of spiritual mind renewal (Read scriptures and daily reading on Temple Care) _____ **ST**-I used the tool of faith____ **ST**-I used the tool of support_____
ST-I used the tool of prayer____   **ST**-I used the tool of repentance ___
Exercise (10+ minutes) ___
ST-I used the tool of spiritual fasting – yes/no; juice fast-yes/no
SP-I'm being honest about and coping with my food temptations _____
SP-I ate more than what I needed _____

"...do you not know your body is the temple of the Holy Spirit who is in you..."
1 Corinthians 6:19

Week Four–Day 26-Thursday
God's Word on Gluttony
Luke 16:19-31

I believe that God has placed this very powerful passage on my heart, for me, and possibly for you. Below, the words of our Lord Jesus reflect another angle from which each and every one of us may be challenged to look at the issue of food. Let us begin by reading the text in its entirety.

19 There was a certain rich man, which was clothed in purple and fine linen, and fared sumptuously every day:

20 And there was a certain beggar named Lazarus, which was laid at his gate, full of sores,

21 And desiring to be fed with the crumbs which fell from the rich man's table: moreover the dogs came and licked his sores.

22 And it came to pass, that the beggar died, and was carried by the angels into Abraham's bosom: the rich man also died, and was buried;

23 And in hell he lift up his eyes, being in torment, and seeth Abraham afar off, and Lazarus in his bosom.

24 And he cried and said, Father Abraham, have mercy on me, and send Lazarus, that he may dip the tip of his finger in water, and cool my tongue; for I am tormented in this flame.

25 But Abraham said, Son, remember that thou in thy lifetime receive thy good things, and likewise Lazarus evil things: but now he is comforted, and thou art tormented.

26 And beside all this, between us and you there is a great gulf fixed: so that they which would pass from hence to you cannot; neither can they pass to us, that would come from thence.

27 Then he said, I pray thee therefore, father, that thou would send him to my father's house:

28 For I have five brethren; that he may testify unto them, lest they also come into this place of torment.

29 Abraham said unto him, They have Moses and the prophets; let them hear them.

30 And he said, Nay, father Abraham: but if one went unto them from the dead, they will repent.

31 And he said unto him, If they hear not Moses and the prophets, neither will they be persuaded, though one rose from the dead.

KJV

We see that this rich man lived a life of abundance and convenience. He wore the attire of princes, which was the expensive, very precious material called Purple. Some also say that he had fine "night-linen" and "day-linen". This man received his material wealth through honest means, and he did not show that he exceeded what his wealth could provide. And even though he "fared sumptuously every day," our Lord does not suggest that this man engaged in excessive eating or gluttony. It's believed that he had "all the varieties and dainties that nature and art could supply" and well dressed servants for him and his many guests. His sin was not of gluttony in the sense of eating, yet it does show a form of gluttony. As stated earlier, gluttony is about having an "excessive appetite" and giving into it. This rich man showed an excessive appetite in accumulating much for himself and his pleasure with no desire to share anything of his (i.e. his food) with those who really needed it. His sin was saying, in essence, "All of my possessions are for me," and consequently he was not really concerned about others.

Question: How can we in the United States have so many overweight and obese individuals who are literally killing themselves and dying prematurely yet also have hundreds of streets full of hungry/malnourished men, women and children? How can this be? What's the cause? The answer is sin or transgression from God's Will/Word. The ancient, spiritual truth from God's Word has encouraged us from the beginning of time to live lives that show our love for our God, our fellow man and ourselves. We're asked to focus on all three. "If a brother or sister is without clothing and in need of daily food and one of you say to them, 'Go in peace, be warmed and be filled,' and yet you do not give them what is necessary for their body, what use is that?" James 3:11

What do you have an "excessive appetite" for? Is it food when all around you hungry people occupy this space of a world in which we all live? Is it clothing and shoes when all around you are people with tattered clothes and bare feet? Is it for homes and lots of cash in your pocket when all around you are homeless and penniless people? Is it even for love and attention from your family/friends by wanting them to constantly meet your needs when all around you are neglected, unloved, uncared for people?

Write about what you tend to have an excessive appetite for. Write about the pros and cons of it and how you can show God more thankfulness for the ways in which He provides for your appetite/needs now and how you can bless others with some of it.

_____
_____
_____
_____

How did the Holy Spirit try to influence your temple care today?_____
How did your flesh want to respond?_____
How did you respond?_____

GOD DESIRES A PEOPLE WHOSE CHARACTER REVEALS A SPIRIT FREE FROM THE BONDAGE OF GLUTTONY.

F.I.R.E

FRESH FRUIT   * NATURAL OILS/FATS
****
                                               *
                                               *
****
FRESH VEGETABLES (CAN BE STEAMED)   *NATURAL SWEETNERS
                                               *
                                               *
****
GRAINS   * MEAT/SEAFOOD/BEANS/NUTS
                                               *
                                               *
****
COOKED FRUIT   *COOKED VEGETABLES
                                               *
                                               *
****
PROCESSED FOODS   *PROCESSED LIQUIDS
                                               *
                                               *
****

ST-I used the tool of spiritual mind renewal (Read scriptures and daily reading on Temple Care) _____ **ST**-I used the tool of faith_____ **ST**-I used the tool of support_____
ST-I used the tool of prayer_____ **ST**-I used the tool of repentance ___
Exercise (10+ minutes) ___
ST-I used the tool of spiritual fasting – yes/no; juice fast-yes/no
SP-I'm being honest about and coping with my food temptations _____
SP-I ate more than what I needed _____

"...do you not know your body is the temple of the Holy Spirit who is in you..."
1 Corinthians 6:19

Week Four–Day 27-Friday
God's Word on Gluttony
Ruth 2:14 and Genesis 43:16

"It was customary among the ancient Hebrews, as among their contemporaries in the East in classical lands, to have but two meals a day." (International Standard Bible Encyclopedia, 1996).

The following information is presented not in an attempt to establish a new recommended eating schedule (like the well known 3x a day breakfast, lunch and dinner or the current 4-6 meals a day). This information is presented to simply allow some to see that many of our ancestors ate only 2 meals a day and fared fine with that schedule. Some of us may not only be eating too much food at one sitting but may also eat too often throughout the day. Some say that the first meal for the ancient Hebrews/Christians was about noontime. This was after one had put in some work during the morning hours and the heat of the day was increased (sometimes that time varied due to one's status and occupation).

Luke 14:16, Mark 6:35, Matt. 14:15 and Luke 9:12

The second meal of the day was usually around the setting of the sun, when the work for the day was complete and often times family members came together.

I am not recommending a certain number of times for daily food intake because I believe that our individual differences should play a part in the activity. To truly know what is best for *your* system means that *you* have to come to *know yourself more intimately.* Yes, intimately, meaning that you have to be open with and attentive toward yourself and your body. For instance, I have learned that often when I want to eat during late evening or night hours, it is because I'm tired or fatigued and not hungry. I've also noticed, since my teen years, that eating after 7 or 8 p.m. often negatively affects my sleep and/or bother my stomach. I also know that I'm naturally hungry in the morning (since I don't usually eat late at night) and that fruit or oatmeal and lots of fluids (for breakfast) are perfect to get my system working and eliminating well. Additionally, my sinuses do not respond well to dairy products, so I eat them seldom and use more organic brown rice and occasionally goat's milk based products as substitutes. Remember, it's good to have rules yet we must not ignore what our individual bodily systems are saying to us and work with instead of against them.

What are some times throughout the day that your body appears to respond negatively to food?

_____

Although you may like them, make a list of the foods which your body tends to respond negatively. Also, write down *how* your body tends to respond to these foods.

_____
_____
_____

Try This Out

It's been recommended to drink a glass of water first, when you are feeling hungry (particularly when you don't feel as if you should be hungry, like fairly soon after a meal). This is because many people misinterpret their thirst cues for hunger cues. "Water even eliminated late night hunger pangs for most dieters, according to a study at the University of Washington" (Natural Health, July/August, 2004). Chewing gum can also replace the desire to have something in your mouth or to taste something. I used to have a basket of loose gum in my living room. For some individuals a better place for your gum is in the kitchen!).

How did the Holy Spirit try to influence your temple care today?_____

How did your flesh want to respond?_____

How did you respond?_____

F.I.R.E

FRESH FRUIT   * NATURAL OILS/FATS
****
                                               *
                                               *
****
FRESH VEGETABLES (CAN BE STEAMED)   *NATURAL SWEETNERS
                                               *
                                               *
****
GRAINS   * MEAT/SEAFOOD/BEANS/NUTS
                                               *
                                               *
****
COOKED FRUIT   *COOKED VEGETABLES
                                               *
                                               *
****
PROCESSED FOODS   *PROCESSED LIQUIDS
                                               *
                                               *
****

ST-I used the tool of spiritual mind renewal (Read scriptures and daily reading on Temple Care) _____ **ST-I used the tool of faith**_____ **ST-I used the tool of support**_____
ST-I used the tool of prayer_____ **ST-I used the tool of repentance** ___
Exercise (10+ minutes) ___
ST-I used the tool of spiritual fasting – yes/no; juice fast-yes/no
SP-I'm being honest about and coping with my food temptations _____
SP-I ate more than what I needed_____

"...do you not know your body is the temple of the Holy Spirit who is in you..."
1 Corinthians 6:19
Week Four–Day 28-Saturday
Summary
<u>God's Word on Gluttony</u>

Glutton, what an unattractive word which most of us would rather not be identified with! Yet, all of us have been gluttonous with food at one time or another. What we need to change is our lifestyle of gluttony. God does not call us to perfection each moment of the day. He does call us toward a walk or lifestyle that strives toward perfection only through His power. It's inevitable that when it comes to eating, we will find ourselves overeating or feeling stuffed every once in a while. The key is to strive to eliminate gluttony from our regular, normal style of eating. God has blessed us with so many pleasurable things and experiences! Let's make sure we keep these blessings and experiences in their proper perspective. Meaning we avoid having an excessive appetite for what God created, otherwise, they can become our "gods". And when this happens we no longer allow God, our Creator, to control our lives but rather His creation and our greed it.

How did the Holy Spirit try to influence your temple care today?_____
How did your flesh want to respond?_____
How did you respond?_____

SNACKING: The No Prayer Zone?

As we complete this section, I want to leave you with a thought…and of course, a spiritual challenge. Many snack and nibble throughout the day without thanking God for the food yet when you sit down to eat a meal you then pray. Why is that? Why is a snack not worth praying over? Please, know that my point here is NOT about being "legalistic". I mention this to encourage us to be thoughtful and thankful about everything God has provided us to eat. Hummm, such thoughtfulness may even decrease ones tendency to needlessly snack and nibble. Pray about it and see what God reveals to you.

**GOD DESIRES A PEOPLE WHOSE CHARACTER REVEALS A SPIRIT
FREE FROM THE BONDAGE OF GLUTTONY**

F.I.R.E

FRESH FRUIT   * NATURAL OILS/FATS
****
                                             *
                                             *
****
FRESH VEGETABLES (CAN BE STEAMED)   *NATURAL SWEETNERS
                                             *
                                             *
****
GRAINS   * MEAT/SEAFOOD/BEANS/NUTS
                                             *
                                             *
****
COOKED FRUIT   *COOKED VEGETABLES
                                             *
                                             *
****
PROCESSED FOODS   *PROCESSED LIQUIDS
                                             *
                                             *
****

ST-I used the tool of spiritual mind renewal (Read scriptures and daily reading on Temple Care) _____ **ST**-I used the tool of faith____ **ST**-I used the tool of support_____
ST-I used the tool of prayer____ **ST**-I used the tool of repentance ___
Exercise **(10+ minutes)** ___
ST-I used the tool of spiritual fasting – yes/no; juice fast-yes/no
SP-I'm being honest about and coping with my food temptations _____
SP-I ate more than what I needed _____

Self Regulating Sheet

Looking back on this week's F.I.R.E. forms how did you do?

1. Spiritual mind renewal (reading what the bible says about Temple Care)
How did I rate this week with this spiritual tool? _____
1-10 (1=not well at all) (10= praise God really well!)

2. Faith (actions toward Godly Temple Care)
How did I rate this week with this spiritual tool? _____
1-10 (1=not well at all) (10= praise God really well!)

3. Support (contacting spiritual support partner/s and discuss Temple Care)
How did I rate this week with this spiritual tool? _____
1-10 (1=not well at all) (10= praise God really well!)

4. Prayer (praying to God about any and every issue regarding my Temple Care)
How did I rate this week with this spiritual tool? _____
1-10 (1=not well at all) (10= praise God really well!)

5. Repentance (expressing Godly sorrow and changing my ways through the Holy Spirit)
How did I rate this week with this spiritual tool? _____
1-10 (1=not well at all) (10= praise God really well!)

6. Fasting (not eating for 1 day or 3 dinners and replace with prayer, singing, reading God's Word...)
How did I rate this week with this spiritual tool? _____
1-10 (1=not well at all) (10= praise God really well!)

7. This week the following came easy for me regarding care of my temple?

_____

_____

8. This week the following was very difficult for me regarding caring for my temple?

_____

_____

9. After evaluating my ratings this week, these two spiritual tools (choose the lowest rated ones) are what I need to improve on next week regarding temple care?

_____

_____

God's Word on Temperance
Week Five

"...do you not know your body is the temple of the Holy Spirit who is in you..."
1 Corinthians 6:19

Week Five-Day 29-Sunday
God's Word on Temperance
"But the fruit of the Spirit is love, joy, peace, longsuffering, gentleness, goodness, faith, meekness, <u>temperance</u>; against such there is no law.
Galatians 5:22

Galatians 5:16-23 is a powerful passage that clearly notes the opposition between man's flesh and spirit. It's translated as meaning if man walks in accordance to the flesh or spirit then he is inherently against the other. <u>This is what I consider the true issue regarding the society's "War on Weight": we must seek spiritual guidance to truly combat the works of the flesh because most don't have the discipline to do it alone!</u> Paul lists some of the "works of the flesh" and states that for us to combat them, we must surrender to the "fruit of the Spirit" (the verse for the day). After the beautiful listing of spiritual fruit, he states, "against such there is no law," meaning we can have as much of this fruit as we want! Temperance, the fruit of the Spirit that specifically deals with issues of self-control/self restraint, is what I feel will help us as we continue to understand the spiritual implications regarding ones destructive style of eating.

The Matthew Henry Bible Commentary suggest that this type of self-control that Paul is talking about can only be experienced through the **aid of God's Spirit**. In essence, the mastery of various desires can *only* be attained through the Spirit and not just ones' willpower. This fruit is what TRULY liberates us from destructive desires! I've heard various people (famous people in the media, clients, family members) express that even though they've lost weight they still tend to "obsess", ruminate, or consistently think about their weight! They obsessively fear they'll gain the weight back, they obsess over how they look in their new body, they tend to be preoccupied with other peoples' weight/body and compare them to their own, or they obsess about food! These people, although slimmer, are not liberated! I believe that their will power helped them obtain their weight loss, but they have not capitalized on the Spirit-aided fruit of temperance. **One vice is exchanged for another; they control their eating and weight but they can't control their thoughts about their eating and/or weight.**

I'm finding out more and more each day that God is really about developing a type of spirit in HIS people that more accurately reflects Him. So, the real issue is beyond me trying to perfectly abide by various spiritual principles but that I increasingly learn to fully surrender to God's principles so that they change my very spirit, my very essence.

C.S. Lewis gives a wonderful example in his book "Mere Christianity" (1952) about exemplifying temperate actions versus being a temperate individual. He talks about the "good tennis player" or reliable tennis player who has exceptionally well trained eyes, muscles and nerves due to his or her consistent and persistent practicing of "good shots". This can bring about a certain quality in this individual even off of the tennis court. But, an individual who's a "bad tennis player" may make a "good shot" because he gets mad and hits the ball extra hard. He may even have a good game every now and then but he has not acquired the quality of a reliable tennis player. Lewis states, "We might think that God wanted simply obedience to a set of rules: whereas He really wants people of a particular sort." In addressing weight loss, let's sincerely evoke God's Spirit in aiding us so that we'll more accurately reflect who our God is with a true quality, spirit of temperance.

Weeks ago, I encouraged you to rid your kitchen of man-made food products and purchase God's food (See "Universal Food List" and the "Favorite Foods Created by God"). At this time, I encourage you to reassess your kitchen, filling it with only God created food (and with what is closest to His created food sources). Some people believe that they must depend on willpower alone to resist temptation. However, avoidance, because it helps eliminate temptation, is a key technique in this change process. Avoidance does not reflect poor self-control; in fact, sometimes self-control includes the ability to keep a problem from starting.

List what you need to avoid by getting it out of your kitchen?

How did the Holy Spirit try to influence your temple care today?_____

How did your flesh want to respond?_____

How did you respond?_____

GOD DESIRES A PEOPLE WHOSE CHARACTER REVEALS A SPIRIT OF TEMPERANCE THROUGH GOD'S AID.

F.I.R.E

FRESH FRUIT	* NATURAL OILS/FATS

****
```
                                                *
                                                *
```
****

FRESH VEGETABLES (CAN BE STEAMED)   *NATURAL SWEETNERS
```
                                                *
                                                *
```
****

GRAINS   * MEAT/SEAFOOD/BEANS/NUTS
```
                                                *
                                                *
```
****

COOKED FRUIT   *COOKED VEGETABLES
```
                                                *
                                                *
```
****

PROCESSED FOODS   *PROCESSED LIQUIDS
```
                                                *
                                                *
```
****

ST-I used the tool of spiritual mind renewal (Read scriptures and daily reading on Temple Care) _____   **ST-**I used the tool of faith_____   **ST-**I used the tool of support_____
ST-I used the tool of prayer_____   **ST-**I used the tool of repentance ____
Exercise (10+ minutes) ____
ST-I used the tool of spiritual fasting – yes/no; juice fast-yes/no
SP-I'm being honest about and coping with my food temptations _____
SP-I ate more than what I needed _____
SP-I demonstrated temperance (Spirit-aided self-control) _____

"...do you not know your body is the temple of the Holy Spirit who is in you..."
1 Corinthians 6:19

Week Five–Day 30-Monday
God's Word on Temperance
"According as His divine power hath given unto us all things that pertain unto life and godliness, through the knowledge of Him that hath called us to glory and virtue: Whereby are given unto us exceeding great and precious promises: that by these ye might be partakers of the divine nature, having escaped the corruption that is in the world through lust. And beside this, giving all diligence, add to your faith virtue; and, to virtue knowledge; And to knowledge __temperance; and to temperance__ *patience; and to patience godliness; And to godliness brotherly kindness; and to brotherly kindness charity. For if these things be in you, and abound, they make you that ye shall neither be barren nor unfruitful in the knowledge of our Lord Jesus Christ."*
II Peter 1:3-8

The glory and virtue (excellence) of our Lord and Savior Jesus Christ draws us to reproduce His character in ourselves. Therefore, giving our very mind, body and spirit as an offering to Him to whom we belong is the "all-inclusive goal of Christian living" (Wycliffe, 1990). Ours is a goal of continual spiritual character development. Let us commit not only to weight loss, health, weight gain or to a lifestyle change. Let's commit to tapping into God's divine nature which He wants to share with us! Let's commit to tapping more and more into a crucial fruit of the Spirit called Temperance.

Fake It Until You Make It
An incredible woman and friend of mine, years ago, told me something I cherished as a wide-eyed, college freshman away from home. She said to decide what goal(s) I wanted regarding any area of my life and then to fake it till' I made it! For instance, I "faked" being a successful doctoral student until I actually became one! I "faked" playing the part of a successful doctoral student means that I *studied hard, read a lot, sought out mentors,* and *only hung around other "successful doctoral students"*. In relation to your weight loss and/or improved nutritional health, I suggest you "fake" being successful at weight loss and improving your health! At this point in the program what do you need to do more of and less of to fake success?

At this point in the program if you need to be rejuvenated by God's aid to press on, then contemplate whether you need to fast again to provoke His presence, guidance and strength. You may want to re-read the section "Spiritual Fast" to determine if you need added strength during this portion of the program to do what He is calling you to do. If so, choose and prepare for a specific day this week to engage in your spiritual fast, and talk to your support partner about it.

How did the Holy Spirit try to influence your temple care today?_____

How did your flesh want to respond?_____

How did you respond?_____

GOD DESIRES A PEOPLE WHOSE CHARACTER REVEALS A SPIRIT OF TEMPERANCE THROUGH GOD'S AID.

F.I.R.E

FRESH FRUIT	* NATURAL OILS/FATS

****
*
*
****

FRESH VEGETABLES (CAN BE STEAMED)	*NATURAL SWEETNERS

*
*
****

GRAINS	* MEAT/SEAFOOD/BEANS/NUTS

*
*
****

COOKED FRUIT	*COOKED VEGETABLES

*
*
****

PROCESSED FOODS	*PROCESSED LIQUIDS

*
*
****

ST-I used the tool of spiritual mind renewal (Read scriptures and daily reading on Temple Care) _____ **ST-**I used the tool of faith_____ **ST-**I used the tool of support_____
ST-I used the tool of prayer_____ **ST-**I used the tool of repentance ____
Exercise (10+ minutes) ____
ST-I used the tool of spiritual fasting – yes/no; juice fast-yes/no
SP-I'm being honest about and coping with my food temptations ____
SP-I ate more than what I needed _____
SP-I demonstrated temperance (Spirit-aided self-control) ____

115

"...do you not know your body is the temple of the Holy Spirit who is in you..."
1 Corinthians 6:19

Week Five–Day 31-Tuesday
God's Word on Temperance
"This know also, that in the last days perilous times shall come. For men shall be lovers of their own selves, covetous, boasters, proud, blasphemers, disobedient to parents, unthankful, unholy, Without natural affection, truce-breakers, false accusers, <u>incontinent,</u> fierce, despisers of those that are good, Traitors,, heady, high-minded, lovers of pleasures more than lovers of God; Having a form of godliness, but denying the power thereof: from such turn away.
II Timothy 3:1-5

Often, when immersed in my relationship with God, He shows me that I possess many (if not, at certain times all) of the characteristics stated above. I praise God for giving me such intimate knowledge of myself and His love for me. He grants all of us so much grace & mercy!

As you read the verses above, you came across the word incontinent which is the opposite of self-control; it's the lack of self-control. God desires that we come to understand that when we lack Spirit-aided self-control in various areas of our lives, we are denying His power and are not pleasing to Him.

While writing this workbook, I wanted to title a section "Get over it! It's just a brownie!" Yet, I decided otherwise one Friday evening, after a long, chaotic week. I began to crave my favorite dessert (at the time), brownies and ice cream. I had not been eating my normal intake of sweet fruit daily (which by the way seems to curb my desire to eat unhealthy, overly processed desserts) for that entire week. Therefore, by the weekend, I desperately wanted something sweet even though I'd already exceeded my weekly brownie intake comfort level! So, in an attempt to eliminate the sweet temptation, I quoted one of the easiest, quickest and relevant scripture that came to my mind. *"I can do ALL things through Christ who strengthens me"!* I said it a few more times out loud and even louder: *"I can do ALL things through Christ who strengthens me!"* And something surprising happened! That sweet tooth craving kicked back harder and harder and actually tormented me for the next 30 minutes or so! In this situation, I did not feel relief in quoting scripture, like I had in the past. For a moment, I felt like crying and if you actually do, it's okay because going toe to toe with the flesh, especially when you are feeling tired and weak, is truly very difficult. It can be surprisingly difficult even when it comes to something as "seemingly" insignificant as food. Also, I began to question my own dedication to temple care because I had eaten poorly all week!

To change the tide, I first made sure that it wasn't really hunger calling me and it wasn't since I had recently eaten. Second, I mentally gave myself permission to feel tired after a rough week and recognized that that was why I wanted something sweet to eat. Third, I decided that if that sweet tooth still plague me after I completed #4 then I'd eat a bowl of "Strawberry cereal" (recipe in back of workbook!) instead of brownies and ice cream. The fourth thing I did was jump in a warm bath of water. I recognized that I really needed rest when I kept hearing softly in my mind "You need to go to bed" But I was determined to boost my energy level by eating something sweet and "escape" with something pleasurable. After soaking in the tub, I surprisingly went straight to bed. I had planned on journaling about my struggle with temperance while eating my bowl of cereal but ended up falling asleep, which was what I *really* needed in the first place.

In other cases, I've recommended that if the above stated coping skills do not help, then to again WAIT until true hunger (rather then appetite/cravings) kicks in. During your wait use the tool of prayer, scripture reading, or call someone (i.e. accountability partner). If you still feel tormented about having the brownie (I've been there) then have a bit of brownie remembering to solicit the Holy Spirit's aid in being temperate.

Again, in practicing temperance, so that later it becomes a part of your character, seek God's guidance first (through prayer, scripture reading...)! Next, try hard not to eat until you are hungry. Why? The body is more likely to use the calories you intake because it's physiologically requiring some food due to your hunger. But, the energy from food that is not physiologically needed when you are not hungry is more apt to be stored as fat. Lastly, when you get hungry, choose a healthier food that can still satisfy your tastes (i.e. nuts rather than potato chips if you want something salty, or fresh fruit or a fruit smoothie rather than cake if you want something sweet). And remember to be temperate, even with that which is healthy. I have a friend who chose not to eat a bunch of junk food he was craving yet instead he ate over eight pints of strawberries! Although he made a healthy choice he forgot about the issue of gluttony! And, if you end up overeating anyway, repent if the Spirit was trying to guide you to temperance, make sure you thanked God for the food (we'll discuss later) and immediately get back on the right track...guilt free, freed by God!

Out To Dinner Exercise

Schedule a time to go out with your accountability partner to a restaurant for dinner within the next week or two. Order your favorite meal, God's food preferably (i.e. BQ ribs, baked potato, coleslaw...) on the menu. Then slowly eat half of the meal and take the other half home. If it's an extra large sized meal and you usually eat only half of it, then eat only a third of the meal. Also, make sure that you do not snack on appetizers, breads or tortilla chips. This is an exercise to help break the way one has been conditioned to eat which is in excess. When you return home, complete the following questions.

What were your thoughts during the meal?

_____

_____

What were your feelings during the meal?

_____

_____

What did you learn about yourself and/or your style of eating during the meal or in retrospect?

_____

_____

_____

GOD DESIRES A PEOPLE WHOSE CHARACTER REVEALS A SPIRIT OF TEMPERANCE THROUGH GOD'S AID.

F.I.R.E

FRESH FRUIT   * NATURAL OILS/FATS

****
                                         *
                                         *

****

FRESH VEGETABLES (CAN BE STEAMED)   *NATURAL SWEETNERS
                                         *
                                         *

****

GRAINS   * MEAT/SEAFOOD/BEANS/NUTS
                                         *
                                         *

****

COOKED FRUIT   *COOKED VEGETABLES
                                         *
                                         *

****

PROCESSED FOODS   *PROCESSED LIQUIDS
                                         *
                                         *

****

ST-I used the tool of spiritual mind renewal (Read scriptures and daily reading on Temple Care) _____ **ST**-I used the tool of faith____ **ST**-I used the tool of support_____
ST-I used the tool of prayer____ **ST**-I used the tool of repentance ___
Exercise (10+ minutes) ___
ST-I used the tool of spiritual fasting – yes/no; juice fast-yes/no
SP-I'm being honest about and coping with my food temptations ___
SP-I ate more than what I needed _____
SP-I demonstrated temperance (Spirit-aided self-control) ___

"...do you not know your body is the temple of the Holy Spirit who is in you..."
1 Corinthians 6:19
Week Five-Day 32-Wednesday
<u>God's Word on Temperance</u>
"And when the woman <u>saw</u> that the tree was good for food, and that it was pleasant to the eyes, and a tree to be desired to make one wise, <u>she took</u> of the fruit thereof, <u>and did eat</u>, and gave also unto her husband with her; and he did eat."
Genesis 3:6

Do you think it is by chance that so many people in our society are prematurely ending their lives due to their lack of temple care? Do you think that it's by chance that people are significantly decreasing their quality of life by choosing a lifestyle that promotes diabetes, high blood pressure, obesity...?

Satan is constantly trying to tempt our human nature and overpower our spirit, which is nurtured by and commune's with God's Spirit within us. For many, God's Spirit is the only true way in which we can overcome temptations with food which can lead to premature death and/or a poor quality of life. Let's look at one of two powerful stories that reveal Satan's attempt to use food and mankind's fleshly needs/desires as a means to destroy them.

The first story begins in the book of Genesis. Isn't it interesting that the first sin ever committed by man, in part, had to do with food, from a tree which God prohibited? Subtle, deceitful, Satan used the tangible vehicle of food and the intangible desire to be like God to tempt Eve and Adam to disobey God. The Matthew Henry Commentary notes Eve's steps of transgression.

> "**1.**<u>She saw.</u> A great deal of sin comes in at the eye. Let us not look on that which we are in danger of lusting after, Matthew 5:28. **2.** <u>She took.</u> It was her own act and deed. Satan may tempt, but he cannot force; may persuade us to cast ourselves down, but he cannot cast us down, Matthew 4:6. **3.** <u>She did eat.</u> When she looked perhaps she did not intend to take; or when she took, not to eat; but it ended in that. It is wisdom to stop the first motions of sin, and to leave it off before it be meddled with."

Sometimes, I wonder if Satan, in his cunning, deceitful nature, has deceived many into actually killing themselves through chronic diseases (heart disease, diabetes, strokes, lung cancer...). Or, maybe he has deceived individuals into at least significantly decreasing their quality of life through chronic diseases *by their own hands*.

I remember, years ago, talking to a group of individuals, who wanted to lose weight, about the unique difficulty in dealing with food. They stated that food is one of the only substances in that we cannot totally abstain from. An alcoholic can keep all alcohol out of his or her home and can find new friends who don't drink, and leave the ones who drink behind. In reality, the addictive potential is different with food versus drugs, yet, it is true that regarding food, we all have to eat to live. On a regular basis, we have to ingest food, so we can not totally abstain from it. With this being the case, let us learn to use the spiritual opportunity of becoming temperate, which God intends for us to be and secondarily improve our health. How are you responding to this spiritual opportunity?

Spirit-Aided Self-Control Exercise

What is the food(s)/drink that you ingest that you believe contributes the most to your unsatisfactory weight range and/or health status?   How often do you tend to eat that food/drink?

	Food	**Intake frequency (a week)**	**Portion size (each intake)**
Ex.	Pizza	2x a week	4 slices each intake
Ex.	Dessert	3x a week	1 (large) slice/piece each intake
	_____	_____	_____
	_____	_____	_____
	_____	_____	_____
	_____	_____	_____

What is it about the above listed substances that are so desirable to you? What does God's Spirit often tell you about these substances?

_____

_____

If you reduced how often (frequency) and the size you eat the food(s)/drink you listed, how often could you eat the food and not feel significantly deprived? This week spend more time praying about these substances and practice eating/drinking the substance less this week.

	Food	**Frequency of intake (a week)**	**Portion size**
Ex.	Pizza	1x a week	2 slices
Ex.	Dessert	1x a week	1 medium size
	_____	_____	_____
	_____	_____	_____
	_____	_____	_____
	_____	_____	_____

Discus your experience with being more temperate._____

_____

How did the Holy Spirit try to influence your temple care today?_____

How did your flesh want to respond?_____

How did you respond?_____

GOD DESIRES A PEOPLE WHOSE CHARACTER REVEALS A SPIRIT OF TEMPERANCE THROUGH GOD'S AID.

F.I.R.E

| FRESH FRUIT | * NATURAL OILS/FATS |

****
*
*
****

FRESH VEGETABLES (CAN BE STEAMED)   *NATURAL SWEETNERS
*
*

****

GRAINS   * MEAT/SEAFOOD/BEANS/NUTS
*
*

****

COOKED FRUIT   *COOKED VEGETABLES
*
*

****

PROCESSED FOODS   *PROCESSED LIQUIDS
*
*

****

ST-I used the tool of spiritual mind renewal (Read scriptures and daily reading on Temple Care) _____   **ST**-I used the tool of faith____   **ST**-I used the tool of support_____
ST-I used the tool of prayer____   **ST**-I used the tool of repentance ___
Exercise (10+ minutes) ___
ST-I used the tool of spiritual fasting – yes/no; juice fast-yes/no
SP-I'm being honest about and coping with my food temptations ___
SP-I ate more than what I needed _____
SP-I used temperance (Spirit-aided self-control) _____

"...do you not know your body is the temple of the Holy Spirit who is in you..."
1 Corinthians 6:19
Week Five–Day 33-Thursday
God's Word on Temperance
"And Jesus being full of the Holy Ghost returned from Jordan, and was led by the Spirit into the wilderness, Being <u>forty days tempted of the devil</u>. And in those days <u>he did eat nothing: and when they were ended, <u>he afterward hungered. And the devil said unto him, If thou be the Son of God, command this stone that it be made bread. And Jesus answered him, saying, It is written, That man shall not live by bread alone, but by every word of God."
Luke 4:1-4

This next story, as the one yesterday, will exemplify a point that many of us need to understand more clearly. The point is that Satan seeks opportunities to attack our human nature/flesh in ANY way possible. Do not be so naïve as to how Satan tries to attack us. Wherever he finds lust of the flesh, lust of the eyes or the pride of life is where he attacks us. Wherever he finds an opportunity to break us down spiritually, he'll do so (which can also become our spiritual opportunity for growth if we overcome with God's aid).

Our Lord Jesus was led into the wilderness by the Holy Spirit to be tempted by Satan. Jesus conquered the temptations of the devil where Adam/Eve failed (discussed yesterday). Adam and Eve succumbed to Satan's temptation yet Jesus did not.

Luke arranged the temptations of Jesus starting with ones bodily needs/requirements. Food was what Satan first tried to tempt Jesus with! Adam and Eve and Jesus all tempted with the tangible object of food! Yet, as with us, He was also getting at something deeper then the temptation of food! Satan knew that Jesus had been fasting, and he used the object/vehicle of food to try to get Jesus to *obey him*. Satan appealed to an appropriate desire (the desire to eat for strength and life), yet Satan wanted Jesus to heed to his suggestion to satisfy His own needs. Jesus did not use His power to make things comfortable for Himself/His flesh because He knew that God wanted Him to sharpen His focus on the work God set before Him, and not His own needs.

The point I'd like to draw from this story is that we must remember that Satan will provoke us, any way he can, to live a life that is lacking in self-control. For some of us, Satan has been successfully using food to primarily weaken our walk with and obedience to God, therefore poorly demonstrating the spiritual fruit of temperance and secondarily weaken our bodies.

List your top 3 food related tempting scenarios that you have succumbed to recently and 3 ways to exhibit temperance/self-control over them.

Succumbed to Scenarios	Spirit-aided/controlled Scenarios
EXAMPLE	EXAMPLE
Not hungry yet want something to nibble on	"Nibble" on husband/kids or on a project you've wanted to complete!

1.

2.

3.

How did the Holy Spirit try to influence your temple care today?_____
How did your flesh want to respond?_____
How did you respond?_____

GOD DESIRES A PEOPLE WHOSE CHARACTER REVEALS A SPIRIT OF TEMPERANCE THROUGH GOD'S AID.

F.I.R.E

FRESH FRUIT   * NATURAL OILS/FATS
****
                                                       *
                                                       *
****
FRESH VEGETABLES (CAN BE STEAMED)   *NATURAL SWEETNERS
                                                       *
                                                       *
****
GRAINS   * MEAT/SEAFOOD/BEANS/NUTS
                                                       *
                                                       *
****
COOKED FRUIT   *COOKED VEGETABLES
                                                       *
                                                       *
****
PROCESSED FOODS   *PROCESSED LIQUIDS
                                                       *
                                                       *
****

<u>ST-I used the tool of spiritual mind renewal</u> (Read scriptures and daily reading on Temple Care) _____ **ST**-I used the tool of faith_____ **ST**-I used the tool of support_____
ST-I used the tool of prayer_____ **ST**-I used the tool of repentance ____
Exercise (10+ minutes) ____
ST-I used the tool of spiritual fasting – yes/no; juice fast-yes/no
SP-I'm being honest about and coping with my food temptations ____
SP-I ate more than what I needed _____
<u>SP-I used temperance (Spirit-aided self-control)</u> ____

"...do you not know your body is the temple of the Holy Spirit who is in you..."
1 Corinthians 6:19

Week Five-Day 34-Friday
God's Word on Temperance
"Rejoice in the Lord always: and again I say, Rejoice. Let your <u>moderation</u> be known unto all men. The Lord is at hand.
Philippians 4:5

An observable characteristic that you and I must strive to exhibit, not for show but for God's glory is "moderation". Moderation in this context is believed to mean that one can control or restrain their desires and passions. Barnes' Notes (1997) suggests that in this scripture, one is to avoid "excess of passion, or dress, or eating, or drinking". We Christians are to manage our appetites, tempers and be gentle, good examples, as we wait for God to appear.

What has it felt like for you to practice more temperance/moderation this week?

Continuing to practice the spiritual fruit of temperance will bring what positive changes and why?

GOD DESIRES A PEOPLE WHOSE CHARACTER REVEALS A SPIRIT OF TEMPERANCE THROUGH GOD'S AID.

F.I.R.E

FRESH FRUIT   * NATURAL OILS/FATS
****
                                               *
                                               *
****
FRESH VEGETABLES (CAN BE STEAMED)   *NATURAL SWEETNERS
                                               *
                                               *
****
GRAINS   * MEAT/SEAFOOD/BEANS/NUTS
                                               *
                                               *
****
COOKED FRUIT   *COOKED VEGETABLES
                                               *
                                               *
****
PROCESSED FOODS   *PROCESSED LIQUIDS
                                               *
                                               *
****

ST-I used the tool of spiritual mind renewal (Read scriptures and daily reading on Temple Care) _____ **ST-**I used the tool of faith____ **ST-**I used the tool of support_____
ST-I used the tool of prayer____ **ST-**I used the tool of repentance ___
Exercise (10+ minutes) ___
ST-I used the tool of spiritual fasting – yes/no; juice fast-yes/no
SP-I'm being honest about and coping with my food temptations ___
SP-I ate more than what I needed _____
SP-I used temperance (Spirit-aided self-control)_____

"...do you not know your body is the temple of the Holy Spirit who is in you..."
1 Corinthians 6:19

Week Five-Day 35-Saturday
Summary
God's Word on Temperance

All of us have areas (not just one area) where we need God's aid in developing within us temperance/Spirit-aided self-control. No one is exempt! We have weaknesses, insecurities and frailties, and we need God and His wise instruction to help us grow and improve spiritually. As I mature, I realize more and more that being the spiritually mature being God wants me to be most often develops through simple daily experiences rather than monumental ones. Some simple daily experiences that aid in spiritual growth are possessing a child-like thankfulness in everything, always rejoicing and praying non-stop (I Thessalonians 5:16-18); or esteeming, thinking about, helping and encouraging the people God places on my path (Philippians 2:3); telling others of God's power in my life (Matthew 10:32 & 33), seeking God's Will first in my daily walk rather than my own (Matthew 6:33), and studying the bible (II Tim.2:15). So, even how I eat/drink daily can allow me to nurture the spirit-aided fruit of temperance and consequently impacting my spiritual growth (1 Corinthians 10:31).

How did the Holy Spirit try to influence your temple care today?_____
How did your flesh want to respond?_____
How did you respond?_____

**GOD DESIRES A PEOPLE WHOSE CHARACTER REVEALS A SPIRIT OF
TEMPERANCE THROUGH GOD'S AID.**

F.I.R.E

FRESH FRUIT	* NATURAL OILS/FATS

****
*
*
****

FRESH VEGETABLES (CAN BE STEAMED)   *NATURAL SWEETNERS
*
*

****
GRAINS   * MEAT/SEAFOOD/BEANS/NUTS
*
*

****
COOKED FRUIT   *COOKED VEGETABLES
*
*

****
PROCESSED FOODS   *PROCESSED LIQUIDS
*
*

****

ST-I used the tool of spiritual mind renewal (Read scriptures and daily reading on Temple Care) _____ **ST**-I used the tool of faith____ **ST**-I used the tool of support_____
ST-I used the tool of prayer____   **ST**-I used the tool of repentance ___
Exercise (10+ minutes) ___
ST-I used the tool of spiritual fasting – yes/no; juice fast-yes/no
SP-I'm being honest about and coping with my food temptations ___
SP-I ate more than what I needed _____
SP-I used temperance (Spirit-aided self-control) ____

Self Regulating Sheet

Looking back on this week's F.I.R.E. forms how did you do?

1. Spiritual mind renewal (reading what the bible says about Temple Care)
How did I rate this week with this spiritual tool? _____
1-10 (1=not well at all) (10= praise God really well!)

2. Faith (actions toward Godly Temple Care)
How did I rate this week with this spiritual tool? _____
1-10 (1=not well at all) (10= praise God really well!)

3. Support (contacting spiritual support partner/s and discuss Temple Care)
How did I rate this week with this spiritual tool? _____
1-10 (1=not well at all) (10= praise God really well!)

4. Prayer (praying to God about any and every issue regarding my Temple Care)
How did I rate this week with this spiritual tool? _____
1-10 (1=not well at all) (10= praise God really well!)

5. Repentance (expressing Godly sorrow and changing my ways through the Holy Spirit)
How did I rate this week with this spiritual tool? _____
1-10 (1=not well at all) (10= praise God really well!)

6. Fasting (not eating for 1 day or 3 dinners and replace with prayer, singing, reading God's Word...)
How did I rate this week with this spiritual tool? _____
1-10 (1=not well at all) (10= praise God really well!)

7. This week the following came easy for me regarding care of my temple?

_____

_____

8. This week the following was very difficult for me regarding caring for my temple?

_____

_____

9. After evaluating my ratings this week, these two spiritual tools (choose the lowest rated ones) are what I need to improve on next week regarding temple care?

_____

_____

Tip: Jot down different scriptures on patience and carry them to encourage you as you go through the program.

God's Created Food Source for Man
Week Six

"...do you not know your body is the temple of the Holy Spirit who is in you..."
1 Corinthians 6:19
Week Six -Day 36-Sunday
<u>*God's Created Food Source for Mankind*</u>
"Then <u>God said, "Let the earth sprout vegetation, plants yielding seed, and fruit trees</u> <u>bearing fruit with seed in them after their kind, with seed in them in the earth; and it</u> <u>was so</u>. And the earth brought forth vegetation, plants yielding seed after their kind, and trees bearing fruit with seed in them, after their kind and God saw that it was good."
Genesis 1:11, 12

The book of Genesis, in its magnificent manner, shows us that everything created, originated from the mind of God. On the first day in time, God created the heavens, the earth and light! On the second day, He created the firmament. On the third day, He created vegetation, plants with seeds and fruit. It's a bit odd to me that the line up of spectacular creations such as the sky, the heavens, lights and the earth also includes fruit and vegetables! Yet, I believe that the wonder, goodness, life-sustaining power and importance held in the sky, earth and heavens are *equally* found in the substance that God told Adam is "food for you". Later, God even mentioned meat from animals as another food source which will be discussed in a few days.

Another interesting fact is that God had an orientation for His new beings. After creating the world, He gave them three points of guidance to help them start their new lives in their garden home. First, as husband and wife, they were to fill the earth with babies (an enjoyable request to fulfill!). Second, He gave them rule over every living thing. And third, He told them to eat the food that He had given them. Therefore, I encourage us all to eat solely (or primarily) the food in its purest, most healthful form that God (not man) created and intended for us.

Are there tasty God-given foods you can replace man-made food with? Of course! For example, I love brownies and Godiva White Chocolate Raspberry Ice Cream (I had a certified "sweet tooth") but I don't want to eat it every time I want something sweet. In fact, when I began the Temple Care program (yes, I've gone through the program 3 times) I took pride in knowing that I restricted my "sweets" intake to once a week, on the weekends. And that included all sweet junk food like cookies, pies, ice cream, pancakes, brownies… I would eat fruit throughout the week to satisfy my "sweet tooth" until the weekend. I chose to control the frequency of having sweets and still allowed myself to have them. Yet, *now*, after losing 18 pounds (over a 4 month period) and allowing God's Spirit to truly strengthen my spirit, I have such sweets maybe once every 1-2 months! I *NEVER* thought that I would *EVER* be able to resist processed sweets for so long, but I do! Praise God!

Our taste buds are designed to detect sweet, sour, bitter, salty, umami flavors and possibly water and fat (Wardlow, 2003). God created foods that satisfy all of the above mentioned flavors; therefore it is natural to desire sweet, salty, bitter…foods. It is best for us to primarily satisfy these taste buds with the foods God designed for us. Fortunately, I've found a few healthy replacements (for brownies and ice cream) such as "Strawberry-Blueberry Cereal"! One of my favorite fruit is strawberry, so I cut a good amount up and place in a bowl with a sliced up banana, a handful of blueberries and vanilla rice drink and raw, non-pasteurized honey (or a tablespoon of Sucanat sugar or a zero calorie packet of

Stevia)! I also eat a lot of watermelon and at times fresh pineapple. I eat God-given sweets daily which significantly decreases my desire for man-made sweets. Also eating God-given sweets (like sweet watermelon!) whenever I really want brownies....usually satisfies my craving for sweets in general! And each healthy sweet provides various vitamins, minerals, enzymes and are also designed to boost my immune system, nourish, cleanse and aid my body in elimination (definitely unlike brownies and ice cream)!

Next list the unhealthy foods you enjoy and its healthier replacement (something that is or is closer to God's created food). Also, by this time you have an idea of how much processed foods and drinks you intake a day/week (from your F.I.R.E. forms). So, I encourage you to start decreasing the number of processed foods/drinks you have a day/week.

Unhealthy food/drink   Healthy Replacement Food   &/or   Healthier Preparation
1.
2.
3.
4.
5.

When it comes to successfully replacing negative foods, things, people/influences from our lives I often refer to a parable in Matthew 12:43-45. This parable suggests when you get rid of evil from your life to remember to replace it with that which is good and Godly. If you do not replace the evil with good then the evil will return, possibly with companions (Barnes Notes)! The passage is as follows:

> 43 When the unclean spirit is gone out of a man, he walketh through dry places, seeking rest, and findeth none.44 Then he saith, I will return into my house from whence I came out; and when he is come, he findeth it empty, swept, and garnished.45 Then goeth he, and taketh with himself seven other spirits more wicked than himself, and they enter in and dwell there: and the last state of that man is worse than the first. Even so shall it be also unto this wicked generation.
> KJV

Let us also remember that God created water for us and that it serves many health purposes. Aside from aiding in digestion and absorption of food, water regulates body temperature and blood circulation. It also carries nutrients and oxygen to cells, removes toxins and other wastes, it helps the body metabolize stored fat and can serve as an appetite suppressant (so the old recommendation of drinking a glass before and after a meal *can* be an appetite suppressant for many). I follow the rule of thumb that for every 50 pounds of body weight you carry, drink one quart of water so I drink about 2 ½ quarts of water a day. Following this rule has significantly improved how I digest food and eliminate/cleanse my body/God's temple.

I had a nurse once tell me to think of drinking water as washing clothes. We can place our clothes in the washer and pour detergent into the machine but if I pour just a couple of cups of water in the washer and turn it on my clothes will not get clean. We would need a lot more water to thoroughly wash our clothes and the same with our bodies. We must drink enough water to properly nourish, hydrate, aid organ function, and cleanse our temples effectively. Therefore, drink up! And don't sip it throughout the day, gulp it down, it's good for you!

How did the Holy Spirit try to influence your temple care today?_____

How did your flesh want to respond?_____

How did you respond?_____

Fact: "We operate on about 2 quarts (2 liters) of water daily and must replenish it regularly because the body does not store water per se." (Wardlow)

GOD DESIRES A PEOPLE WHOSE CHARACTER REVEALS A SPIRIT OF WISDOM BY EATING PRIMARILY FROM GOD'S CREATED FOOD SOURCE.

F.I.R.E

FRESH FRUIT   * NATURAL OILS/FATS
****
                                                         *
                                                         *
****

FRESH VEGETABLES (CAN BE STEAMED)   *NATURAL SWEETNERS
                                                         *
                                                         *
****

GRAINS   * MEAT/SEAFOOD/BEANS/NUTS
                                                         *
                                                         *
****

COOKED FRUIT   *COOKED VEGETABLES
                                                         *
                                                         *
****

PROCESSED FOODS   *PROCESSED LIQUIDS
                                                         *
                                                         *
****

ST-I used the tool of spiritual mind renewal (Read scriptures and daily reading on Temple Care) _____ **ST**-I used the tool of faith_____ **ST**-I used the tool of support_____
ST-I used the tool of prayer_____ **ST**-I used the tool of repentance ____ Exercise 10 minutes+ ____ **ST**-I used the tool of spiritual fasting – yes/no; juice fast-yes/no
SP-I'm being honest about and coping with my food temptations ___
SP-I ate more than what I needed _____
SP-I demonstrated temperance (Spirit aided self-control)___
SP-# of food items I ate created by God ____
Water intake _____ SP-# of food items and liquid not created by God_____

"...do you not know your body is the temple of the Holy Spirit who is in you..."
1 Corinthians 6:19

Week Six-Day 37-Monday
God's Created Food Source for Mankind
"Then God said, Behold <u>I have given you every plant yielding seed that is on the surface of all the earth, and every tree which has fruit yielding seed, it shall be food for you:</u> and to every beast of the earth and to every bird of the sky and to everything that moves on the earth which has life, I have given every green plant for food, and it was so."
Genesis 1:29, 30
WHAT EXACTLY IS GOD'S FOOD?

I've noted three "criterion" that may be helpful in choosing God's food. We will look at the foundation, formula and function for food.

Foundation means basis or groundwork (Dictionary.com). The two foundational God given food sources are the earth and animals (nothing genetically engineered or created in laboratories). When looking at the earth as our food source we then think of foods that come from trees, vines, bushes and other earth producing plants. When looking at animals as our food source we then think of foods that come from cows, lambs, goats, fish, turkey, pigs, deer, chicken and animals that live in the water/sea. I usually tell my students that you can generally pick God's food straight from the earth or cut it straight off the animal and eat it (that is after cooking the meat). If this can not be done then man more than likely altered the food in some way which more often then not is less optimal then God intended for us. For instance, are there peanut butter trees? Are there orange juice trees? Are there cracker or pretzel vines? Are there bread bushes? No, those foods are the products of man significantly processing God's food. I believe that if we want to receive the best of what God's given us then we need to stay as close as possible to its original God-given state.

Formula means a prescription of ingredients in fixed proportion (Dictionary.com). God's food contains certain, I believe, divinely prescribed ingredients in perfectly fixed proportion. For instance, we find that most store bought orange juices have approximately 10 teaspoons of sugar per cup. Yet God's fresh orange has this interesting white fibrous stuff all around the orange. That white substance in called "pith". Some say that the pith actually helps to moderate the amount of sugar which comes from the orange! Therefore let's not underestimate the importance of all the elements God has placed in and around His food! Another example is regarding ham and bacon. We know that these meats have been cut straight off of an animal so they meet the "Foundation" criterion. Yet, they have been processed by man in a way other meats aren't. Do you know in what way they've been processed? Exactly, they have been "cured" which involves some form of soaking in a salt/sugar solution which often includes other chemicals like nitrates and nitrites. We see that for many people this salt solution greatly contributes to the elevation of their blood pressure and other unhealthy bodily reactions.

Function means purpose for creation and/or design (Dictionary.com). Now we discussed in "God's Purpose for Food" that it is primarily for "strength". Also, in "God's Intended Perspective on His Food" we learned that God's food is "good for food" meaning "possessing desirable qualities" is "beneficial" and "agreeable". At this time, let's look at some specific functions for which God has created certain foods. For instance, pecan nuts function in the way of providing antioxidants, vitamin E, calcium, magnesium, zinc and fiber. Snap snow peas provide iron, vitamin C, fiber and greatly improves ones immune system. Deer meat provides protein, Selenium, Zinc, Copper, iron and Vitamins B12, B2, B3, and B6. A whole grain like wheat has antioxidants, various B Vitamins, magnesium, iron and fiber. Unfortunately we find that when the formula for much of God's food is changed through processing then the function is consequently altered. For instance, processing a whole grain such as wheat (altering its formula) to make the flour that are in brownies no longer provide the vital nutrients (function) God placed in wheat.

I am constantly running across information in magazines and/or on the television, internet, and radio that reveal research findings that show the great power in God's food! God's food functions in the way of nourishing, healing, calming, stimulating, rejuvenating, cleansing and much more! I am very glad that I don't have to always be knowledgeable about the current research to care for my body/God's temple in the way that He desires. In the Bible, God makes it clear that His food is "good for food". Therefore, I needn't know all of the latest research about His food. I trust that His food not only is good for me but that it has been perfectly designed for my body. In all reality, we will never develop technology advanced enough to completely understand the divine goodness and effects in and caused by God's food.

How did the Holy Spirit try to influence your temple care today?_____

How did your flesh want to respond?_____

How did you respond?_____

GOD DESIRES A PEOPLE WHOSE CHARACTER REVEALS A SPIRIT OF WISDOM BY EATING PRIMARILY FROM HIS CREATED FOOD SOURCE.

F.I.R.E

FRESH FRUIT   * NATURAL OILS/FATS
****
                                               *
                                               *
****
FRESH VEGETABLES (CAN BE STEAMED)   *NATURAL SWEETNERS
                                               *
                                               *
****
GRAINS   * MEAT/SEAFOOD/BEANS/NUTS
                                               *
                                               *
****
COOKED FRUIT   *COOKED VEGETABLES
                                               *
                                               *
****
PROCESSED FOODS   *PROCESSED LIQUIDS
                                               *
                                               *
****

ST-I used the tool of spiritual mind renewal (Read scriptures and daily reading on Temple Care) _____ **ST**-I used the tool of faith____ **ST**-I used the tool of support_____ **ST**-I used the tool of prayer____ **ST**-I used the tool of repentance ___ Exercise ___

ST-I used the tool of spiritual fasting – yes/no; juice fast-yes/no

SP-I'm being honest about and coping with my food temptations ___

SP-I ate more than what I needed _____

SP-I demonstrated temperance (Spirit aided self-control)___

SP-# of food items I ate created by God ____

Water intake ____ **SP-# of food items and liquid not created by God** ____

"...do you not know your body is the temple of the Holy Spirit who is in you..."
1 Corinthians 6:19

Week Six–Day 38-Tuesday
God's Created Food Source for Mankind

Although some may think that the issue of food is unimportant during our walk here on earth, God appears to address the issue during three separate time periods. As our Creator, He thought it important to provide optimal food for our wondrously created bodies to nourish our temples, ultimately for His glory.

These 3 times fall within common periods of biblical history: the *Patriarchal Age*, the *Mosaic Age*, and the *Christian Age*. Of course "creation" began within the Patriarchal Age, which included historical events such as the flood, the story of Joseph and the birth of Moses. Moses' birth transitioned into the second age, the Mosaic Age. This period included events such as the children of Israel's wilderness wandering, the messages of the major and Minor Prophets, the birth of Jesus and his teachings. Lastly, the Christian Age began after the death, burial and resurrection of Jesus the Christ. During this age, events began, such as the first century church on the day of Pentecost in 33AD, and other things, such as the profound descriptors of what true love is and what the fruit of the Spirit looks like (Miller and Stevens, 1992). Today, we will address the Patriarchal Age.

The Patriarchal Age

We are all familiar to some degree with the biblical account of Creation. Moses is the author of this first book of the Bible, Genesis, which means beginning. The first chapter of the book reveals a few incredible things about our Heavenly Father, God. First, that God is omnipotent, all-powerful, and that he created everything by speaking it into existence. No concoction in a lab or even material to work with! Just His vision, His vitality, and His voice! The second point is his true love and concern for all of His creation, particularly man. God made sure that all of man's needs were provided for from the rain so that plants would grow to woman so that man would not be alone. Included in this provision for man, God specifically designed and cultivated food. This food came from the same source from which God created man which is the earth. God also made the food self-propagating in that it would continue to bear after its own kind! This leads me to believe that God intended for the food He created to be a continual supply of nourishment for man for *all time*. It is incredible to think that the banana I just ate came from the original source of banana God created at the beginning of time!

Genesis 1:11, 12, 29, 30, show classes or categories of food that were originally created for us: "plants yielding seed", "fruit trees bearing fruit", and "green plant" or "vegetation". Some theologians reported that there were three different categories of substances produced by the earth (yet today these categories are defined differently). Grass, herbs and trees (fruit) are the categories with two of them (herbs and trees) being designated to be man's food source (Leupold).

Grass is defined as being the "first sprouts of the earth, tender herb, in which the seed is not noticed". This refers to the different kinds of grasses that supply food for the lower animals, not man. Grass yields seed, yet the specific mentioning of seed is made only regarding "herbs," which are noted as one of God's intended food sources for man. It's believed that herb refers to something like seed-bearing pod, which make the seed more visible as being a substance in and of it. Herb is defined as "the more mature herbage, in which the seed is the most striking characteristic; the larger description of plants and vegetables." This broad class name is believed to include everything in between grass and trees (that have noticeable seed) and all of the various grains. The second food category, fruit tree, is also believed to be used in a broad sense. This would include trees that bear fruit, trees yielding nuts and cones and bushes that produce berries (Baker). Fruit trees appear to be described as having a specific nature meaning bears fruit. It also describes a certain characteristic, which is that it possesses seed in the very fruit. Finally, its outer appearance is above the ground.

All three categories address two factors, the structure and the seed. The structure of grass is green blade, the herb is the stalk and the tree is the woody texture. Regarding the seed, the grass has inconspicuous seed, the herb has conspicuous seed and in the fruit, the seed in enclosed in it, which makes it conspicuous. Again, the scriptures show the power in these substances through their ability to multiply their kind (Leupold). I often think that habitually ingesting man-made food may be "counter to God's wisdom". I'm not saying that brownies are evil or that you are evil if you eat brownies! **What I am saying is that most of God's food multiplies itself, which shows an element of living energy! Our bodies operate best with these live food sources.** Yes, we can enjoy what some people call "dead", highly processed food sources yet hopefully not in our regular food intake.

5 New Veggies & 3 New Fruit!

This exercise is always fun! Include on your grocery list to look for 5 new vegetables and 3 new fruit to purchase next time you go grocery shopping. You do not have to purchase large amounts, 5 small vegetables would be fine. And you may prefer trying just one of the individual fruit rather than purchasing amounts of fruit. Select food that you don't usually eat and/or have never eaten! Pair your new vegetable with your favorite meat, seafood, grain or legume/bean for dinner and enjoy more of the different foods *God has created for you!*

How did the Holy Spirit try to influence your temple care today?_____
How did your flesh want to respond?_____
How did you respond?_____

GOD DESIRES A PEOPLE WHOSE CHARACTER REVEALS A SPIRIT OF WISDOM BY EATING PRIMARILY FROM GOD'S GIVEN FOOD SOURCE.

F.I.R.E

FRESH FRUIT   * NATURAL OILS/FATS
****
                                               *
                                               *
****
FRESH VEGETABLES (CAN BE STEAMED)   *NATURAL SWEETNERS
                                               *
                                               *
****
GRAINS   * MEAT/SEAFOOD/BEANS/NUTS
                                               *
                                               *
****
COOKED FRUIT   *COOKED VEGETABLES
                                               *
                                               *
****
PROCESSED FOODS   *PROCESSED LIQUIDS
                                               *
                                               *
****

ST-I used the tool of spiritual mind renewal (Read scriptures and daily reading on Temple Care) _____ **ST**-I used the tool of faith_____ **ST**-I used the tool of support_____
ST-I used the tool of prayer_____ **ST**-I used the tool of repentance ____ Exercise ____
ST-I used the tool of spiritual fasting – yes/no; juice fast-yes/no
SP-I'm being honest about and coping with my food temptations ____
SP-I ate more than what I needed _____
SP-I demonstrated temperance (Spirit aided self-control)___
SP-# of food items I ate created by God ____
Water intake ____ **SP-# of food items and liquid not created by God** ____

"...do you not know your body is the temple of the Holy Spirit who is in you..."
1 Corinthians 6:19

Week Six-Day 39-Wednesday
God's Created Food Source for Man
"Every moving thing that is alive shall be food for you; I give all to you, as I gave the green plant."
Genesis 9:3-4

Continuing with the Patriarchal Age, we see that God allowed man to eat meat. Whether man was vegetarian prior to the fall of Adam and Eve is debated. Some say that, originally, God did not formally exclude animals as food believing that man's assigned dominion over them could have meant that man could choose to use them as a food source. Others say that man best not add to what is said regarding God's intention for food and that man had no instruction from God saying that he could partake of animals as meat until after the flood (Genesis 9:3). Baker stated, "If men before the flood ever ate the meat of beasts, they did so without divine sanction."

Scholars have given differing explanations for why they believe God may have later added meat to man's food plan. One explanation is that man's strength possibly decreased after the flood. Due to all of the difficult and physically draining events surrounding the flood and the land for so many years, some say that man needed more nourishment than the earth could provide. Another explanation is that God continued to show His goodness and mercy toward man by allowing man to broaden his dietary intake. Who knows why God said what He said, but we know that He did allow it. Also, in Genesis 9:3, we see no distinction at this time between clean or unclean meat. Man could eat anything that lived and moved. The only stipulation was that the animal not be eaten with its blood in it. Basically, this means that an animal's blood was to be drained before it was eaten.

I believe that we must be more vigilant about how animals (which God gave us dominion over) are to be treated before we consume them. Hormone pumped animals being raised in overcrowded, disease infested facilities is not only bad for the animals but, I believe, in the long run is not good for us. Basically, we consume what they consume! For instance, lately there have been health reports recommending that we avoid certain seafood/fish due to them being laden with toxic chemicals *that we* dump into the ocean! Due to our poor stewardship (and sometimes just exertion of foolish dominion) we poison the animals that God has given us to oversee and then ingest them and become poisoned ourselves.

Some individuals suggest that eating meat (red meat) is not good for us, yet I do not agree based on God's Word. I do believe that some individuals have *so sorely violated* various spiritual principles for years, particularly with red meat (gluttony, lack of temperance, disregard of God's entire created food source or poor balance of God's fruits, vegetables, and grains), that now their bodies may respond negatively to red meat. If the meat is fresh, the animal is raised healthily (as discussed earlier) and is pure of chemicals (i.e. nitrates, nitrites, uncured...) then I believe that it can be a beneficial part of a *balanced* dietary intake. It's best to buy whole meat with it's natural skin and fat...how God intended.

Check F.I.R.E.

As I mentioned earlier, many individuals lack balance in their food intake. This exercise is to help you become more aware of, and change if necessary, your dietary imbalance. Randomly flip through your workbook and make note of the healthy categories that are lacking on your completed F.I.R.E. forms. Write down what you need to add more or less of in your daily diet.

_____

_____

_____

_____

_____

_____

How did the Holy Spirit try to influence your temple care today?_____

How did your flesh want to respond?_____

How did you respond?_____

GOD DESIRES A PEOPLE WHOSE CHARACTER REVEALS A SPIRIT OF WISDOM BY EATING PRIMARILY FROM GOD'S GIVEN FOOD SOURCE.

F.I.R.E

FRESH FRUIT * NATURAL OILS/FATS
****
*
*
****
FRESH VEGETABLES (CAN BE STEAMED) *NATURAL SWEETNERS
*
*
****
GRAINS * MEAT/SEAFOOD/BEANS/NUTS
*
*
****
COOKED FRUIT *COOKED VEGETABLES
*
*
****
PROCESSED FOODS *PROCESSED LIQUIDS
*
*
****

ST-I used the tool of spiritual mind renewal (Read scriptures and daily reading on Temple Care) _____ **ST**-I used the tool of faith____ **ST**-I used the tool of support_____
ST-I used the tool of prayer____ **ST**-I used the tool of repentance ___ Exercise ___
ST-I used the tool of spiritual fasting – yes/no; juice fast-yes/no
SP-I'm being honest about and coping with my food temptations ___
SP-I ate more than what I needed _____
SP-I demonstrated temperance (Spirit aided self-control) ____
SP-# of food items I ate created by God __
Water intake ____ **SP-# of food items and liquid not created by God** ____

"...do you not know your body is the temple of the Holy Spirit who is in you..."
1 Corinthians 6:19

Week Six-Day 40-Thursday
God' Created and Intended Food Source for Man
Leviticus 11 and Deuteronomy 14

The Mosaic Age

During the Mosaic period, man, in general, could still eat of herbs, trees (in a very broad sense) and animals. Only the children of Israel were asked at this time to distinguish between "clean" and "unclean" meats. God clearly spelled out in our two chapters for the day the guidelines between the edible creature and the creature that was not to be eaten.

According to some theologians there is no English word that can accurately describe the true meaning of "unclean" as it is spoken in Leviticus 11. It does not appear to be synonymous with the word "holy," which is what many have thought in the past. Being "clean" or "unclean" appears to one's society or community, and holiness seems to relate more to God. There is still debate as to whether or not uncleanness in Leviticus solely related to morality, rules of hygiene or an established, very detailed pattern that gave order and clarity to the life journey of the Israelite. The word improper may best describe what unclean meant. Basically improper means that something is atypical in ones society or against convention but it is not an issue of sin or immorality. As to why some animals were deemed clean and others unclean is another issue of debate. Many say that in Leviticus, some of the unclean animals (i.e. pig) were sacred in other religions. And so, the Israelites were to remain distinctly different from men who worshipped others than God (pagan worshippers) by not ingesting or having any part of their idol sacrifices. I must stress that the Israelites, during this time, saw every aspect of their lives as pertaining to God (because God did) and His religion, and food was no exception (Matthew Henry Commentary).

It is said that Leviticus was God's legal document, or law, and Deuteronomy has been translated as meaning "this is the repetition of the Law". Primarily, some of the laws, which Moses wrote about earlier, were to be reiterated and, in some cases, elaborated upon for the new generation of Israelites. Others say that the repeating of the law regarding the catalyst which brought about the dividing into clean and unclean in the book of Deuteronomy may have changed. Originally, some said that certain animals were seen as sacred or totems, so no one could eat them. Yet, later, other possible reasons were given such as 1). Society as a whole gradually saw some foods as more pleasant or edible than others 2). Sanitation 3). To be holy and separated as God's chosen people, the Israelites were not to partake of the animals that were part of pagan rituals or idolatry (Baker). Deuteronomy 14:3-21 is very similar to Leviticus 11:2-23.

Nectar from Heaven...Literally!

Since we are covering what God's Word says about the food He has created, I'd like to see how you have been doing on your juice fast? Remember, this is our weekly fast that focuses on using God's food at a more concentrated level to improve our health? To be able to ingest more vegetables and fruits by juicing a large amount of "live" vegetable and fruit allows our temples to experience a very nourishing, cleansing, restorative process. Just think of the cumulative impact if you continue having a juice fast, once a week, for an entire year! By doing this you would have intentionally cleaned and rested your digestive system for 52 days!

I believe that because of our constant bombardment of toxins from overly processed foods, polluted air, chemically laden water, soaps, lotions…that our bodies accumulate these chemicals and cause what I call the "Sludge Factor"! These substances can burden our bodies so much that our immune systems, metabolisms, organs, etc. can be slowed down and kept from operating at their fullest, God-given potential. Hopefully you have been using God's "live" food in a concentrated form (weekly) to decrease some of the sludge in your body. Consequently, your body will be able to work more efficiently.

How did the Holy Spirit try to influence your temple care today?_____

How did your flesh want to respond?_____

How did you respond?_____

GOD DESIRES A PEOPLE WHOSE CHARACTER REVEALS A SPIRIT OF WISDOM BY EATING PRIMARILY FROM GOD'S GIVEN FOOD SOURCE

F.I.R.E

FRESH FRUIT   * NATURAL OILS/FATS
****
                                                  *
                                                  *
****
FRESH VEGETABLES (CAN BE STEAMED)   *NATURAL SWEETNERS
                                                  *
                                                  *
****
GRAINS   * MEAT/SEAFOOD/BEANS/NUTS
                                                  *
                                                  *
****
COOKED FRUIT   *COOKED VEGETABLES
                                                  *
                                                  *
****
PROCESSED FOODS   *PROCESSED LIQUIDS
                                                  *
                                                  *
****

ST-I used the tool of spiritual mind renewal (Read scriptures and daily reading on
Temple Care) _____ **ST**-I used the tool of faith____ **ST**-I used the tool of support_____
ST-I used the tool of prayer____ **ST**-I used the tool of repentance ___ Exercise ___
ST-I used the tool of spiritual fasting – yes/no; juice fast-yes/no
SP-I'm being honest about and coping with my food temptations ___
SP-I ate more than what I needed _____
SP-I demonstrated temperance (Spirit aided self-control) ___
SP-# of food items I ate created by God ___
Water intake ____ SP-# of food items and liquid not created by God ____

"...do you not know your body is the temple of the Holy Spirit who is in you..."
1 Corinthians 6:19

Week Six-Day 41-Friday
God' Created and Intended Food Source for Man
Acts 10 & 1 Timothy 4:3-5

Christian Age

The book of Acts primarily tells how the church began and how the early disciples of Jesus, being led by the Holy Spirit, spread the Gospel to the world: it was no longer limited to the Jewish nation.

One day, about noontime, Peter needed some privacy to spend time praying to God. He was on the roof of the house where he was staying with little external distraction so that He could better communicate with his Lord. After a while, Peter started to get hungry yet had to wait until the food was prepared (more than likely this would have been his 1st meal for the day). And, as he was waiting, "he fell into a trance". This is similar to a deep meditative state where one is not really exercising control over their thoughts but is in a deep, relaxed state. Peter at this time was open to receive lessons and understanding from God. Upon doing this, Peter received the following vision three times in a row. First the heavens opened up to show a sheet being lowered to the ground. On this sheet were all kinds of animals and a voice said aloud, "Rise, Peter, kill and eat." Peter's conscience was disturbed because he obeyed the old law meaning he only ate clean meat, yet in his dream unclean/common meat was presented on the sheet. But then Peter heard "What God hath cleansed, that call thou not common." Again, this particular vision played out three times (Matthew Henry Commentary and Barnes Notes).

Primarily, the dream was to reveal that there was no longer a distinction between the Jews and the Gentiles. The Gentiles would receive similar privileges (new law) that were once only for the Jews (Galatians 3:26-29). Secondarily, God expressed that Paul was to no longer reject the food God at one time declared unclean (under the old law) but to realize that now whatever God declared as clean is clean (new law). From this point forward, throughout the Christian age, there was no distinction of clean and unclean food for God's followers.

1 Timothy 4:3-5 is as follows, ***"Forbidding to marry, and commanding to abstain from meats, which God hath created to be received with thanksgiving of them which believe and know the truth. For every creature of God is good, and nothing to be refused, if it be received with thanksgiving: For it is sanctified by the word of God and prayer."*** According to this passage, men were told to understand that meat was created by God and therefore is good for the nourishment of man. Meat in this context is said to specifically mean flesh of animals rather than food in general. At the time of this writing some religious individuals believed that eating meat (particularly certain meat at certain times of the year) was to be forbidden. "The fact that God had created them (plants and animal flesh for food) was proof that they were not to be regarded as evil, and that it was not to be considered as a religious duty to abstain from them." (Barnes Notes, 1997) I find it interesting that this particular commentary expounded on verse 4 by saying that every creature is good as God has created it. "As man perverts them, it is no longer proper to call

them the 'creation of God,' and they may be injurious in the highest degree." (Barnes Notes, 1997)

Let's Give It A Try!

Either today and/or tomorrow try to eat only God-given food all day! See what it is like to eat and drink that which God has given you and try to have it as close to its original form as possible. Steam and/or cook your favorite God-given items or eat them fresh and then write about your experience below. For example, for breakfast I had *fresh* oatmeal (see "Overnight Oatmeal" recipe in Appendices) and lots of water. I became hungry again mid-afternoon and had a spring salad with some walnut pieces, raisins, red onions, avocado slices and my homemade Rosemary vinaigrette dressing along with ½ bag of popcorn (with real butter) and lots more water throughout the afternoon. Later that evening I ate BQ Ribs and about half of a sweet potato and a handful of raw baby carrots.

On _____ (choose a day), I will complete the exercise described above and write about my experience.

_____
_____
_____
_____
_____
_____

How did the Holy Spirit try to influence your temple care today?_____
How did your flesh want to respond?_____
How did you respond?_____

GOD DESIRES A PEOPLE WHOSE CHARACTER REVEALS A SPIRIT OF WISDOM BY EATING PRIMARILY FROM GOD'S GIVEN FOOD SOURCE.

F.I.R.E

FRESH FRUIT   * NATURAL OILS/FATS
****
                                               *
                                               *
****
FRESH VEGETABLES (CAN BE STEAMED)   *NATURAL SWEETNERS
                                               *
                                               *
****
GRAINS   * MEAT/SEAFOOD/BEANS/NUTS
                                               *
                                               *
****
COOKED FRUIT   *COOKED VEGETABLES
                                               *
                                               *
****
PROCESSED FOODS   *PROCESSED LIQUIDS
                                               *
                                               *
****

ST-I used the tool of spiritual mind renewal (Read scriptures and daily reading on Temple Care) _____ **ST**-I used the tool of faith____ **ST**-I used the tool of support_____
ST-I used the tool of prayer____ **ST**-I used the tool of repentance ___ Exercise ___
ST-I used the tool of spiritual fasting – yes/no; juice fast-yes/no
SP-I'm being honest about and coping with my food temptations ___
SP-I ate more than what I needed _____
SP-I demonstrated temperance (Spirit aided self-control) ___
SP-# of food items I ate created by God ___
Water intake ____ SP-# of food items and liquid not created by God ____

"...do you not know your body is the temple of the Holy Spirit who is in you..."
1 Corinthians 6:19

Week Six-Day 42-Saturday
Summary
<u>*God's Created and Intended Food Source for Man*</u>

God created man, and He created food for man. God's provision (food) has been specifically designed to meet man's need for strength and nourishment. I believe that God knew that the food He created for man would be compatible with the system/body/temple of man. We always try to make eating healthy difficult, yet it's easy to see that what God designed, fruits, grains, vegetables, and nuts in their whole, complete, non-processed, uncooked, good, perfect state, is what man needs. Also, eating meat of animals was allowed. Unfortunately, man often pumps our animals/meat with hormones and antibiotics. Also they raise these animals in disease infested environments. We need to take a more active stand to encourage grass and grain fed animals. We need to discourage the use of hormones and antibiotics and make sure the environment in which our produce is grown is healthy and disease free. We also need to encourage greater improvements regarding fruit and vegetables being grown from the earth and the enrichment of our soil. Furthermore, I believe that the use of laboratory manipulated and grown fruits and vegetables (genetically engineered) should be discouraged and petitioned against.

Can scientists or mankind fully explain if or why there may be a connection between man coming from the soil and his food also coming from the soil? No. Yet, we do see clearly that the majority of God's created food is from the earth and man also is from the earth (Genesis 1:11 & I Corinthians 15:47). Only God can explain why He created the two from this source. Still, He thought that which comes from the earth is fit, necessary and complete/perfect in providing man with the nourishment necessary for man's uniquely created body/God's temple.

Once again, God created food (similarly to man and animals) with the potential to multiply or bring forth after its own kind. What a tremendous hint for man! God wanted His food source, which was developed during the beginning/creation to be the same food source for us in the 21st century! He created a food substance that is self-perpetuating! In fact, the self perpetuating elements that are in fruits, vegetables, nuts and grains are precisely what our bodies/temples need to perpetuate proper growth, health, and elimination.

How did the Holy Spirit try to influence your temple care today?_____

How did your flesh want to respond?_____

How did you respond?_____

GOD DESIRES A PEOPLE WHOSE CHARACTER REVEALS A SPIRIT OF WISDOM BY EATING PRIMARILY FROM GOD'S GIVEN FOOD SOURCE.

Self Regulating Sheet

Looking back on this week's F.I.R.E. forms how did you do?

1. Spiritual mind renewal (reading what the bible says about Temple Care)
How did I rate this week with this spiritual tool? _____
1-10 (1=not well at all) (10= praise God really well!)

2. Faith (actions toward Godly Temple Care)
How did I rate this week with this spiritual tool? _____
1-10 (1=not well at all) (10= praise God really well!)

3. Support (contacting spiritual support partner/s and discuss Temple Care)
How did I rate this week with this spiritual tool? _____
1-10 (1=not well at all) (10= praise God really well!)

4. Prayer (praying to God about any and every issue regarding my Temple Care)
How did I rate this week with this spiritual tool? _____
1-10 (1=not well at all) (10= praise God really well!)

5. Repentance (expressing Godly sorrow and changing my ways through the Holy Spirit)
How did I rate this week with this spiritual tool? _____
1-10 (1=not well at all) (10= praise God really well!)

6. Fasting (not eating for 1 day or 3 dinners and replace with prayer, singing, reading God's Word…)
How did I rate this week with this spiritual tool? _____
1-10 (1=not well at all) (10= praise God really well!)

7. This week the following came easy for me regarding care of my temple?

_____

_____

8. This week the following was very difficult for me regarding caring for my temple?

_____

9. After evaluating my ratings this week, these two spiritual tools (choose the lowest rated ones) are what I need to improve on next week regarding temple care?

_____

_____

Tip: Jot down more scriptures on patience and carry them to encourage you as you go through the program.

God's Intended Purpose for Food
Week Seven

"...do you not know your body is the temple of the Holy Spirit who is in you..."
1 Corinthians 6:19

Week Seven-Day 43-Sunday
<u>*God's Intended Purpose for Food*</u>
"But he himself went a day's journey into the wilderness, and came and sat down under a juniper tree; and he requested for himself that he might die, and said, 'it is enough; now, O Lord, take my life, for I am not better than my fathers.' And he lay down and slept under a juniper tree; and behold, there was an angel touching him, and he said to him, 'Arise, eat.' Then he looked and behold, there was at his head a bread cake baked on hot stones, and a jar of water. So he ate and drank and lay down again. And the angel of the Lord came again a second time and touched him and said, 'Arise, eat, because the journey is too great for you.' <u>So he arose and ate and drank, and went in the strength of that food forty days and forty nights to Horeb, the mountain of God."</u>
I Kings 19:4-8

From this reading, what would you say is God's intended purpose for food?

_____

An interesting thing happened to me a few years ago at dinner, something I never experienced so saliently before. I went down to the buffet dinner at a hotel I was staying in with the purpose in my heart to care for my body/God's temple in a way that reflects God. I ate healthy, natural, God-created foods and nothing more. I also had a satisfying portion size of food. When I finished eating, I watched others go up for seconds, and so I asked myself if I was still hungry. But, what was odd was that I could not feel where I was regarding my level of hunger. I did notice this, I realized I wasn't hungry and that that was not the usually required feeling I needed to determine whether I would continue eating. It became clearer to me that the required feeling that often determined whether I'd have seconds (or thirds), was if I wasn't full or stuffed. You know, did I have more room in my stomach to comfortably eat more was the question. There was this vast, unknown land between being hungry and being full. Because I was in this numb-like state (neither hungry nor full), I felt nothing, which made it even easier for me to seek my full feeling. My full feeling was a feeling which gave me a very clear indication that I should stop eating. Wanting to use God's food for the purpose He intended, I needed to condition myself to equate feeling "nothing" (neither hungry nor full) to satiation or satisfaction *and* that this is a good state to be in.

A friend of mine told me that she was gaining weight and wanted to lose it. She also told me that she only ate when she was hungry. I asked her how many times she ate that day and she said four times. I asked her if she could rate from 0 (not hungry) to 10 (very hungry) where she rated each of the four times she ate. She said morning was an 8, early afternoon was a 6, mid-afternoon was a 4 and late evening was a 7. I then asked her if she snacked or nibbled any time during the day (which she had) then what would she rate that snack on the scale before she snacked/nibbled. She said she was about a 1 or 2 on the scale (remember she originally said she ate only when she was hungry)! I then asked her what she considered was a rating range of true hunger, need nourishment/strength.. She said 6-10, which then quickly helped her to realize that when she ate mid-afternoon and snacked she wasn't really hungry. She decided that she would try not to eat unless she was a 6 or 7 on the hunger scale and then at that time not snack but rather sit down and have a meal. I follow the same principle, if I'm not hungry enough to sit down and eat a meal than I will usually pass on feeding myself excessively and not put any food in my mouth. This exercise helped her to realize that whenever she wanted something to eat didn't always mean that she was truly hungry or need strength.

Take your time and complete the exercise below (use one word descriptors) to better determine when you are really hungry. Again the purpose for which God intended hunger is for strength.

When I am not hungry I feel? (rating=0)   When I am truly hungry I feel? (rating=10_

_____   _____

_____   _____

_____   _____

 What do you assign as your personal hunger rating which will help guide you to eat for God's intended purpose? _____

How did the Holy Spirit try to influence your temple care today?_____
How did your flesh want to respond?_____
How did you respond?_____

GOD DESIRES A PEOPLE WHOSE CHARACTER REVEALS A SPIRIT OF HONORING GOD'S FOOD SOURCE AND WHO USE IT FOR GOD'S INTENDED PURPOSE.

F.I.R.E

FRESH FRUIT	* NATURAL OILS/FATS

****
*
*
****

FRESH VEGETABLES (CAN BE STEAMED)	*NATURAL SWEETNERS

*
*
****

GRAINS	* MEAT/SEAFOOD/BEANS/NUTS

*
*
****

COOKED FRUIT	*COOKED VEGETABLES

*
*
****

PROCESSED FOODS	*PROCESSED LIQUIDS

*
*
****

ST-I used the tool of spiritual mind renewal (Read scriptures and daily reading on Temple Care) _____ **ST**-I used the tool of faith_____ **ST**-I used the tool of support_____
ST-I used the tool of prayer_____ **ST**-I used the tool of repentance ___ Exercise ___
ST-I used the tool of spiritual fasting – yes/no; juice fast-yes/no
SP-I'm being honest about and coping with my food temptations ___
SP-I ate more than what I needed _____
SP-I demonstrated temperance (Spirit aided self-control) _____
SP-# of food items I ate created by God _____
Water intake _____ **SP**-# of food items and liquid not created by God _____
SP-# of times I ate for the purpose of hunger _____
SP-# of times I ate to cope with spiritual/emotional/physical issues _____

"...do you not know your body is the temple of the Holy Spirit who is in you..."
1 Corinthians 6:19

Week Seven-Day 44-Monday
God's Intended Purpose for Food
"And immediately there fell from his eyes something like scales, and he regained his sight, and he arose and was baptized; and <u>he took food and was strengthened.</u>"
Acts 9:18, 19

"Two drives influence our desire to eat and thus take in food/drink energy: hunger and appetite"(Wardlow, 2003). *Hunger* is driven by physiological needs because the body needs fuel for energy/strength. *Appetite* is usually psychologically driven, stimulated by external or internal/emotional cues. We can often have an appetite for something yet not be hungry. Some of the external cues can be simply the presence of others eating, the media, the time of day, and social cues. Some internal cues can be influencing you to want to taste a certain flavor or feel a certain texture in your mouth. Feeling tired, bored, sad, happy, or empty can also influence you to want certain foods (Wardlow, 2003).

Some Good News!
"Satiety (a feeling of satisfaction) associated with consuming a meal may actually reside primarily in our psychological frame of mind. We become accustomed to a certain amount of food at a meal. Providing less than that amount leaves us wanting more. One way to put this observation into practice for weight-control purposes is to train the eye to expect less food by slowly decreasing serving sizes. Our appetites then readjust as we expect less food" (Wardlow, 2003).

Also, if we chew our food more thoroughly we'll find that we'll eat less (because we are giving our brain the time it needs to register a feeling of satiety). Although it seems odd to say this as a reminder, I must say that one purpose for teeth is to thoroughly break down our food for proper digestion, and I believe this ultimately affects our food absorption and it being metabolized correctly. Now we know this but don't often practice it. Try to chew approximately 20-30 times a bite depending on the food substance. Give it a try for the rest of the program and you'll find that you'll develop the habit of chewing your food more properly.

Question: Does hunger or appetite drive your style of eating the most throughout the day?

_____

Begin this exercise in the morning, and carry the workbook with you to complete throughout the day.

Hunger-Appetite Exercise

The time of day that I truly felt <u>hungry</u>:   **What I wanted and ate at that time?**

_____   _____
_____   _____
_____   _____
_____   _____
_____   _____

The time of day when I felt my <u>appetite</u>:   **What I wanted and did at that time?**

_____   _____
_____   _____
_____   _____
_____   _____
_____   _____

GOD DESIRES A PEOPLE WHOSE CHARACTER REVEALS A SPIRIT OF HONORING GOD'S FOOD SOURCE AND WHO USE IT FOR GOD'S INTENDED PURPOSE.

F.I.R.E

FRESH FRUIT   * NATURAL OILS/FATS
****
                                               *
                                               *
****
FRESH VEGETABLES (CAN BE STEAMED)   *NATURAL SWEETNERS
                                               *
                                               *
****
GRAINS   * MEAT/SEAFOOD/BEANS/NUTS
                                               *
                                               *
****
COOKED FRUIT   *COOKED VEGETABLES
                                               *
                                               *
****
PROCESSED FOODS   *PROCESSED LIQUIDS
                                               *
                                               *
****

ST-I used the tool of spiritual mind renewal (Read scriptures and daily reading on
Temple Care) _____   **ST**-I used the tool of faith_____   **ST**-I used the tool of support_____
ST-I used the tool of prayer_____   **ST**-I used the tool of repentance ____ Exercise ____
ST-I used the tool of spiritual fasting – yes/no; juice fast-yes/no
SP-I'm being honest about and coping with my food temptations ____
SP-# of times I ate more than what I needed _____
SP-I demonstrated temperance (Spirit aided self-control) ____
SP-# of food items I ate created by God ____
Water intake ____   **SP**-# of food items and liquid not created by God ____
SP-# of times I ate for the purpose of hunger ____
SP-# of times I ate to cope with spiritual/emotional/physical issues _____

How did the Holy Spirit try to influence your temple care today?_____
How did your flesh want to respond?_____
How did you respond?_____

"...do you not know your body is the temple of the Holy Spirit who is in you..."
1 Corinthians 6:19

Week Seven-Day 45-Tuesday-
God's Intended Purpose of Food
"Now they found an Egyptian in the field and brought him to David, and gave him bread and he ate, and they provided him water to drink. And they gave him a piece of fig cake and two clusters of raisins, and <u>he ate; then his spirit revived</u>. For he had not eaten bread or drunk water for three days and three nights."
I Samuel 30:11, 12
&
"Blessed art thou, O land, when thy king is the son of nobles, and thy princes <u>eat in due season, for strength, and not for drunkenness</u>!"
Ecclesiastes 10:17

In this passage, Solomon states how blessed a land and its people are when their rulers are temperate. They eat during the right season, which shows restraint over their appetites and passions. Also in this scripture Solomon mentions that such wise rulers understand the true purpose of food is for strength rather than addictive pleasures (Matthew Henry's Commentary, 1991). Often we do not eat "during the right season" for instance; we snack, nibble and taste all throughout the day. Unfortunately, many of us are using God's created food (and man's created food) as a perpetual source of self-stimulation/pleasure. How could this apply to you?

_____

_____

<u>When I am hungry I feel?</u>   <u>When I am full I feel?</u>

_____   _____

_____   _____

_____   _____

Now, in between the 2 columns above write about how you feel when you are in the middle meaning your body has fulfilled its purpose for eating which is for strength and nourishment. Remember this feeling to help guide you in knowing when to start and stop eating in a way that truly cares for the temple God has given you and His Spirit resides in.

Write about your experience throughout the day, focusing on how you approached eating until you were no longer hungry and yet not full. Also you'll recognize your hunger more accurately the less you eat between meals!

How did the Holy Spirit try to influence your temple care today?_____
How did your flesh want to respond?_____
How did you respond?_____

GOD DESIRES A PEOPLE WHOSE CHARACTER REVEALS A SPIRIT OF HONORING GOD'S FOOD SOURCE AND WHO USE IT FOR GOD'S INTENDED PURPOSE.

F.I.R.E

FRESH FRUIT   * NATURAL OILS/FATS
****
                                               *
                                               *
****
FRESH VEGETABLES (CAN BE STEAMED)   *NATURAL SWEETNERS
                                               *
                                               *
****
GRAINS   * MEAT/SEAFOOD/BEANS/NUTS
                                               *
                                               *
****
COOKED FRUIT   *COOKED VEGETABLES
                                               *
                                               *
****
PROCESSED FOODS   *PROCESSED LIQUIDS
                                               *
                                               *
****

ST-I used the tool of spiritual mind renewal (Read scriptures and daily reading on Temple Care) _____ **ST**-I used the tool of faith_____ **ST**-I used the tool of support_____
ST-I used the tool of prayer_____ **ST**-I used the tool of repentance ____ Exercise ____
ST-I used the tool of spiritual fasting – yes/no; juice fast - yes/no
SP-I'm being honest about and coping with my food temptations ____
SP-# of times I ate more than what I needed _____
SP-I demonstrated temperance (Spirit aided self-control) ____
SP-# of food items I ate created by God _____
Water intake _____ **SP**-# of food items and liquid not created by God _____
SP-# of times I ate for the purpose of hunger _____
SP-# of times I ate to cope with spiritual/emotional/physical issues _____

"…do you not know your body is the temple of the Holy Spirit who is in you…"
1 Corinthians 6:19

Week Seven-Day 46-Wednesday
God's Intended Purpose of Food
"All things are lawful for me, but not all things are profitable. All things are lawful for me, but I will not be mastered by anything. <u>Food is for the stomach, and the stomach is for food</u>; but God will do away with both of them. Yet the body is not for immorality, but for the Lord, and the Lord is for the body.
I Corinthians 6:12, 13

Now up to this point we have looked at scriptures that support the fact that the purpose of food is primarily for strengthening the body when it needs sustenance. So I ask, "When you eat, are you eating to provide your body strength and health or are you trying to receive something else?" Along those lines, I think the Corinthian scripture (I Corinthians 6:13) is very interesting. Paul (in this context) briefly states that food is for the stomach and the stomach for food and that God will eventually do away with both. Question: How many times have you eaten because you were sad, happy, anxious, bored, or confused? We've heard professionals talk about emotional eating and how unhealthy it can be for us. Yet the Word of God pointed out the true purpose for food long, long ago. Food was designed to primarily nourish our temples and not fulfill other needs. Our bellies/intestines break down and release food substances into our bodies/blood stream, and this ultimately strengthens our temples. The problem enters the picture when food is eaten outside of the purpose for which God designed it. The Jamieson, Fausset and Brown Commentary (1997) so accurately states, "Unlawful things ruin thousand: "lawful" things (unlawfully used), ten thousands."

A friend called me the other night and shared that her eating had "gotten out of control" and asked if I could get a food plan together for her. Immediately, I asked her what stressors were occurring in her life, and she started mentioning a few "benign" things but then began expressing some pretty big issues that would call for her to make some significant changes in her life. I gave her the exercise for today to complete. She recognized that she was using food to meet a need in which it was not intended to meet. She also realized that if she started to use the temporary pleasure of eating food as a coping skill, then her problems would definitely increase, hence, her feeling "out of control".

Eating food outside of God's intended purpose (i.e. using it as a coping mechanism) is as distorted as getting into a car wreck, leaving your car in the middle of the street and hobbling over to a local fast food restaurant to order fries and a shake. Instead of coping with the situation directly/appropriately by going out to talk to the arriving police officer about the incident, one uses food to "cope" with the situation. This form of coping is actually a distraction which diffuses the degree of focus and power you can have in directly dealing with the situation. Although a ridiculous example, *in essence* it is what thousands and thousands of people do everyday when they use food as a coping tool! Now, I can't deny resorting to a brownie once or twice when I was feeling sad, bored, tired/fatigued…, but I can say that I now involve myself in more conscious, direct coping skills (spoken about in God's word) to help me deal appropriately with life situations.

Coping with the Real Problem

1. I am currently eating to deal with discomfort (not hunger) in the following areas: (Check one)

Emotional ("I *feel* like having a brownie", stress, boredom, anger, jealousy, "feel unappreciated") _____

Relationship(s)/Social (God, spouse, friends, kids) _____

Physical (chronic pain, fatigue/need more &/or better sleep) _____

Vocation (struggle with having a meaningful life, "want more for my life",) _____

Past issues (i.e. neglect, physical, sexual, emotional abuse)

2. Write out in <u>detail</u> the #1 problem that influences you to eat in an unhealthy way.

_____

_____

_____

3. Usually, when one is struggling or having a problem, an emotion or various emotions are also experienced. What is the emotion (or emotions) which you experience during your #1 problem discussed above?

_____

_____

_____

4. How have you been dealing with the problem so far (besides eating)?

_____

_____

_____

_____

5. How does the reality of Ephesians 6:11 & 12 relate to your problem?

_____

_____

_____

6. Discuss the spiritual tools (prayer, searching scriptures, talking to spiritual leaders/support, fasting, repentance, faith) you've used in the past to help you through difficulties.

_____

_____

_____

7. Have you used all of the spiritual tools you've used with past difficulties to handle your problem and emotion regarding the care of your temple (#1 and #2)? Why or why not?

_____

_____

_____

8. What bothers you the most about your problem and how you've been handling it?

_____

_____

_____

_____

9. List ALL of the new ways in which you could handle this problem (no matter how ridiculous they may sound).

_____
_____
_____
_____

10. What do you believe God has been telling you about this situation up to this point? Also, what direction has He been leading you toward?

_____
_____
_____
_____
_____

11. Do you have any scriptural support for your previous answer? If so then write about it.

_____
_____
_____
_____

12. What can you do TODAY (rather than eat) to more directly and appropriately deal with the problem you have that has been affecting your temple care?

_____
_____
_____
_____

Go over this same exercise and continue too pray and add more information as God's Spirit increasingly guides you. As I stated earlier in the workbook, God is not a God of riddles but has a Will for our lives. He wants you to follow Him, so *He will show you which way to go*. It's just up to you to follow through with His Will when He reveals it.

My Personal Struggle

After completing this last exercise I realized that a couple of times a week I inappropriately desire certain foods as a "pick me up". In reality though, I actually need to sit and/or lie down, not be picked up! Now, when I'm feeling tired and want to eat, when I'm not really hungry and needing food for strength, I sit down, listen to my breathing and shut my eyes for a few minutes. Usually after a good rest or nap, focused breathing *and* prayer to God about the situation, I no longer want to eat. So, you see, I'm continually learning (like you) how to deal with the REAL issue rather than resort to eating inappropriately.

Write down one reason why you eat outside of God's intended purpose for food.

_____

Now for the rest of the program focus on dealing with the REAL issue. Also focus on using a spiritual tool or more as a way to cope rather than resort to eating.

GOD DESIRES A PEOPLE WHOSE CHARACTER REVEALS A SPIRIT OF HONORING GOD'S FOOD SOURCE AND WHO USE IT FOR GOD'S INTENDED PURPOSE.

F.I.R.E

FRESH FRUIT   * NATURAL OILS/FATS
****
                                               *
                                               *
****
FRESH VEGETABLES (CAN BE STEAMED)   *NATURAL SWEETNERS
                                               *
                                               *
****
GRAINS   * MEAT/SEAFOOD/BEANS/NUTS
                                               *
                                               *
****
COOKED FRUIT   *COOKED VEGETABLES
                                               *
                                               *
****
PROCESSED FOODS   *PROCESSED LIQUIDS
                                               *
                                               *
****

ST-I used the tool of spiritual mind renewal (Read scriptures and daily reading on Temple Care) _____ **ST**-I used the tool of faith____ **ST**-I used the tool of support_____
ST-I used the tool of prayer____ **ST**-I used the tool of repentance ___ Exercise ___
ST-I used the tool of spiritual fasting – yes/no; juice fast - yes/no
SP-I'm being honest about and coping with my food temptations ___
SP-# of times I ate more than what I needed _____
SP-I demonstrated temperance (Spirit aided self-control) ____
SP-# of food items I ate created by God ____
Water intake ____ **SP**-# of food items and liquid not created by God ____
SP-# of times I ate for the purpose of hunger ____
SP-# of times I ate to cope with spiritual/emotional/physical issues _____

How did the Holy Spirit try to influence your temple care today?_____
How did your flesh want to respond?_____
How did you respond?_____

"...do you not know your body is the temple of the Holy Spirit who is in you..."
1 Corinthians 6:19

Week Seven-Day 47-Thursday
<u>God's Intended Purpose of Food</u>
<u>"All things are lawful for me, but not all things are profitable. All things are lawful</u>
<u>for me, but I will not be mastered by anything.</u> Food is for the stomach, and the
stomach is for food; but God will do away with both of them. Yet the body is not for
immorality, but for the Lord, and the Lord is for the body.
I Corinthians 6:12, 13

When we look back at the beginning of 1 Corinthians 6:12 we see Paul expressing that he would not be mastered by anything. I do not believe that our God created food and drink to master over his highest creation…you and me. Paul was attempting to warn Christians about carrying the popular phase at that time, "All things are lawful unto me", to far. He was concerned that possessing such a mind set could set one up to be in bondage to a deceitful, crafty individual or ones own fleshly appetite. Yes, Christ has made Christians free, free from the bondage of sin, through his death! Yet, Paul says that he would never allow his liberty or freedom to put him under the power of a bodily appetite. "Though all meats were supposed lawful, he would not become a glutton or a drunkard. And much less would he abuse the maxim of lawful liberty to countenance the sin of fornication." (Matthew Henry Commentary, 1991).

A similar concept is prevalent in our time today! Some people say to me "Well, I'm going to die of something, so I'm going to eat the way I want to and enjoy it!" Yet the question is, "Are you, as a child of God improperly under the power of something, using it outside of its purpose? Paul suggests that we are not to be under the power of a bodily appetite. A good friend of mine came to the realization that she was under the power of a particular soft drink, primarily due to its caffeine. Whenever she was dragging in energy she would grab that soft drink (very regularly) to improve her "performance". She used the drink to keep her on her toes and in doing so she developed an addiction to the caffeine and sugar. She felt mastered by the drink because when she didn't have it she believed she didn't function well and experienced withdrawal headaches and fatigued. Fortunately, in faith she began to fervently use the tools of prayer, repentance, mind renewal through the scriptures and Christian support. She asked God to strengthen and energize her whenever she felt weak, tired and wanted to depend on the soft drink for deliverance. She found that God was waiting on her to ask Him for help and He consistently met her needs! I must mention that she also practiced something else in faith to help her with fatigue which was that she got more rest based on her personal needs. Today she determines when she is going to have her favorite soft drink which is usually in moderation on weekends. Through God's aid she is no longer "mastered" by a soft drink!

"The 'power' ought to be in the hands of the believer, not in the thing which he uses; else his liberty is forfeited-he ceases to be his own master." (Jamieson, Fausset and Brown, 1997)

What food substance and/or drink do you feel powerless too?

_____   _____

_____   _____

_____   _____

_____   _____

      What spiritual steps can you began to take to no longer be mastered by the above mentioned item(s)?

_____

_____

How did the Holy Spirit try to influence your temple care today?_____

How did your flesh want to respond?_____

How did you respond?_____

F.I.R.E

FRESH FRUIT   * NATURAL OILS/FATS

****

                           *

                           *

****

FRESH VEGETABLES (CAN BE STEAMED)   *NATURAL SWEETNERS

                           *

                           *

****

GRAINS   * MEAT/SEAFOOD/BEANS/NUTS

                           *

                           *

****

COOKED FRUIT   *COOKED VEGETABLES

                           *

                           *

****

PROCESSED FOODS   *PROCESSED LIQUIDS

                           *

                           *

****

ST-I used the tool of spiritual mind renewal (Read scriptures and daily reading on Temple Care) _____ **ST**-I used the tool of faith____ **ST**-I used the tool of support_____
ST-I used the tool of prayer____ **ST**-I used the tool of repentance ___ Exercise ___
ST-I used the tool of spiritual fasting – yes/no; juice fast - yes/no
SP-I'm being honest about and coping with my food temptations ___
SP-# of times I ate more than what I needed _____
SP-I demonstrated temperance (Spirit aided self-control) ____
SP-# of food items I ate created by God ____
Water intake ____ **SP**-# of food items and liquid not created by God ____
SP-# of times I ate for the purpose of hunger ____
SP-# of times I ate to cope with spiritual/emotional/physical issues _____

"...do you not know your body is the temple of the Holy Spirit who is in you..."
1 Corinthians 6:19

Week Seven-Day 48-Friday
God's Intended Purpose of Food
"All things are lawful for me, but not all things are profitable. All things are lawful for me, but I will not be mastered by anything. Food is for the stomach, and the stomach is for food; but God will do away with both of them. Yet the body is not for immorality, but for the Lord, and the Lord is for the body.
I Corinthians 6:12, 13

At this point, I want to address Paul's comment above about God destroying the belly (temple) and food. This small statement says so much! You see, dear reader, your spirit is destined to live forever, yet your body (temple) and food are temporary and will perish by God's own hand! It is amazing to think that all of our lower appetites and sensations will be destroyed by death and such needs/experiences, the earth and what it manifests will be destroyed by fire. In fact, at the coming of Christ, our natural bodies/temples will be changed from corruptible flesh to incorruptible spirit (1Corinthians 15:44-53)! **With this being the case, when we immortal beings choose to become enslaved to that which is temporary, we've forgotten (or never really knew) whom we are (spiritual identity crisis!)!** Remember, we were created in God's image, an incorruptible/eternal spirit who God loves indescribably!

Also, not only are we eternal, immortal spirits, but those who have repented and are baptized believers also have another spirit within them! Acts 2:38 says ***"Then Peter said unto them, Repent, and be baptized every one of you in the name of Jesus Christ for the remission of sins, and ye shall receive the gift of the Holy Spirit."*** The Bible tells us that this Spirit, the Holy Spirit, "instructs, regenerates, sanctifies, and comforts believers" (The New Unger's Bible Dictionary, 1988). So, we even have a greater power within to help us conquer the bondage of the flesh and its appetite. I believe that we, ultimately as spiritual beings, need to stop listening to the world, which tells us that pampering our fleshly appetites (often to its destruction) is what makes life enjoyable and worth living. **Sure, it's healthy to enjoy food, yet I believe to become a slave to that which is perishable actually diminishes some of our immortal presence and power here on earth.**

How did the Holy Spirit try to influence your temple care today?_____

How did your flesh want to respond?_____

How did you respond?_____

GOD DESIRES A PEOPLE WHOSE CHARACTER REVEALS A SPIRIT OF HONORING GOD'S FOOD SOURCE AND USE IT FOR GOD'S INTENDED PURPOSE.

F.I.R.E

FRESH FRUIT   * NATURAL OILS/FATS

****

                                                       *

                                                       *

****

FRESH VEGETABLES (CAN BE STEAMED)   *NATURAL SWEETNERS

                                                       *

                                                       *

****

GRAINS   * MEAT/SEAFOOD/BEANS/NUTS

                                                       *

                                                       *

****

COOKED FRUIT   *COOKED VEGETABLES

                                                       *

                                                       *

****

PROCESSED FOODS   *PROCESSED LIQUIDS

                                                       *

                                                       *

****

ST-I used the tool of spiritual mind renewal (Read scriptures and daily reading on Temple Care) _____ **ST**-I used the tool of faith____ **ST**-I used the tool of support_____
ST-I used the tool of prayer____ **ST**-I used the tool of repentance ___ Exercise ___
ST-I used the tool of spiritual fasting – yes/no; juice fast - yes/no
SP-I'm being honest about and coping with my food temptations ___
SP-# of times I ate more than what I needed _____
SP-I demonstrated temperance (self-control) ____
SP-# of food items I ate created by God ____
Water intake ____ **SP**-# of food items and liquid not created by God ____
SP-# of times I ate for the purpose of hunger ____
SP-# of times I ate to cope with spiritual/emotional/physical issues _____

"...do you not know your body is the temple of the Holy Spirit who is in you..."
1 Corinthians 6:19
Week Seven-Day 49-Saturday-Summary
God's Intended Purpose of Food

As we can see there are quite a few scriptural references which reveal that the true purpose of food was and still is to primarily strengthen the body. We are to provide our bodies food substances so that it can function properly with strength. Years ago, I worked with a young lady who was diagnosed with anorexia nervosa. During the height of her illness, she was unable to push her vacuum cleaner across her floor because she deprived herself of food so much that she lacked strength. Of course, this is not what God has intended for us and praise God, she was able to, with much work, change the way she cared for her temple.

On the other hand, what about those who sit at the table eating until they can't move? Or, what about those who mindlessly pop food (healthy or unhealthy) into their mouths when they are not truly hungry? Or what about those who just "have a taste for something salty/sweet" and just have to have it even though they are not hungry? Let's continue to remind ourselves of the primary God-given reason for food and practice this spiritual reality.

We also looked at how Paul determined that he would not allow himself to be mastered by his fleshly appetite! He fought against being mastered by food, drink and fornication. What an inspiring goal! Remember you are an immortal spirit so live your life like it and continually break those bonds of temporary, perishable temptations!

GOD DESIRES A PEOPLE WHOSE CHARACTER REVEALS A SPIRIT OF HONORING GOD'S FOOD SOURCE AND WHO USE IT FOR GOD'S INTENDED PURPOSE.

F.I.R.E

FRESH FRUIT   * NATURAL OILS/FATS
****
                                                     *
                                                     *
****
FRESH VEGETABLES (CAN BE STEAMED)   *NATURAL SWEETNERS
                                                     *
                                                     *
****
GRAINS   * MEAT/SEAFOOD/BEANS/NUTS
                                                     *
                                                     *
****
COOKED FRUIT   *COOKED VEGETABLES
                                                     *
                                                     *
****
PROCESSED FOODS   *PROCESSED LIQUIDS
                                                     *
                                                     *
****

ST-I used the tool of spiritual mind renewal (Read scriptures and daily reading on Temple Care) _____ **ST**-I used the tool of faith____ **ST**-I used the tool of support_____
ST-I used the tool of prayer____
ST-I used the tool of repentance ___ Exercise ___
ST-I used the tool of spiritual fasting – yes/no; juice fast - yes/no
SP-I'm being honest about and coping with my food temptations ___
SP-# of times I ate more than what I needed _____ **SP**-I demonstrated temperance (Spirit aided self-control) __
SP-# of food items I ate created by God _____ Water intake ____
SP-# of food items and liquid not created by God ____
SP-# of times I ate for the purpose of hunger ____
SP-# of times I ate to cope with spiritual/emotional/physical issues _____

Self Regulating Sheet

Looking back on this week's F.I.R.E. forms how did you do?

1. Spiritual mind renewal (reading what the bible says about Temple Care)
How did I rate this week with this spiritual tool? _____
1-10 (1=not well at all) (10= praise God really well!)

2. Faith (actions toward Godly Temple Care)
How did I rate this week with this spiritual tool? _____
1-10 (1=not well at all) (10= praise God really well!)

3. Support (contacting spiritual support partner/s and discuss Temple Care)
How did I rate this week with this spiritual tool? _____
1-10 (1=not well at all) (10= praise God really well!)

4. Prayer (praying to God about any and every issue regarding my Temple Care)
How did I rate this week with this spiritual tool? _____
1-10 (1=not well at all) (10= praise God really well!)

5. Repentance (expressing Godly sorrow and changing my ways through the Holy Spirit)
How did I rate this week with this spiritual tool? _____
1-10 (1=not well at all) (10= praise God really well!)

6. Fasting (not eating for 1 day or 3 dinners and replace with prayer, singing, reading God's Word...)
How did I rate this week with this spiritual tool? _____
1-10 (1=not well at all) (10= praise God really well!)

7. This week the following came easy for me regarding care of my temple?

_____

_____

8. This week the following was very difficult for me regarding caring for my temple?

_____

9. After evaluating my ratings this week, these two spiritual tools (choose the lowest rated ones) are what I need to improve on next week regarding temple care?

_____

_____

God's Intended Purpose for Food
Week Eight

"...do you not know your body is the temple of the Holy Spirit who is in you..."
1 Corinthians 6:19
Week Eight-Day 50-Sunday
<u>**God's Intended Perspective on His Created Food**</u>
"And <u>God saw all that He had made, and behold, it was very good.</u>"
Genesis 1:31

I like how the Adam Clarke's Commentary (1996) sums up "it was very good" keeping in mind that all of God's creation (including His food) is being commented upon. "...for everything was formed to the utmost perfection of its nature so that nothing could be added or diminished without encumbering the operations of matter and spirit on the one hand, or rendering them inefficient to the end proposed on the other; and God has so done all these marvelous works as to be glorified in all, by all, and through all."

Carbohydrates, carbohydrates--bad, bad, bad! Well, that's the diet craze at this moment, yet food with carbohydrates is not our problem. Fresh, sweet, delicious mangos, bananas, and pineapples, which have what some would consider a significant amount of carbohydrates in them, were created by God and are "very good" for us. Also, filling, tasty sweet potatoes, white potatoes, and kidney beans have been created by God and are "very good" for us. Many of these foods provide us with a wonderful source of energy, fiber and water (which many Americans are in need of) and provide essential nutrients that God has specifically intended for our bodies. *Carbohydrates are not the problem; having a soul that craves for and regularly submits to processed, and proven unhealthy food (which contradicts the wisdom of God) is the problem.*

There are various levels of processing foods, yet for the most part, the closer our food is to its original God-given state, the better health benefits (and weight loss) we'll experience. The more you can find meat that is taken directly from the animal without much processing (fresh chicken breasts versus chicken fingers), the better. I tend to get about 50% of my produce fresh and 50% frozen. Fresh and frozen fruits and vegetables have undergone some form of processing yet they have less loss of nutrients and are pretty close to their original form than most processed foods.

1 Tim 4:4 reads, *"For every creature of God is good, and nothing to be refused, if it be received with thanksgiving..."* I find it very interesting that a particular commentary expounded on 1 Timothy 4:4 by saying that every creature is good as God has created it yet, "As man perverts them, it is no longer proper to call them the 'creation of God,' and they may be injurious in the highest degree." (Barnes Notes, 1997)

List some of God's food, in their most pure and natural form and then list their more processed derivatives, created by man.

God's Food	*Processed Form*
Peanuts	Peanut Butter

172

How did the Holy Spirit try to influence your temple care today?_____

How did your flesh want to respond?_____

How did you respond?_____

GOD DESIRES A PEOPLE WHOSE CHARACTER REVEALS A SPIRIT OF APPRECIATION FOR AND POSITIVE MINDSET REGARDING HIS CREATED FOOD.

F.I.R.E

FRESH FRUIT   * NATURAL OILS/FATS

****

                                       *

                                       *

****

FRESH VEGETABLES (CAN BE STEAMED)   *NATURAL SWEETNERS

                                       *

                                       *

****

GRAINS   * MEAT/SEAFOOD/BEANS/NUTS

                                       *

                                       *

****

COOKED FRUIT   *COOKED VEGETABLES

                                       *

                                       *

****

PROCESSED FOODS   *PROCESSED LIQUIDS

                                       *

                                       *

****

<u>ST-I used the tool of spiritual mind renewal</u> (Read scriptures and daily reading on Temple Care) _____ **ST**-I used the tool of faith____ **ST**-I used the tool of support_____
ST-I used the tool of prayer____ **ST**-I used the tool of repentance ___ Exercise ___
ST-I used the tool of spiritual fasting – yes/no; juice fast – yes/no
SP-I'm being honest about and coping with my food temptations ___
SP-# of times I ate more than what I needed _____
SP-I demonstrated temperance (Spirit aided self-control) ____
SP-# of food items I ate created by God ____
Water intake ____ **SP**-# of food items and liquid not created by God ____
SP-# of times I ate for the purpose of hunger ____
SP-# of times I ate to cope with spiritual/emotional/physical issues _____
SP-<u>My perspective about God's food and man-made food is becoming more correct (yes/no)</u>____

"...do you not know your body is the temple of the Holy Spirit who is in you..."
1 Corinthians 6:19
Week Eight-Day 51-Monday
God's Intended Perspective on His Created Food
"And the <u>earth brought forth vegetation, plants yielding seed after their kind, and trees bearing fruit, with seed in them</u>, after their kind; and <u>God saw that it was good</u>."
Genesis 1:12

The International Standard Bible Encyclopedia states that the word "good" used in reference to God's created food is "possessing desirable qualities" is "beneficial" and "agreeable".

Choose one meal made of God's food from your Favorite Food list and *really* observe and appreciate the natural food God has provided for you. Preferably eat alone, just you and God. Notice the flavor, texture (in mouth and in hand), and the smell, all the while giving thanks to your heavenly Father for His provision. God saw that the food he created "was good" how do you see it? Write about your thoughts and feelings throughout your meal.

_____

GOD DESIRES A PEOPLE WHOSE CHARACTER REVEALS A SPIRIT OF APPRECIATION FOR AND POSITIVE MINDSET REGARDING HIS CREATED FOOD.

F.I.R.E

FRESH FRUIT   * NATURAL OILS/FATS
****
                                               *
                                               *
****
FRESH VEGETABLES (CAN BE STEAMED)   *NATURAL SWEETNERS
                                               *
                                               *
****
GRAINS   * MEAT/SEAFOOD/BEANS/NUTS
                                               *
                                               *
****
COOKED FRUIT   *COOKED VEGETABLES
                                               *
                                               *
****
PROCESSED FOODS   *PROCESSED LIQUIDS
                                               *
                                               *
****

ST-I used the tool of spiritual mind renewal (Read scriptures and daily reading on Temple Care) _____   **ST**-I used the tool of faith____   **ST**-I used the tool of support_____
ST-I used the tool of prayer____   **ST**-I used the tool of repentance ___ Exercise ___
ST-I used the tool of spiritual fasting – yes/no; juice fast - yes/no
SP-I'm being honest about and coping with my food temptations ___
SP-# of times I ate more than what I needed ___
SP-I demonstrated temperance (Spirit aided self-control) ____
SP-# of food items I ate created by God ____
Water intake ____   **SP**-# of food items and liquid not created by God ____
SP-# of times I ate for the purpose of hunger ____
SP-# of times I ate to cope with spiritual/emotional/physical issues _____
SP-_My perspective about God's food and man-made food is becoming more correct (yes/no)_____

"…do you not know your body is the temple of the Holy Spirit who is in you…"
1 Corinthians 6:19

Week Eight-Day 52-Tuesday
God's Intended Perspective on His Created Food
"And the Lord God planted a garden toward the east, in Eden; and there He placed the man whom He had formed. And out of the ground <u>the Lord God caused to grow every tree that is pleasing to the sight and good for food</u>…"
Genesis 2:8, 9

One of the most pleasing breakfast (or dessert) sights for me is a bowl full of cut strawberries, 1 banana and blueberries in rice drink (mixed with raw honey or Stevia). It's such a healthy, wholesome, vitamin-packed dish, AND it's delicious! It's awesome how God created many foods in such a way as to attract them to us visually. Today, I challenge you to take extra time noticing how our Heavenly Father designed fresh fruits, vegetables, nuts, and grains from the earth for you. Spend time savoring the flavors (using herbs to enhance flavors if you'd like), textures, smells and/or colors that God, in His Genius, created, from nothing, into the perfect food source for your body/His Temple.

As the scripture says, God created substances that are pleasant to look at and "good for food". Question: is what you are eating "*good* for food" or just food? I believe that God's food in general, tends to do a few things extremely well. God's food will naturally nourish, cleanse, heal, and eliminate. Today, I'd like for you to focus on foods that are packed with natural vitamins, minerals, carbohydrates, protein, antioxidants, water, and fat/oil. I encourage you to focus on these natural substances rather than the synthetic/processed ones. For instance, you can get protein from a synthetic, processed protein bar or from a nice cut Rib eye (one of my favorites) or from a salad with kidney beans combined with sweet corn tossed in it. Additionally, many other health benefits come from these protein sources of God's.

God would never create the type of food that man creates because He loves us to much!
NOT EVERYTHING IS "GOOD FOR FOOD"!

How did the Holy Spirit try to influence your temple care today?_____
How did your flesh want to respond?_____
How did you respond?_____

GOD DESIRES A PEOPLE WHOSE CHARACTER REVEALS A SPIRIT OF APPRECIATION FOR AND POSITIVE MINDSET REGARDING HIS CREATED FOOD.

F.I.R.E

FRESH FRUIT   * NATURAL OILS/FATS
****

                                              *
                                              *
****

FRESH VEGETABLES (CAN BE STEAMED)   *NATURAL SWEETNERS
                                              *
                                              *

****

GRAINS   * MEAT/SEAFOOD/BEANS/NUTS
                                              *
                                              *

****

COOKED FRUIT   *COOKED VEGETABLES
                                              *
                                              *

****

PROCESSED FOODS   *PROCESSED LIQUIDS
                                              *
                                              *

****

ST-I used the tool of spiritual mind renewal (Read scriptures and daily reading on
Temple Care) _____   **ST**-I used the tool of faith____   **ST**-I used the tool of support_____
ST-I used the tool of prayer____   **ST**-I used the tool of repentance ___ Exercise ___
ST-I used the tool of spiritual fasting – yes/no; juice fast - yes/no
SP-I'm being honest about and coping with my food temptations ___
SP-# of times I ate more than what I needed ___
SP-I demonstrated temperance (Spirit aided self-control)___
SP-# of food items I ate created by God _____ Water intake _____
SP-# of food items and liquid not created by God ____   SP-# of times I ate for the purpose
of hunger _____   SP-# of times I ate to cope with spiritual/emotional/physical issues _____
*SP-**My perspective about God's food and man-made food is becoming more correct
(yes/no)____**

"...do you not know your body is the temple of the Holy Spirit who is in you..."
1 Corinthians 6:19

Week Eight-Day 53-Wednesday
God's Intended Perspective on His Created Food
"When <u>the woman saw that the tree was good for food</u>, and that <u>it was a delight to the eyes</u>..."
Genesis 3:6

Continuing with yesterday's theme "good for food," I'd like to clarify a point. Just because we can eat or ingest something does not mean that it is "good for food". For instance, I can boil paper, sprinkle salt on it and eat it, yet, although edible, it is not "good for food". Now although the example I just mentioned is not normally ingested, we do ingest things that are comparable/equivalent in its food value, and the only difference is that what we eat "tastes good".

When preparing the section on "Temptation" I came across a powerful explanation that I'd like to address in this section. In looking at the word "enticed" from James 1:14 the Matthew Henry's Commentary states the following:

> "The word translated enticed signifies being wheedled and beguiled by allurements and deceitful representations of things, exelkomenos kai deleazomenos. There is a great deal of violence done to conscience and to the mind by the power of corruption: and there is a great deal of cunning and deceit and flattery in sin to gain us to its interests. The force and power of sin could never prevail, were it not for its cunning and guile."

The part of this interpretation which interests me is the "violence" that is done to our conscience and "deceitful representations of things" that tempt us to do things that actually harm us! You read about and hear about certain food substances that are consistently found to harm our health over a period of time that is man-made. They harm our health by leading us to experience being overweight or obese, to having high blood pressure, high cholesterol, sluggish immune systems, constipation, diverticulitis, food allergy symptoms, heart disease, some forms of cancer...!

Can you list some of these man-made foods that you may eat that are believed to harm your temple?

_____   _____   _____
_____   _____   _____
_____   _____   _____

What are some of the "deceitful representations" of these substances/products?

_____   _____   _____
_____   _____   _____
_____   _____   _____

GOD DESIRES A PEOPLE WHOSE CHARACTER REVEALS A SPIRIT OF APPRECIATION FOR AND POSITIVE MINDSET REGARDING HIS CREATED FOOD.

F.I.R.E

FRESH FRUIT   * NATURAL OILS/FATS
****
                                             *
                                             *
****
FRESH VEGETABLES (CAN BE STEAMED)   *NATURAL SWEETNERS
                                             *
                                             *
****
GRAINS   * MEAT/SEAFOOD/BEANS/NUTS
                                             *
                                             *
****
COOKED FRUIT   *COOKED VEGETABLES
                                             *
                                             *
****
PROCESSED FOODS   *PROCESSED LIQUIDS
                                             *
                                             *
****

ST-I used the tool of spiritual mind renewal (Read scriptures and daily reading on Temple Care) _____ **ST**-I used the tool of faith____ **ST**-I used the tool of support_____
ST-I used the tool of prayer____ **ST**-I used the tool of repentance ___ Exercise ___
ST-I used the tool of spiritual fasting – yes/no; juice fast - yes/no
SP-I'm being honest about and coping with my food temptations ___
SP-# of times I ate more than what I needed ___
SP-I demonstrated temperance (Spirit aided self-control) ___
SP-# of food items I ate created by God _____ Water intake ____
SP-# of food items and liquid not created by God ____
SP-# of times I ate for the purpose of hunger ____
SP-# of times I ate to cope with spiritual/emotional/physical issues _____
SP-<u>My perspective about God's food and man-made food is becoming more correct (yes/no)</u>____

How did the Holy Spirit try to influence your temple care today?_____
How did your flesh want to respond?_____
How did you respond?_____

"...do you not know your body is the temple of the Holy Spirit who is in you..."
1 Corinthians 6:19

Week Eight-Day 54-Thursday
God's Intended Perspective on His Created Food
***"For everything created by God is good, and nothing is to be rejected, if it is received
with gratitude; for it is sanctified by means of the word of God and prayer."***
I Timothy 4:4, 5

Choose five favorite foods created by God. Investigate and then list all of their
health benefits that you can find! Check the Internet, books, magazines--anything that
can give you the information you need. Also, add newly found favorite foods on your
Favorite Foods Created by God list at anytime. Notice how the food which God has
created is truly good for food.

<u>*Example*</u>

<u>*God's Food=Good*</u>	<u>*Health Benefits*</u>
Pistachio Nuts	Excellent for protein, calcium, thiamin
	Vitamin A & E for strong immune system
	Helps decrease fatigue
	Small amount of magnesium, phosphorous, irons and zinc

1._____   _____
                                                                 _____

2._____   _____

3._____   _____

4._____   _____

5._____   _____

F.I.R.E

FRESH FRUIT   * NATURAL OILS/FATS
****
                                               *
                                               *
****
FRESH VEGETABLES (CAN BE STEAMED)   *NATURAL SWEETNERS
                                               *
                                               *
****
GRAINS   * MEAT/SEAFOOD/BEANS/NUTS
                                               *
                                               *
****
COOKED FRUIT   *COOKED VEGETABLES
                                               *
                                               *
****
PROCESSED FOODS   *PROCESSED LIQUIDS
                                               *
                                               *
****

ST-I used the tool of spiritual mind renewal (Read scriptures and daily reading on Temple Care) _____ **ST**-I used the tool of faith____ **ST**-I used the tool of support_____
ST-I used the tool of prayer____ **ST**-I used the tool of repentance ___ Exercise ___
ST-I used the tool of spiritual fasting – yes/no; juice fast – yes/no
SP-I'm being honest about and coping with my food temptations ___
SP-# of times I ate more than what I needed __
SP-I demonstrated temperance (Spirit aided self-control) ___
SP-# of food items I ate created by God _____ Water intake ____
SP-# of food items and liquid not created by God ____
SP-# of times I ate for the purpose of hunger ____
SP-# of times I ate to cope with spiritual/emotional/physical issues _____
*SP-**My perspective about God's food and man-made food is becoming more correct (yes/no)____***

How did the Holy Spirit try to influence your temple care today?_____
How did your flesh want to respond?_____
How did you respond?_____

"...do you not know your body is the temple of the Holy Spirit who is in you..."
1 Corinthians 6:19

Week Eight-Day 55-Friday
God's Intended Perspective on His Created Food
Book of Song of Solomon

The most romantic, passionate book of the Bible, Song of Solomon, is such a pleasure to read and learn about. You may be wondering why I chose it for a workbook regarding temple care. Well, in this book of the Bible, I see how the author often uses healthy, natural foods as a symbol of what is pure, pleasurable and good in a couple's relationship as they anticipate marriage. "Apples", "cinnamon" "spice", "sweet fruit", "pomegranates", and "dripping milk and honey" are the foods described in this sensual poem of love. So, in addressing how to see God's food, many of us need to flip the switch (change our thinking) and see the tantalizing beauty in God's food. You can do it! You can decide what to put and focus on in your soul (thinking, mind, will...)!

Buy some healthy food (by this time I hope that you have a refrigerator full of it!), eat it throughout the day and write about your findings! In other words, write about the ways in which you experience pleasure from eating God's food (for instance, I could write that I love the juiciness of an almost overly ripe Red Pear). If you are married and find that this exercise is stimulating some lawful desires in you, then share your findings with your spouse. You may find that even a spouse who doesn't want to do this program may very willingly participate in this exercise!

_____

_____

_____

_____

_____

_____

GOD DESIRES A PEOPLE WHOSE CHARACTER REVEALS A SPIRIT OF APPRECIATION FOR AND POSITIVE MINDSET REGARDING HIS CREATED FOOD.

How did the Holy Spirit try to influence your temple care today?_____

How did your flesh want to respond?_____

How did you respond?_____

F.I.R.E

FRESH FRUIT   * NATURAL OILS/FATS
****
                                               *
                                               *
****
FRESH VEGETABLES (CAN BE STEAMED)   *NATURAL SWEETNERS
                                               *
                                               *
****
GRAINS   * MEAT/SEAFOOD/BEANS/NUTS
                                               *
                                               *
****
COOKED FRUIT   *COOKED VEGETABLES
                                               *
                                               *
****
PROCESSED FOODS   *PROCESSED LIQUIDS
                                               *
                                               *
****

ST-I used the tool of spiritual mind renewal (Read scriptures and daily reading on Temple Care) _____ **ST**-I used the tool of faith____ **ST**-I used the tool of support_____
ST-I used the tool of prayer____ **ST**-I used the tool of repentance ___ Exercise ___
ST-I used the tool of spiritual fasting – yes/no; juice fast - yes/no
SP-I'm being honest about and coping with my food temptations ___
SP-# of times I ate more than what I needed ____
SP-# of times I demonstrated temperance (self-control) __
SP-# of food items I ate created by God ____ Water intake ____
SP-# of food items and liquid not created by God ____
SP-# of times I ate for the purpose of hunger ____
SP-# of times I ate to cope with spiritual/emotional/physical issues _____
SP-My perspective about God's food and man-made food is becoming more correct (yes/no)____

"...do you not know your body is the temple of the Holy Spirit who is in you..."
1 Corinthians 6:19

Week Eight-Day 56-Saturday
Summary
God's Intended Perspective on His Created Food

The scriptures in Genesis reflect how God viewed the food that He created. Many people view food categories such as vegetables as being nasty, unlikable, bland or just plain boring. Yet, if we are to take on God's view, we must recognize, acknowledge and come to believe that His food is good. Good in every sense-- it's delicious, pleasant, and excellently designed for our bodies! This doesn't mean that you must learn to like every vegetable. Yet, I encourage you to learn to like and eat as much of God's food as you can and less and less of man's food! You see, having a positive perspective on God's created food for us continues to develop our character into one that respects His provision for our lives and this glorifies Him. **Primarily, eating and appreciating God's food reveals our trust in His wisdom about what is best for us. It also reflects a practical appreciation of how He provides for our *every* need.**

Explore new foods that God has created! Believe me, there's a lot more out there than broccoli, carrots and lettuce (see Universal Food List). If we truly come to believe this spiritual principle, seeing the goodness in God's food, then we'd be more likely to eat *and* enjoy it.

Lastly, in 1Timothy 4:4, we see that everything which God created is good. Particularly, in this context, Timothy is referring to food and marriage (yes, *God, not man,* created marriage). Again, everything which God created, including His food, is good!

GOD DESIRES A PEOPLE WHOSE CHARACTER REVEALS A SPIRIT OF APPRECIATION FOR AND POSITIVE MINDSET REGARDING HIS CREATED FOOD.

How did the Holy Spirit try to influence your temple care today?_____
How did your flesh want to respond?_____
How did you respond?_____

F.I.R.E

FRESH FRUIT   * NATURAL OILS/FATS
****
              *
              *
****
FRESH VEGETABLES (CAN BE STEAMED) *NATURAL SWEETNERS
              *
              *
****
GRAINS   * MEAT/SEAFOOD/BEANS/NUTS
              *
              *
****
COOKED FRUIT   *COOKED VEGETABLES
              *
              *
****
PROCESSED FOODS   *PROCESSED LIQUIDS
              *
              *
****

ST-I used the tool of spiritual mind renewal (Read scriptures and daily reading on Temple Care) _____ **ST**-I used the tool of faith____ **ST**-I used the tool of support_____
ST-I used the tool of prayer____ **ST**-I used the tool of repentance ___ Exercise ___
ST-I used the tool of spiritual fasting yes/no; juice fast - yes/no
SP-I'm being honest about and coping with my food temptations ___
SP-# of times I ate more than what I needed ___
SP-I demonstrated temperance (Spirit aided self-control) ___
SP-# of food items I ate created by God ____
Water intake ____ **SP**-# of food items and liquid not created by God ____
SP-# of times I ate for the purpose of hunger ____
SP-# of times I ate to cope with spiritual/emotional/physical issues _____
SP-_My perspective about God's food and man-made food is becoming more correct (yes/no)_____

Self Regulating Sheet

Looking back on this week's F.I.R.E. forms how did you do?

1. Spiritual mind renewal (reading what the bible says about Temple Care)
How did I rate this week with this spiritual tool? _____
1-10 (1=not well at all) (10= praise God really well!)

2. Faith (actions toward Godly Temple Care)
How did I rate this week with this spiritual tool? _____
1-10 (1=not well at all) (10= praise God really well!)

3. Support (contacting spiritual support partner/s and discuss Temple Care)
How did I rate this week with this spiritual tool? _____
1-10 (1=not well at all) (10= praise God really well!)

4. Prayer (praying to God about any and every issue regarding my Temple Care)
How did I rate this week with this spiritual tool? _____
1-10 (1=not well at all) (10= praise God really well!)

5. Repentance (expressing Godly sorrow and changing my ways through the Holy Spirit)
How did I rate this week with this spiritual tool? _____
1-10 (1=not well at all) (10= praise God really well!)

6. Fasting (not eating for 1 day or 3 dinners and replace with prayer, singing, reading God's Word...)
How did I rate this week with this spiritual tool? _____
1-10 (1=not well at all) (10= praise God really well!)

7. This week the following came easy for me regarding care of my temple?
_____
_____

8. This week the following was very difficult for me regarding caring for my temple?
_____
_____

9. After evaluating my ratings this week, these two spiritual tools (choose the lowest rated ones) are what I need to improve on next week regarding temple care?
_____
_____

Tip: Jot down more scriptures on patience and carry them to encourage you as you go through the program.

God's Word on Thanksgiving
Week Nine

"…do you not know your body is the temple of the Holy Spirit who is in you…"
1 Corinthians 6:19

Week Nine-Day 57-Sunday
God's Word on Thanksgiving and Blessing
"…and <u>He took the seven loaves and the fish</u>; and <u>giving thanks</u>, He broke them and started giving them to the disciples, and the disciples in turn, to the multitudes."
Matthew 15:36

Honestly, I am unable to explain the spiritual impact having a thankful spirit toward God for providing His food for us has on *our being*. Yet, I believe that it's similar (yet more profound) to when parents teach their children the good manners of saying, "thank you," when someone thinks enough to give them something. A child thinks that it's a formality or that it is what you do when you are a good girl/boy. Yet, parents are instilling a deeper character building value within the child that will last a lifetime and this value reflects the type of parenting the child received! I hope that it becomes clear that God wants and deserves a people who acknowledge their true dependency on Him and the things He provides for them. As James states, ***"Every good gift and perfect gift is from above and cometh down from the Father of lights with whom there is no variableness, neither shadow of turning."***

The Matthew Henry Commentary states that, "Giving thanks to God is a proper way of craving a blessing from God." And when we come to ask and receive further mercy, we ought to give thanks for the mercies we have received." What an honorable practice for God's people.

How has God blessed you so far regarding your temple care or your weight loss since you have started this program and have you thanked him for it? Why or why not?

Are there more blessings that you desire God to give you regarding your temple care? If so, what are they?

GOD DESIRES A PEOPLE WHOSE CHARACTER REVEALS A SPIRIT OF THANKSGIVING FOR HIS PROVISION.

How did the Holy Spirit try to influence your temple care today?_____
How did your flesh want to respond?_____
How did you respond?_____

F.I.R.E

FRESH FRUIT	* NATURAL OILS/FATS

****

*
*

****

FRESH VEGETABLES (CAN BE STEAMED)   *NATURAL SWEETNERS
*
*

****

GRAINS   * MEAT/SEAFOOD/BEANS/NUTS
*
*

****

COOKED FRUIT   *COOKED VEGETABLES
*
*

****

PROCESSED FOODS   *PROCESSED LIQUIDS
*
*

****

ST-I used the tool of spiritual mind renewal (Read scriptures and daily reading on Temple Care) _____   **ST**-I used the tool of faith____   **ST**-I used the tool of support_____
ST-I used the tool of prayer____   **ST**-I used the tool of repentance ___ Exercise ___
ST-I used the tool of spiritual fasting – yes/no; juice fast - yes/no
SP-I'm being honest about and coping with my food temptations ___
SP-# of times I ate more than what I needed ___
SP-I demonstrated temperance (Spirit aided self-control)
SP-# of food items I ate created by God _____   Water intake ____
SP-# of food items and liquid not created by God ____
SP-# of times I ate for the purpose of hunger ____
SP-# of times I ate to cope with spiritual/emotional/physical issues _____
SP-My perspective about God's food and man-made food is becoming more correct _____
SP-Today I've thanked God for His provision, blessing and my health _____

"...do you not know your body is the temple of the Holy Spirit who is in you..."
1 Corinthians 6:19

Week Nine-Day 58-Monday
God's Word on Thanksgiving and Blessing
"As soon as you enter the city you will find him before he goes up to the high place to eat, for the people will not eat until he comes, because <u>he must bless the sacrifice;</u> afterward those who are invited will eat"
1 Samuel 9:13

This passage speaks of Saul (soon to be king of Israel at that time) as he looked for the prophet Samuel. Whether a common, daily meal or a religious assembly, this passage makes note of an important act which is asking a blessing over our food. The Matthew Henry Commentary suggests that we must ask that our food benefits us, continuing to recognize that God is the provider of our food and the true power within the food He's created. Let's strive to be humble before God and recognize our dependency upon Him. In doing so, we'll have an opportunity to feed our spirit before we feed our flesh.

What are your feelings about requesting God's blessing on your food?

GOD DESIRES A PEOPLE WHOSE CHARACTER REVEALS A SPIRIT OF THANKSGIVING FOR HIS PROVISION.

GRACE!

When I was in my mid-twenties I was blessed to work at a heart center and work in a program that implemented Dr. Dean Ornish's work. Dr. Ornish through his pioneering work showed the world that coronary artery disease could not only be stopped but also reversed! He found that through simple life-style changes such as yoga, a low-fat diet, stress management/meditation, smoking cessation and exercise one could not only experience increased health and vitality but also reverse their atherosclerosis! Atherosclerosis means *"a condition in which fatty material is deposited along the walls of arteries. This fatty material thickens, hardens, and may eventually block the arteries"* (Dictionary.com).

Dear reader, this information reminds me about the mind boggling amount of grace God bestows on all of us! A person who has *abused* their body to the point of their arteries being clogged with "fat" (which limits the amount of blood flow) can actually *open up* those narrowing arteries again! That's **GRACE!** God's amazing grace can allow you to regain a significant portion of your health and mercifully keep you from receiving the full penalty of your abusive behavior through simple lifestyle changes! God's grace and mercy *can* bring you through! So as we become more cognizant of the importance of having a thankful spirit regarding God's daily food provision let's thank Him for how He is graciously restoring our health (in various ways) through the Temple Care program!

F.I.R.E

FRESH FRUIT	* NATURAL OILS/FATS

****
```
                                          *
                                          *
```
****

FRESH VEGETABLES (CAN BE STEAMED)	*NATURAL SWEETNERS

```
                                          *
                                          *
```
****

GRAINS	* MEAT/SEAFOOD/BEANS/NUTS

```
                                          *
                                          *
```
****

COOKED FRUIT	*COOKED VEGETABLES

```
                                          *
                                          *
```
****

PROCESSED FOODS	*PROCESSED LIQUIDS

```
                                          *
                                          *
```
****

ST-I used the tool of spiritual mind renewal (Read scriptures and daily reading on Temple Care) _____ **ST**-I used the tool of faith____ **ST**-I used the tool of support_____
ST-I used the tool of prayer____ **ST**-I used the tool of repentance ___ Exercise ___
ST-I used the tool of spiritual fasting – yes/no; juice fast - yes/no
SP-I'm being honest about and coping with my food temptations ___
SP-# of times I ate more than what I needed __
SP-I demonstrated temperance (Spirit aided self-control) ___
SP-# of food items I ate created by God _____ Water intake _____
SP-# of food items and liquid not created by God ____
SP-# of times I ate for the purpose of hunger _____
SP-# of times I ate to cope with spiritual/emotional/physical issues _____
SP-My perspective about God's food and man-made food is becoming more correct _____
SP-Today I've thanked God for His provision, blessing and my health _____

How did the Holy Spirit try to influence your temple care today?_____
How did your flesh want to respond?_____
How did you respond?_____

"...do you not know your body is the temple of the Holy Spirit who is in you..."
1 Corinthians 6:19

Week Nine-Day 59-Tuesday
<u>God's Word on Thanksgiving and Blessing</u>
*<u>"He who observes the day, observes it for the Lord, and **he who eats, does so for the Lord, for he gives thanks to God, and he who eats not, to the Lord he does not eat, and gives thanks to God."**</u>*
Romans 14:6

According to Romans chapter 14, we see that the Christians in Rome were in conflict over what Paul considered trivial matters. They were in conflict over issues, such as whether or not to observe Jewish holidays or not since Christ abolished the ceremonial days (except the Lord's Day and Lord's Supper) and whether one should eat all types of meat (clean and unclean as discussed earlier), recognizing that God abolished the old Mosaic Law, which only allowed the eating of clean meat. In this context, Paul is saying not to focus on who is right or wrong on these issues. **They were challenged by Paul to recognize that if everyone was sincerely seeking God's acceptance and thanking God in his or her actions then that would keep them from focusing on trivial matters amongst them.**

Do you focus more on the health issues of others than your own? Are you getting lost in the right or wrong of health concerns with someone else but *refuse to live what God is asking of you regarding your health?* Answer the above questions if they apply to you.

Snacking: The No Blessing Zone?

Why don't most people pray for the food they snack or nibble on? Does a snack not need "blessing" or are we not thankful for what we nibble on? I've recommended to a few individuals who snack and nibble when they aren't hungry (experience gluttony) to pray before they put anything in their mouths. We usually talk about the importance of asking God's blessing over everything we put into our mouths and/or to give thanks for all food/drink provision. Often Temple Care members tell me that once they start praying over <u>everything</u> they eat that they don't snack and nibble as much as before. It can be an effective accountability tool! Others feel uncomfortable praying for God's blessing over food and/or drink that is toxic and no good for them. Humm, give it a try and see how God's Spirit speaks to you!

GOD DESIRES A PEOPLE WHOSE CHARACTER REVEALS A SPIRIT OF THANKSGIVING FOR HIS PROVISION.

How did the Holy Spirit try to influence your temple care today?_____

How did your flesh want to respond?_____

How did you respond?_____

FRESH FRUIT   * NATURAL OILS/FATS
****
                                          *
                                          *
****

FRESH VEGETABLES (CAN BE STEAMED)   *NATURAL SWEETNERS
                                          *
                                          *
****

GRAINS   * MEAT/SEAFOOD/BEANS/NUTS
                                          *
                                          *
****

COOKED FRUIT   *COOKED VEGETABLES
                                          *
                                          *
****

PROCESSED FOODS   *PROCESSED LIQUIDS
                                          *
                                          *
****

ST-I used the tool of spiritual mind renewal (Read scriptures and daily reading on Temple Care) _____ **ST**-I used the tool of faith____ **ST**-I used the tool of support_____
ST-I used the tool of prayer____ **ST**-I used the tool of repentance ___ Exercise ___
ST-I used the tool of spiritual fasting – yes/no; juice fast - yes/no
SP-I'm being honest about and coping with my food temptations ___
SP-# of times I ate more than what I needed ____
SP-I demonstrated temperance (Spirit aided self-control) __
SP-# of food items I ate created by God ____ Water intake ____
SP-# of food items and liquid not created by God ____
SP-# of times I ate for the purpose of hunger ____
SP-# of times I ate to cope with spiritual/emotional/physical issues _____
SP-My perspective about God's food and man-made food is becoming more correct ____
SP-Today I've thanked God for His provision, blessing and my health ____

"...do you not know your body is the temple of the Holy Spirit who is in you..."
1 Corinthians 6:19

Week Nine-Day 60-Wednesday
God's Word on Thanksgiving and Blessing
"For every creature of God, is good, and nothing to be refused, if it be received with thanksgiving: For it is sanctified by the word of God and prayer."
1 Timothy 4: 4 and 5

This passage was intended to help guide Christians and keep them from naively wandering away from God's wisdom and teachings toward the beliefs of individuals who weren't following God. Paul said that some people would "depart from the faith" (1 Timothy 4:1) if they said that certain people were holy or special because they did not marry or eat meat (Matthew Henry Commentary). Yet, Christians should continually trust that everything God created (discussed earlier) is good and that we must always be thankful for such blessings. We should thankfully recognize that God's food will be sanctified, or set apart, for our temple through the Word of God and prayer. He gives us the permission and freedom to enjoy His created food which is proper for our bodies. Can you imagine what our health would be like if God created nothing for our sustenance and we only had whatever man could conjure up? Human beings would kill themselves with good tasting toxins, kind of like what many are doing now! Let's always give God thanks for His magnificent food!

What does the part of today's verse that says, "For it is sanctified by the Word of God and prayers" mean to you? Feel free to consult your bible commentaries.

GOD DESIRES A PEOPLE WHOSE CHARACTER REVEALS A SPIRIT OF THANKSGIVING FOR HIS PROVISION.

How did the Holy Spirit try to influence your temple care today? _____
How did your flesh want to respond? _____
How did you respond? _____

F.I.R.E

FRESH FRUIT	* NATURAL OILS/FATS

****

*
*

****

FRESH VEGETABLES (CAN BE STEAMED)   *NATURAL SWEETNERS
*
*

****

GRAINS   * MEAT/SEAFOOD/BEANS/NUTS
*
*

****

COOKED FRUIT   *COOKED VEGETABLES
*
*

****

PROCESSED FOODS   *PROCESSED LIQUIDS
*
*

****

ST-I used the tool of spiritual mind renewal (Read scriptures and daily reading on Temple Care) _____ **ST**-I used the tool of faith_____ **ST**-I used the tool of support_____
ST-I used the tool of prayer_____ **ST**-I used the tool of repentance ___ Exercise ___
ST-I used the tool of spiritual fasting – yes/no; juice fast - yes/no
SP-I'm being honest about and coping with my food temptations ___
SP-# of times I ate more than what I needed ___
SP-I demonstrated temperance (Spirit aided self-control) __
SP-# of food items I ate created by God _____ Water intake _____
SP-# of food items and liquid not created by God _____
SP-# of times I ate for the purpose of hunger _____
SP-# of times I ate to cope with spiritual/emotional/physical issues _____
SP-My perspective about God's food and man-made food is becoming more correct _____
SP-Today I've thanked God for His provision, blessing and my health _____

"...do you not know your body is the temple of the Holy Spirit who is in you..."
1 Corinthians 6:19

Week Nine-Day 61-Thursday
God's Word on Thanksgiving and Blessing
"Therefore I encourage you to take some food, for this is for your preservation; for not a hair from the head of any of you shall perish. And having said this, <u>he took bread and gave thanks to God in the presence of all</u>; and he broke it and began to eat."
Acts 27:35

We are told that about 276 people were stressed out when they and Paul had eaten very little over a 14-day period. Primarily, these individuals did not want to eat because they thought that they were going to die at sea as they cruised toward Rome. Yet, at this difficult time, Paul was breaking what bread they did have and giving thanks for it! He not only engaged in his normal dialogue of thanksgiving (in the midst of a crisis) to God but also showed an example of his thankfulness by thanking God in the presence of all who were on the boat. Paul did not do this to be a show off or to appear more righteous than others but to show his shameless devotion, dependency and thanksgiving to God and invite others to share in it also (Matthew Henry Commentary, 1991).

When you eat in public, do you pray for show for whomever you are eating with, out of tradition or for the eyes of the nearby strangers? Discuss.

What is your experience like when praying in public (you praying or others praying for or with you)? Please don't feel shameful about what your answer could be. Just be honest about your personal response(s) and know that many other people feel that way too.

If, you struggle or feel uncomfortable about praying in public, what could you ask God to help you with regarding this experience?

GOD DESIRES A PEOPLE WHOSE CHARACTER REVEALS A SPIRIT OF THANKSGIVING FOR HIS PROVISION.

How did the Holy Spirit try to influence your temple care today? _____
How did your flesh want to respond? _____
How did you respond? _____

F.I.R.E

FRESH FRUIT   * NATURAL OILS/FATS
****
                                                     *
                                                     *
****
FRESH VEGETABLES (CAN BE STEAMED)   *NATURAL SWEETNERS
                                                     *
                                                     *
****
GRAINS   * MEAT/SEAFOOD/BEANS/NUTS
                                                     *
                                                     *
****
COOKED FRUIT   *COOKED VEGETABLES
                                                     *
                                                     *
****
PROCESSED FOODS   *PROCESSED LIQUIDS
                                                     *
                                                     *
****

ST-I used the tool of spiritual mind renewal (Read scriptures and daily reading on Temple Care) _____ **ST**-I used the tool of faith____ **ST**-I used the tool of support_____
ST-I used the tool of prayer____ **ST**-I used the tool of repentance ___ Exercise ___
ST-I used the tool of spiritual fasting – yes/no; juice fast - yes/no
SP-I'm being honest about and coping with my food temptations ___
SP-# of times I ate more than what I needed ____
SP-I demonstrated temperance (Spirit aided self-control)__
SP-# of food items I ate created by God ____ Water intake ____
SP-# of food items and liquid not created by God ____
SP-# of times I ate for the purpose of hunger ____
SP-# of times I ate to cope with spiritual/emotional/physical issues _____
SP-My perspective about God's food and man-made food is becoming more correct ____
SP-Today I've thanked God for His provision, blessing and my health ____

"...do you not know your body is the temple of the Holy Spirit who is in you..."
1 Corinthians 6:19

Week Nine-Day 62-Friday
God's Word on Thanksgiving and Blessing
"But Jesus said unto them, They need not depart; give ye them to eat. And they say unto him, We have here but five loaves, and two fishes. And he said, Bring them hither to me. And he commanded the multitude to sit down on the grass, and took the five loaves, and the two fishes, and looking up to heaven, <u>he blessed, and brake, and gave the loaves to his disciples, and the disciples to the multitude.</u>"
Matthew 14:16-19

Christ showed such love for man by blessing the food he miraculously manifested. Jesus' blessing meant that he prayed that the food he was about to give to the multitude would benefit (bless) their bodies. As Jesus was concerned, we to must be concerned about evoking God's blessing on the food that we eat so it will benefit our bodies/God's temple.

What are your thoughts about what is stated above?

_____

_____

How did the Holy Spirit try to influence your temple care today? _____

How did your flesh want to respond? _____

How did you respond? _____

GOD DESIRES A PEOPLE WHOSE CHARACTER REVEALS A SPIRIT OF THANKSGIVING FOR HIS PROVISION.

F.I.R.E

FRESH FRUIT   * NATURAL OILS/FATS
****
                                           *
                                           *
****
FRESH VEGETABLES (CAN BE STEAMED)   *NATURAL SWEETNERS
                                           *
                                           *
****
GRAINS   * MEAT/SEAFOOD/BEANS/NUTS
                                           *
                                           *
****
COOKED FRUIT   *COOKED VEGETABLES
                                           *
                                           *
****
PROCESSED FOODS   *PROCESSED LIQUIDS
                                           *
                                           *
****

ST-I used the tool of spiritual mind renewal (Read scriptures and daily reading on Temple Care) _____ **ST**-I used the tool of faith_____ **ST**-I used the tool of support_____
ST-I used the tool of prayer_____ **ST**-I used the tool of repentance ___ Exercise ___
ST-I used the tool of spiritual fasting – yes/no; juice fast - yes/no
SP-I'm being honest about and coping with my food temptations ___
SP-# of times I ate more than what I needed _____
SP-I demonstrated temperance (self-control) __
SP-# of food items I ate created by God _____ Water intake _____
SP-# of food items and liquid not created by God _____
SP-# of times I ate for the purpose of hunger _____
SP-# of times I ate to cope with spiritual/emotional/physical issues _____
SP-My perspective about God's food and man-made food is becoming more correct _____

SP-Today I've thanked God for His provision, blessing and my health _____

"...do you not know your body is the temple of the Holy Spirit who is in you..."
1 Corinthians 6:19

Week Nine-Day 63-Saturday-Summary
God's Word on Thanksgiving and Blessing

To have a spirit of thanksgiving toward God requires much humility, particularly today in this independent, self-sufficient; "I am the master of my own ship" society in which we live. What an opportunity for spiritual growth! To approach the great I AM in humble appreciation, without showing off for others or fearing what other people may think, in a spirit of thanksgiving for the food He provides us is the kind of spirit that glorifies and pleases Him!

> **"Know ye that the LORD he is God: it is he that hath made us, and not we ourselves; we are his people, and sheep of his pasture. <u>Enter into his gates with thanksgiving, and into his courts with praise: <u>be thankful unto him, and bless his name</u>.</u> For the LORD is good; his mercy is everlasting; and his truth endureth to all generations."**
> **Psalms 100:3, 4, 5**

F.I.R.E

FRESH FRUIT   * NATURAL OILS/FATS
****
                                               *
                                               *
****
FRESH VEGETABLES (CAN BE STEAMED)   *NATURAL SWEETNERS
                                               *
                                               *
****
GRAINS   * MEAT/SEAFOOD/BEANS/NUTS
                                               *
                                               *
****
COOKED FRUIT   *COOKED VEGETABLES
                                               *
                                               *
****
PROCESSED FOODS   *PROCESSED LIQUIDS
                                               *
                                               *
****

ST-I used the tool of spiritual mind renewal (Read scriptures and daily reading on Temple Care) _____   **ST**-I used the tool of faith_____   **ST**-I used the tool of support_____
ST-I used the tool of prayer_____   **ST**-I used the tool of repentance ___ Exercise ___
ST-I used the tool of spiritual fasting yes/no; juice fast - yes/no
SP-I'm being honest about and coping with my food temptations ___
SP-# of times I ate more than what I needed ___
SP-I demonstrated temperance (Spirit-aided self control) ___
SP-# of food items I ate created by God _____ Water intake _____
SP-# of food items and liquid not created by God _____
SP-# of times I ate for the purpose of hunger _____
SP-# of times I ate to cope with spiritual/emotional/physical issues _____
SP-My perspective about God's food and man-made food is becoming more correct _____
SP-Today I've thanked God for His provision, blessing and my health _____

How did the Holy Spirit try to influence your temple care today? _____
How did your flesh want to respond? _____
How did you respond? _____

Self Regulating Sheet

Looking back on this week's F.I.R.E. forms how did you do?

1. Spiritual mind renewal (reading what the bible says about Temple Care)
How did I rate this week with this spiritual tool? _____
1-10 (1=not well at all) (10= praise God really well!)

2. Faith (actions toward Godly Temple Care)
How did I rate this week with this spiritual tool? _____
1-10 (1=not well at all) (10= praise God really well!)

3. Support (contacting spiritual support partner/s and discuss Temple Care)
How did I rate this week with this spiritual tool? _____
1-10 (1=not well at all) (10= praise God really well!)

4. Prayer (praying to God about any and every issue regarding my Temple Care)
How did I rate this week with this spiritual tool? _____
1-10 (1=not well at all) (10= praise God really well!)

5. Repentance (expressing Godly sorrow and changing my ways through the Holy Spirit)
How did I rate this week with this spiritual tool? _____
1-10 (1=not well at all) (10= praise God really well!)

6. Fasting (not eating for 1 day or 3 dinners and replace with prayer, singing, reading God's Word...)
How did I rate this week with this spiritual tool? _____
1-10 (1=not well at all) (10= praise God really well!)

7. This week the following came easy for me regarding care of my temple?
_____
_____

8. This week the following was very difficult for me regarding caring for my temple?
_____

9. After evaluating my ratings this week, these two spiritual tools (choose the lowest rated ones) are what I need to improve on next week regarding temple care?
_____
_____

TEMPLE CARE REVIEW

"LET'S PUT IT ALL TOGETHER!"

WEEK TEN

"...do you not know your body is the temple of the Holy Spirit who is in you..."
1 Corinthians 6:19

Week Ten-Day 64-Sunday
Temple Care Review
God's Created Image--You!
Write out your favorite spiritual principle scripture from week 2 and its book, chapter and verse.

_____

_____

_____

Write out something that was said during the reading from week 2 that has moved your spirit and inspires you to continue to better care for your temple?

_____

_____

_____

How did the Holy Spirit try to influence your temple care today? _____
How did your flesh want to respond? _____
How did you respond? _____

F.I.R.E

FRESH FRUIT   * NATURAL OILS/FATS
****
                                               *
                                               *
****
FRESH VEGETABLES (CAN BE STEAMED)   *NATURAL SWEETNERS
                                               *
                                               *
****
GRAINS   * MEAT/SEAFOOD/BEANS/NUTS
                                               *
                                               *
****
COOKED FRUIT   *COOKED VEGETABLES
                                               *
                                               *
****
PROCESSED FOODS   *PROCESSED LIQUIDS
                                               *
                                               *
****

ST-I used the tool of spiritual mind renewal (Read scriptures and daily reading on Temple Care) _____ **ST**-I used the tool of faith_____ **ST**-I used the tool of support_____
ST-I used the tool of prayer_____ **ST**-I used the tool of repentance ___ Exercise ___
ST-I used the tool of spiritual fasting – yes/no; juice fast - yes/no
SP-I'm being honest about and coping with my food temptations ___
SP-# of times I ate more than what I needed ___
SP-I demonstrated temperance (Spirit-aided self control) ___
SP-# of food items I ate created by God _____ Water intake _____
SP-# of food items and liquid not created by God ____
SP-# of times I ate for the purpose of hunger _____
SP-# of times I ate to cope with spiritual/emotional/physical issues _____
SP-My perspective about God's food and man-made food is becoming more correct _____
SP-Today I've thanked God for His provision, blessing and my health _____

"...do you not know your body is the temple of the Holy Spirit who is in you..."
1 Corinthians 6:19

Week Ten-Day 65-Monday
Temple Care Review
God's Word on Temptation
Write out your favorite spiritual principle scripture from week 3 and its book, chapter and verse.

_____
_____
_____

Write out something that was said during the reading from week 3 that has moved your spirit and inspires you to continue to better care for your temple?

_____
_____
_____

How did the Holy Spirit try to influence your temple care today? _____
How did your flesh want to respond? _____
How did you respond? _____

F.I.R.E

FRESH FRUIT   * NATURAL OILS/FATS

****
                                            *
                                            *
****

FRESH VEGETABLES (CAN BE STEAMED)   *NATURAL SWEETNERS
                                            *
                                            *
****

GRAINS   * MEAT/SEAFOOD/BEANS/NUTS
                                            *
                                            *
****

COOKED FRUIT   *COOKED VEGETABLES
                                            *
                                            *
****

PROCESSED FOODS   *PROCESSED LIQUIDS
                                            *
                                            *
****

ST-I used the tool of spiritual mind renewal (Read scriptures and daily reading on Temple Care) _____ **ST**-I used the tool of faith____ **ST**-I used the tool of support_____
ST-I used the tool of prayer____   **ST**-I used the tool of repentance ___ Exercise ___
ST-I used the tool of spiritual fasting – yes/no; juice fast - yes/no
SP-I'm being honest about and coping with my food temptations ___
SP-# of times I ate more than what I needed ___
SP-I demonstrated temperance (self-control) ___
SP-# of food items I ate created by God _____ Water intake ____
SP-# of food items and liquid not created by God ____
SP-# of times I ate for the purpose of hunger ____
SP-# of times I ate to cope with spiritual/emotional/physical issues _____
SP-My perspective about God's food and man-made food is becoming more correct ____
SP-Today I've thanked God for His provision, blessing and my health ___

"...do you not know your body is the temple of the Holy Spirit who is in you..."
1 Corinthians 6:19

Week Ten-Day 66-Tuesday
Temple Care Review
God's Word on Gluttony

Write out your favorite spiritual principle scripture from week 4 and its book, chapter and verse.

_____

_____

_____

Write out something that was said during the reading from week 4 that has moved your spirit and inspires you to continue to better care for your temple?

_____

_____

_____

How did the Holy Spirit try to influence your temple care today? _____

How did your flesh want to respond? _____

How did you respond? _____

F.I.R.E

FRESH FRUIT   * NATURAL OILS/FATS
****
                                               *
                                               *
****
FRESH VEGETABLES (CAN BE STEAMED)   *NATURAL SWEETNERS
                                               *
                                               *
****
GRAINS   * MEAT/SEAFOOD/BEANS/NUTS
                                               *
                                               *
****
COOKED FRUIT   *COOKED VEGETABLES
                                               *
                                               *
****
PROCESSED FOODS   *PROCESSED LIQUIDS
                                               *
                                               *
****

ST-I used the tool of spiritual mind renewal (Read scriptures and daily reading on Temple Care) _____ **ST**-I used the tool of faith____ **ST**-I used the tool of support_____

ST-I used the tool of prayer____ **ST**-I used the tool of repentance ___ Exercise ___

ST-I used the tool of spiritual fasting yes/no; juice fast - yes/no

SP-I'm being honest about and coping with my food temptations ___

SP-# of times I ate more than what I needed ___

SP-I demonstrated temperance (Spirit-aided self control) ___

SP-# of food items I ate created by God _____ Water intake _____

SP-# of food items and liquid not created by God ____

SP-# of times I ate for the purpose of hunger ____

SP-# of times I ate to cope with spiritual/emotional/physical issues _____

SP-My perspective about God's food and man-made food is becoming more correct ____

SP-Today I've thanked God for His provision, blessing and my health ____

"...do you not know your body is the temple of the Holy Spirit who is in you..."
1 Corinthians 6:19
Week Ten-Day 67-Wednesday
Temple Care Review
God's Word on Temperance

Write out your favorite spiritual principle scripture from week 5 and its book, chapter and verse.

_____

_____

_____

Write out something that was said during the reading from week 5 that has moved your spirit and inspires you to continue to better care for your temple?

_____

_____

_____

What is one thing that God's Spirit said to you today during this Temple Care review week to influence you to better care for your temple, His place of holy residence?

_____

How did you respond?

_____

F.I.R.E

FRESH FRUIT   * NATURAL OILS/FATS
****
                                              *
                                              *
****
FRESH VEGETABLES (CAN BE STEAMED)   *NATURAL SWEETNERS
                                              *
                                              *
****
GRAINS   * MEAT/SEAFOOD/BEANS/NUTS
                                              *
                                              *
****
COOKED FRUIT   *COOKED VEGETABLES
                                              *
                                              *
****
PROCESSED FOODS   *PROCESSED LIQUIDS
                                              *
                                              *
****

ST-I used the tool of spiritual mind renewal (Read scriptures and daily reading on Temple Care) _____ **ST**-I used the tool of faith____ **ST**-I used the tool of support_____

ST-I used the tool of prayer____ **ST**-I used the tool of repentance ___ Exercise ___

ST-I used the tool of spiritual fasting – yes/no; juice fast - yes/no

SP-I'm being honest about and coping with my food temptations ___

SP-# of times I ate more than what I needed ___

SP-I demonstrated temperance (Spirit-aided self control) ___

SP-# of food items I ate created by God ____ Water intake ____

SP-# of food items and liquid not created by God ____

SP-# of times I ate for the purpose of hunger ____

SP-# of times I ate to cope with spiritual/emotional/physical issues _____

SP-My perspective about God's food and man-made food is becoming more correct ____

SP-Today I've thanked God for His provision, blessing and my health ____

"...do you not know your body is the temple of the Holy Spirit who is in you..."
1 Corinthians 6:19

Week Ten-Day 68-Thursday
Temple Care Review
God' Created and Intended Food Source for Man
Write out your favorite spiritual principle scripture from week 6 and its book, chapter and verse.

_____
_____
_____

Write out something that was said during the reading from week 6 that has moved your spirit and inspires you to continue to better care for your temple?

_____
_____
_____

How did the Holy Spirit try to influence your temple care today? _____

How did your flesh want to respond? _____

How did you respond? _____

F.I.R.E

FRESH FRUIT   * NATURAL OILS/FATS
****
                                                 *
                                                 *
****

FRESH VEGETABLES (CAN BE STEAMED)   *NATURAL SWEETNERS
                                                 *
                                                 *

****
GRAINS   * MEAT/SEAFOOD/BEANS/NUTS
                                                 *
                                                 *

****
COOKED FRUIT   *COOKED VEGETABLES
                                                 *
                                                 *

****
PROCESSED FOODS   *PROCESSED LIQUIDS
                                                 *
                                                 *

****

ST-I used the tool of spiritual mind renewal (Read scriptures and daily reading on Temple Care) _____ **ST**-I used the tool of faith____ **ST**-I used the tool of support_____
ST-I used the tool of prayer____ **ST**-I used the tool of repentance ___ Exercise ___
ST-I used the tool of spiritual fasting yes/no; juice fast - yes/no
SP-I'm being honest about and coping with my food temptations ___
SP-# of times I ate more than what I needed ___
SP-I demonstrated temperance (self-control) ___
SP-# of food items I ate created by God _____ Water intake _____
SP-# of food items and liquid not created by God ____
SP-# of times I ate for the purpose of hunger ____
SP-# of times I ate to cope with spiritual/emotional/physical issues _____
SP-My perspective about God's food and man-made food is becoming more correct ____
SP-Today I've thanked God for His provision, blessing and my health ____

"...do you not know your body is the temple of the Holy Spirit who is in you..."
1 Corinthians 6:19

Week Ten-Day 69-Friday
__Temple Care Review__
__God's Intended Purpose for Food__

Write out your favorite spiritual principle scripture from week 7 and its book, chapter and verse.

_____
_____
_____

Write out something that was said during the reading from week 7 that has moved your spirit and inspires you to continue to better care for your temple?

_____
_____
_____

How did the Holy Spirit try to influence your temple care today? _____
How did your flesh want to respond? _____
How did you respond? _____

F.I.R.E

FRESH FRUIT   * NATURAL OILS/FATS

****
*
*
****

FRESH VEGETABLES (CAN BE STEAMED)   *NATURAL SWEETNERS
*
*

****

GRAINS   * MEAT/SEAFOOD/BEANS/NUTS
*
*

****

COOKED FRUIT   *COOKED VEGETABLES
*
*

****

PROCESSED FOODS   *PROCESSED LIQUIDS
*
*

****

ST-I used the tool of spiritual mind renewal (Read scriptures and daily reading on Temple Care) _____ **ST**-I used the tool of faith_____ **ST**-I used the tool of support_____

ST-I used the tool of prayer_____ **ST**-I used the tool of repentance ___ Exercise ___

ST-I used the tool of spiritual fasting yes/no; juice fast - yes/no

SP-I'm being honest about and coping with my food temptations ___

SP-# of times I ate more than what I needed ___

SP-I demonstrated temperance (Spirit-aided self control) ___

SP-# of food items I ate created by God _____ Water intake _____

SP-# of food items and liquid not created by God _____

SP-# of times I ate for the purpose of hunger _____

SP-# of times I ate to cope with spiritual/emotional/physical issues _____

SP-My perspective about God's food and man-made food is becoming more correct _____

SP-Today I've thanked God for His provision, blessing and my health _____

"...do you not know your body is the temple of the Holy Spirit who is in you..."
1 Corinthians 6:19
Week Ten-Day 70-Saturday
__Temple Care Review__
__God's Intended Perspective on His Created Food__
Write out your favorite spiritual principle scripture from week 8 and its book, chapter and verse.

_____

_____

_____

Write out something that was said during the reading from week 8 that has moved your spirit and inspires you to continue to better care for your temple?

_____

_____

_____

How did the Holy Spirit try to influence your temple care today? _____
How did your flesh want to respond? _____
How did you respond? _____

&
__Temple Care Review__
__God's Word on Thanksgiving and Blessing__
Write out your favorite spiritual principle scripture from week 9 and its book, chapter and verse.

_____

_____

_____

_____

Write out something that was said during the reading from week 9 that has moved your spirit and inspires you to continue to better care for your temple?

_____

_____

_____

How did the Holy Spirit try to influence your temple care today? _____
How did your flesh want to respond? _____
How did you respond? _____

F.I.R.E

FRESH FRUIT   * NATURAL OILS/FATS
****
                                               *
                                               *
****
FRESH VEGETABLES (CAN BE STEAMED)   *NATURAL SWEETNERS
                                               *
                                               *
****
GRAINS   * MEAT/SEAFOOD/BEANS/NUTS
                                               *
                                               *
****
COOKED FRUIT   *COOKED VEGETABLES
                                               *
                                               *
****
PROCESSED FOODS   *PROCESSED LIQUIDS
                                               *
                                               *
****

ST-I used the tool of spiritual mind renewal (Read scriptures and daily reading on Temple Care) _____ **ST**-I used the tool of faith____ **ST**-I used the tool of support_____

ST-I used the tool of prayer____ **ST**-I used the tool of repentance ___ Exercise ___

ST-I used the tool of spiritual fasting – yes/no; juice fast - yes/no

SP-I'm being honest about and coping with my food temptations ___

SP-# of times I ate more than what I needed ___

SP-I demonstrated temperance (Spirit-aided self control) ___

SP-# of food items I ate created by God _____ Water intake ____

SP-# of food items and liquid not created by God ____

SP-# of times I ate for the purpose of hunger ____

SP-# of times I ate to cope with spiritual/emotional/physical issues _____

SP-My perspective about God's food and man-made food is becoming more correct ____

SP-Today I've thanked God for His provision, blessing and my health ____

Self Regulating Sheet

Looking back on this week's F.I.R.E. forms how did you do?

1. Spiritual mind renewal (reading what the bible says about Temple Care)
How did I rate this week with this spiritual tool? ____
1-10 (1=not well at all) (10= praise God really well!)

2. Faith (actions toward Godly Temple Care)
How did I rate this week with this spiritual tool? ____
1-10 (1=not well at all) (10= praise God really well!)

3. Support (contacting spiritual support partner/s and discuss Temple Care)
How did I rate this week with this spiritual tool? ____
1-10 (1=not well at all) (10= praise God really well!)

4. Prayer (praying to God about any and every issue regarding my Temple Care)
How did I rate this week with this spiritual tool? ____
1-10 (1=not well at all) (10= praise God really well!)

5. Repentance (expressing Godly sorrow and changing my ways through the Holy Spirit)
How did I rate this week with this spiritual tool? ____
1-10 (1=not well at all) (10= praise God really well!)

6. Fasting (not eating for 1 day or 3 dinners and replace with prayer, singing, reading God's Word...)
How did I rate this week with this spiritual tool? ____
1-10 (1=not well at all) (10= praise God really well!)

7. This week the following came easy for me regarding care of my temple?

_____

_____

8. This week the following was very difficult for me regarding caring for my temple?

_____

9. After evaluating my ratings this week, these two spiritual tools (choose the lowest rated ones) are what I need to improve on next week regarding temple care?

_____

_____

The next page is for you to carry with you or post somewhere so that you can see it, memorize it and say aloud every day.

"...do you not know your body is the temple of the Holy Spirit who is in you..."
1 Corinthians 6:19

SUCCESS SHEET!

Spiritual Tools   Favorite scripture or sentence from each Spiritual Tool reading

_____   _____
                 _____

_____   _____
                 _____

_____   _____
                 _____

_____   _____
                 _____

_____   _____

Write out your 9 favorite spiritual principle scriptures/passages (just transfer from your past week's assignment) that helps you to better care for your temple through dependency on God and His Word.

1. _____

2. _____

3. _____

4. _____

5. _____

6. _____

7. _____

8. _____

9. _____

"...do you not know your body is the temple of the Holy Spirit who is in you..."
1 Corinthians 6:19

MAINTENANCE PLAN

On average, by following the program, people typically lose a few pounds a month. And this weight is what I consider "solid" weight in that it's not primarily water weight but fat and waste. So when, through Spirit aided patience, you reach your goal, it's very simple to maintain.

The one day a week in which you were once juice fasting can now be a day of eating whole uncooked fruit, vegetables, salads and homemade, lightly cooked vegetable soup (among the cooked foods include baked potato or sweet potato). A natural homemade vinaigrette (Sweet Garlic) is in the recipe section that maintains all of its vitamins, minerals and other health benefits due to no pasteurization. Or exercise some creativity and make your own or jump on the internet and find a salad dressing recipe you'd like to try. Also continue drinking lots of water, again I drink about 1 quart of water every 50 pounds I weigh. There are some great recipes to try for this day such as "Healthy Mush" or "Split-cado" and more.

Regularly monitoring how much you weigh is important to maintain the weight you have lost! If you weigh in about 1 time a week you can avoid the "I didn't know I had gained 10 pounds!" statement. If you gain outside of your **goal range** (less restrictive than **goal weight**) then just have your healthy juice fast, on your usually scheduled fast day that week. If you've kept within your weight range then it usually takes only 1-2 weeks (each week fasting only 1 day or fasting during 3 dinners) to get back to your goal range. Also continue to maintain a moderate exercise routine.

Below is an example of the "live" foods (has its full, God-given health potential) I ate during my one day a week maintenance day. I tend to continue using the more intense, focused prayer time and communication with God on this day as when engaged in a "spiritual fast".

F.I.R.E

FRESH FRUIT   * NATURAL OILS/FATS
****
WATERMELON (LOTS!)—MANGO—STRAWBERRIES BUTTER*
BANANA—AVOCADO   *Homemade chicken stock (with vegetables)
****

FRESH VEGETABLES (CAN BE STEAMED)   *NATURAL SWEETNERS
CARROTS-ONIONS-BEETS-CELERY   *
FROZEN SWEET PEAS
****

GRAINS   * MEAT/SEAFOOD/BEANS/NUTS
                                                    *
                                                    *

****

COOKED FRUIT   *COOKED VEGETABLES
                                                    *BAKED POTATO
                                                    *

****

PROCESSED FOODS   *PROCESSED LIQUIDS
                                                    *
                                                    *

****

ST-I used the tool of spiritual mind renewal (Read scriptures and daily reading on Temple
Care) _**Y**____   **ST**-I used the tool of faith__**Y**__   **ST**-I used the tool of support___**Y**__
ST-I used the tool of prayer__**Y**__   **ST**-I used the tool repentance _**0**_Exercise _**Y**_
ST-I used the tool of spiritual fasting–**yes**/no-juice fast-yes/no
SP-# of times I ate more than what I needed _**0**_
SP-I demonstrated temperance (Spirit-aided self control) _**Y**_
SP-# of food items I ate created by God __**6**__Water intake _**2-1/2 quarts**__   Exercise _**N**_
SP-# of food items and liquid not created by God __**0**__
SP-# of times I ate for the purpose of hunger __**4**__
 SP-# of times I ate to cope with spiritual/emotional/physical issues __**0**___

CONGRATULATIONS!

Dear Reader,

Thank God! You have made it! I hope and pray that you have learned and grown from the Temple Care Program. My desire for you is to grow in spiritual knowledge and character so that it impacts your practical, everyday care of your body/God's temple. Many of us have naively and/or carelessly overlooked some of the very practical teachings from the Word of God that are designed to change our lives in every aspect (i.e. health). Please pray for me, as I pray for you, to continue to grow in intimacy with our God so that we can't help but reflect Him in our mundane, routine areas of life to that which is significant and fabulous! Allowing God's Spirit (which is in us, don't forget!), and His Spiritual Tools which include His Word to change our very character is the only way we can genuinely be the people He wants us to be. Let's continually strive to manifest the deep truths and principles from God's Word into our daily lives, and we'll live lives reflecting Godly Temple Care!

Love,

Sonja

P.S. Okay, program over…hopefully not! I sincerely recommend that you start the program again. Yes, that's right! I've found with all of my support groups, so far, that by the end of the program many people feel like they were just beginning to grasp the total Temple Care program! Due to the program addressing various biblical principles (rather than a simple eat less calories plan) people need to go through it a few times to really allow God's Word to transform their minds! May God, our Father, be with you!

*As with any program, we must assess the progress that has been made from when you began the program. With this being the case, I need you to complete the following material (Temple Care Questionnaire and Goals/Commitment Contract). Please do not look at how you previously answered the questions on these same forms, which you completed at the beginning of the program.

After you have completed the following forms feel free to compare them to the forms you previously completed ten weeks ago.

SECTION THREE

Post-Assessment

Post-Program Temple Care Questionnaire
Instructions: Answer each question to your best ability, and circle the number that
fits your experience most accurately.

Circle your answer.
1. I take care of my body as God's temple when it comes to eating nutritionally?
   1-hardly ever 2-sometimes 3-most of the time 4-almost all of the time

2. In my kitchen, I have more fresh or frozen God-created food than boxed,
   bagged or canned processed foods.
   1-hardly ever 2-sometimes 3-most of the time 4-almost all of the time

3. I experience the spiritual fruit of temperance (self-control) when it comes to
   eating right on a daily basis.
   1-hardly ever 2-sometimes 3-most of the time 4-almost all of the time

4. Yesterday, at least ____ percent of the food I ate was uncooked or steamed
   vegetables.
   1-zero   2-twenty-five   3-fifty   4-seventy-five

5. Yesterday, at least____percent of the food I ate was fresh fruit.
   1-zero   2-twenty-five   3-fifty percent   4-seventy-five

6. Yesterday, I ate only when I was hungry.
   1-not at all   2-some of the day   3-most of the day   4-all day long

7. I have people in my life who are good examples as to how to eat in a way that is
   in accordance to God's will.
   1-no   4-yes

8. There is someone I have (or can have) regular contact with that is a good
   example of the nutritional/health changes I want to make.
   1-not   4-yes

9. I can have direct or indirect contact with the person stated above.
   1-almost never 2-once a week 3-twice a week 4-three +times a week

10. I have a role model whose life in general inspires me to change my nutritional
    habits. I can be exposed to him or her.
    1-once a week 2-twice a week 3-three times a week 4-four + times a week

11. I tend to eat to temporarily soothe my emotions ("I just *feel* like eating...", or
    stress, boredom, depression...).
    1- almost all of the time   2- most of the time   3-sometimes   4-hardly ever

12. I want better health, so I take action daily toward living a healthy lifestyle.
1-hardly ever   2-sometimes   3-most of the time   4-almost all of the time

13. I tend to be preoccupied with my weight, my eating habits, or feelings of guilt regarding my eating habits.
1-hardly ever 2-sometimes   3-most of the time   4-almost all of the time

14 I understand how God wants me to view myself and my temple/body.
1-hardly ever 2-sometimes 3-most of the time   4-almost all of the time

15 I understand how God wants me to view the food He has created.
1-hardly ever 2-sometimes   3-most of the time   4-almost all of the time

16. I live in an environment where me changing my style of eating is supported or at least attainable.
1-not at all   2-sometimes 3-most of the time   4-almost all the time

17. I have a good body image based on God's Word.
1-hardly ever 2-sometimes   3-most of the time   4-almost all of the time

18. In general, I eat only when I'm hungry.
1-hardly ever 2-sometimes 3-most of the time   4-almost all of the time

19. I try to lose weight through diets that sometimes concern me regarding whether or not they are healthy for my temple/body.
1- almost all of the time   2- most of the time   3-sometimes   4-hardly ever

20. Even if I'm no longer hungry, I eat until my plate is clean.
1- almost all of the time   2- most of the time   3-sometimes   4-hardly ever

21. I have purposefully fasted.
1-no   4-yes

22. I have fasted for spiritual reasons.
1-hardly ever 2-sometimes   3-most of the time   4-almost all of the time

23. Within the past month, I've had a stomachache and have eaten anyway.
1- almost all of the time   2- most of the time   3-sometimes   4-hardly ever

24. I have a health-related issue that is primarily caused by my style of eating.
1-yes   4-no

25. I have a health-related issue that is not caused by my style of eating but is worsened by my style of eating.
1-yes   4-no

26. I compare my body shape, size and/or weight to others.
1- almost all of the time   2- most of the time   3-sometimes   4-hardly ever

27. Through God, I feel as if I can truly lose weight and can keep it off throughout my lifetime.
1-hardly ever 2-sometimes   3-most of the time   4-almost all of the time

28. I tend to feel helpless regarding eating certain foods and/or to eating too much food.
1- almost all of the time   2- most of the time   3-sometimes   4-hardly ever

29. My rating on how often I am obsessed/preoccupied with weight and/or food.
1- almost all of the time   2- most of the time   3-sometimes   4-hardly ever

30. I plan to work hard to be healthier.
1-hardly ever 2-sometimes 3-most of the time   4-almost all of the time

31. As a religious person, I feel that eating is one of the few pleasures I can engage in.
1- almost all of the time   2- most of the time   3-sometimes   4-hardly ever

32. I ask God to bless my food so that it will nourish and cleanse my body in the way in which He intended it too.
1-hardly ever 2-sometimes   3-most of the time   4-almost all of the time

33. I see many of the vegetables that God created as being the perfect fuel for my body and tasting good.
1-hardly ever 2-sometimes   3-most of the time   4-almost all of the time

34. I see many of the fruit that God created as being the perfect fuel for my body and tasting good.
1-hardly ever 2-sometimes   3-most of the time   4-almost all of the time

35. I see the meat that God created as being the perfect fuel for my body and tasting good.
1-hardly ever 2-sometimes   3-most of the time   4-almost all of the time

36. I eat to provide my body health and strength and not to satisfy emotional/spiritual deficits.
1-hardly ever 2-sometimes   3-most of the time   4-almost all of the time

37. I understand the difference between my own hunger drive versus my appetite.
1-hardly ever 2-sometimes   3-most of the time   4-almost all of the time

38.   I understand what <u>God's created food</u> means.
        1-hardly ever 2-sometimes   3-most of the time   4-almost all of the time

39.   I intentionally contact/ask others to help and support me with my weight loss/weight goals.
        1-hardly ever 2-sometimes   3-most of the time   4-almost all of the time

40.   I see overly processed food in a positive way (i.e. soda, brownies, chips…)
        1- almost all of the time   2- most of the time   3-sometimes   4-hardly ever

41.   Within this past month, even when my body has needed food, I have severely deprived myself of eating in an attempt to lose weight.
        1- most of the month 2- often   3- a little bit   4- not at all

42.   Within this past month, I have vomited, used laxatives and/or diuretics in an attempt to lose weight.
        1- most of the month 2- often   3- a little bit   4- not at all

43.   I have a bowel movement at least every day.
        1-hardly ever 2-sometimes   3-most of the time   4-almost all of the time

44.   I glorify God through how I care for the temple/body He has given me, particularly regarding   how I eat.
        1-hardly ever 2-sometimes   3-most of the time   4-almost all of the time

45.   According to the scriptures, I truly understand what caring for my temple means.
        1-not really   2-a little bit   3-for the most part   4-yes, I do

46.   I have a biblical understanding of what temptation means.
        1-not really   2-a little bit   3-for the most part   4-yes, I do

47.   I have an understanding of how temptation can influence my temple care.
        1-not really   2-a little bit   3-for the most part   4-yes, I do

48.   I understand the good that can come from my temptations.
        1-not really   2-a little bit   3-for the most part   4-yes, I do

Calculate your total score for all 48 questions. Total Score = _____

Compare your total score from the first week of the program to your current score 8 weeks later.
        Total Score-Day 1 _____
        Current Score-Day 70 _____
                Discuss the difference between the scores

Post-Program Goals/Contract Commitment Form

Please answer the following questions.

Are you closer to your original goal now then when you began the program and if so in what way(s)?

_____

_____

If you have not accomplished your goal, after completing this program, what would you say is the #1 reason why this is so? Look over your program material, especially your 10 weekly Self Regulating Forms and/or your F.I.R.E. forms to gain a better understanding of what could be getting in your way.

_____

_____

What is the #2 reason of you not completing your goal?

_____

_____

Age _____

Height _____

My weight today is_____

   My BMI today is _____

Do you believe that you have successfully practiced the skills in the program? Yes/No
Why or why not?

_____

_____

 Might you further benefit from going back through the ten week program to continue improving upon your spiritual development? Yes/No
Discuss

_____

_____

SECTION FOUR

Appendices

Appendix A
Food Intake Recognition Evaluation (F.I.R.E.) Form

All of the activities in this workbook, including F.I.R.E., are geared toward teaching you to become what some researchers call self-regulators which is basically a quality that high achievers possess. I want you to achieve your goal(s) of losing and/or maintaining weight and/or improving your nutritional health. Yet, remember this program is about depending on God's Spirit to help you and then you do the best you can to help you.

McGraw found that the most high-achieving students are self-regulatory learners (Santrock, 2003), and I believe that the same is true for adults who want to change their behaviors. First, they set goals to continue expanding their knowledge and motivation/interest. In Temple Care we increase our spiritual/biblical knowledge, therefore correcting and replacing our worldly knowledge. Second, these achievers are aware of their feelings and have appropriate coping skills to handle them. In Temple Care, we use spiritual "coping" skills (spiritual tools) to help us deal with our feelings and difficult challenges. Third, they regularly check how they are progressing toward their goal which is what we do throughout the program. Fourth, they are flexible enough to revise their actions toward their goals based on their progress or lack of progress. Lastly, they evaluate the challenges that arise and adapt to them (Santrock, 2003). We also practice the last two self-regulating techniques throughout the workbook.

The F.I.R.E. form is about helping you to experience a certain type of "self-regulation" so that you will achieve your goals. Again, throughout this program it's not about you self-regulating on your own! You will be evoking the aide of God's Spirit! Remember the section on "Temperance" which means Spirit-aided self-control? I want you to monitor, evaluate and revise a few very important components of your program. In looking at the F.I.R.E. forms you'll see that I want you to monitor your actual food intake. You'll record the individual items you've eaten, whether you have eaten the food item raw, steamed or cooked. Also you will record whether the food item is primarily in its natural state (is in its God given form) or highly processed form (changed significantly from its "straight from the earth" form or "straight from the animal form").

F.I.R.E

FRESH FRUIT   * NATURAL OILS/FATS
****

WATERMELON-ONIONS-GARLIC   *BUTTER*
TOMATOES-BANANA-KIWI   *
****

FRESH VEGETABLES (LIGHT STEAMING)   *NATURAL SWEETNERS
CARROT JUICE (JUICER)–SPINACH   *
BROCCOLI-MIXED VEGETABLES   *
****

GRAINS   * MEAT/SEAFOOD/BEANS/NUTS
EZEKIEL 4:9-ENGLISH MUFFIN   *PECANS*
                                               BAKED SALMON PATTIES

****

COOKED/DRIED FRUIT   *COOKED VEGETABLES
RAISINS   *
                                                            *

****

PROCESSED FOODS   *PROCESSED LIQUIDS
                                               RASBERRY VINAIGRETTE (& BRAGG'S APPLE CIDER
                                               *   VINAIGRETTE)
****

ST-I used the tool of spiritual mind renewal (Read scriptures and daily reading on Temple Care) yes **ST**-I used the tool of faith yes **ST**-I used the tool of support   no
ST-I used the tool of prayer yes **ST**-I used the tool of repentance no
ST-I used the tool of spiritual fasting – yes/**no;** juice fast – yes/**no**
SP-I ate more than what I needed no
SP-I demonstrated temperance (self-control) yes

Note: This is not a complete food list so if you know of a food that needs to be added (and is God's created food in its original state) then add it to your personal food list.

Meat

Beef
Pork
Lamb
Goat
Poultry
Venison

Seafood

Fish

Bass
Blowfish
Cod
Eel
Flounder
Haddock
Halibut
Mahi Mahi
Monkfish
pike
Salmon
Shark
Snapper
Sole
Swordfish
Tilefish
Trout
Tuna
White Fish

Shellfish

Crustaceans

Crab
Crayfish
Lobster
Shrimp

Mollusks

Abalone
Clam
Mussel
Octopus

Oyster
Snail
Squid
Scallop
Caviar
Uni

Beans/Meat (these dry beans and peas or *included in the meat food group* and some are also in the vegetable group)

Adzuki Beans
Pink Beans
Small Red Beans
Dark Red Kidney
Black Beans
Light Red Kidney Beans
Navy Beans
Baby Lima Beans
Black Eyed Beans (Peas)
Cranberry Beans
Pinto Beans
Northern White Beans
Garbanzo Beans (Chick Peas)
Lentils (Beluga, Red, Green, Split, French…)

Vegetable

Alfalfa sprouts
Artichoke
Arugula
Asparagus
Aubergine (UK) = Eggplant (US)
Avocado
Beans and Peas

Adzuki beans
Bean sprouts
Black beans
Borlotti beans
Broad beans
Butter beans
Green beans
Red kidney beans
Lentils
Lima beans
Mung beans
Navy beans
Runner beans
Soybeans
Peas

Breadfruit

Broccoflower (a hybrid)
Broccoli
Cabbage
  Brussel sprouts
Calabrese
Capsicum
Cauliflower
Celery
Chard
Chinese leaves (UK) or Bok Choi (US)
Cilantro
Collard greens
Cucumber
Endive
Fiddleheads (young coiled fern leaves)
Frisee
Garbanzos, or ceci beans
Gem squash
Green pepper
Kale
Kohlrabi
Lemongrass
Lettuce
Maize (UK) = Corn (US) (actually a grain)
Mangetout
Mushrooms (actually a fungus, not a plant)
Mustard greens
Nettles
New Zealand spinach
Okra
Onion family
  Chives
  Garlic
  Leek
  Onion
  Shallot
  Spring onion (UK)
    Scallion
Parsley
Patty pans
Radicchio
Red pepper
Rhubarb
Root vegetables
  Beetroot (UK) =or Beet (US)
  Carrot

Celeriac
Daikon
Ginger
Parsnip
Radish
Swede (UK) or Rutabaga (US)
Turnip
Wasabi
White radish

Skirret
Snap peas
Spinach
Squashes
Acorn squash
Butternut squash
Courgette (UK) or Zucchini (US)
Cucumber
Marrow (UK) or Squash (US)
Pumpkin
Spaghetti squash

Sweet corn (actually a grain)
Tat soi
Tomato (actually a fruit, but treated as a vegetable)
Tubers
Jicama
Jerusalem artichoke
Potato
Sweet potato
Taro
Yam

Watercress

Fruit

Apple and crabapple
Chokeberry
Haw, the fruit of the hawthorn
Juneberry or saskatoon
Medlar
Pear, European and Asian species
Quince
Rowan or mountain ash
Sorb or sorb apple, the fruit of the service tree
Apricot
Cherry, sweet, sour, and wild species
Plum, of which there are several domestic and wild species; dried plums are called prunes
Peach

Nectarine (variant of the Peach)
Blackberry, of which there are many species and hybrids, such as dewberry, boysenberry, and loganberry
Raspberry, several species
Cloudberry
Wineberry
Bearberry
Bilberry or whortleberry
Blueberry
Cranberry
Crowberry
Huckleberry
Lingonberry
Barberry
Currant red, black, and white types
Elderberry
Gooseberry
Honeysuckle: the berries of some species (called honeyberries) are edible, others are poisonous
Nannyberry or sheepberry
Seaberry or sea buckthorn
Cornelian cherry
Goumi
Jujube
Kiwi fruit or Chinese gooseberry
Loquat
Kumquat
Persimmon,
Buffaloberry which grows wild in the prairies of Canada
Chokeberry which is cultivated in Canada
Pawpaw
Persimmon,
Prickly pear
Saguaro
Muskmelons
    Melon
    Cantaloupe
    Honeydew
Sunberry
Watermelon
Rhubarb
Strawberry
Fig
Grape, called raisin, sultana, or currant when dried
Pomegranate
Date

Mulberry
Citron
Pummelo (Pomello) predecessor of the Grapefruit
Grapefruit
Key Lime
Lemon
Lime (an important hybrid of the Key Lime and the Citron)
Mandarin, clementine, tangelo, tangerine,
Orange
Ugli fruit, a hybrid
Guava
Longan
Lychee
Passion fruit
Akee
Banana
Plantain a starchy variant of the Banana
Breadfruit
CamuCamu
Carambola also called star fruit
Cempedak
Custard apple also called cherimoya
Coconut
Durian
Guarana
Jackfruit also called *nangka*
Langsat also called longkong or duku
Mamoncillo also known as the quenepa or genip
Mango
Mangosteen
Papaya
Pineapple
Rambutan
Rose apple also called Malay apple
Salak also called snakefruit
Sapodilla also called chiku
Soursop
Tamarind

Grain

Amaranth (actually herb yet used as a grain)
Barley
Buckwheat
Corn also Flint and Sweet Corn
Farro
Flaxseed
Job's Tears

Kamut
Millet
Oats
Quinoa
Rice
Rye
Sorghum
Spelt
Teff
Triticale (man-made, crossbreeding of wheat)
Wheat
Wild Rice

Nuts/Seeds

Almond
Apricot Kernel
Brazil
Cashew
Chestnut
Pine
Corn
Hazel
Macadamia
Lotus seed
Mustard seed
Pecan
Pepita
Pistachio
Poppy seed
Pumpkin seed
Sesame Seed
Sunflower Seed
Walnut

Natural Sweetener

Stevia (a bit controversial so do your own research)
Truvia
Unpasterized Honey
Molasses
Sucanat
Maple Syrup
Brown Rice Syrup

Appendix C
Sonja's Favorite Food's Created by God

Fruits

Strawberries	Plums	Avocados	Kiwi	Grapes
Bananas	Watermelons	Coconuts		Cherries
Pears	Tomatoes	Peaches		Pineapple

Vegetables

Greens (mustard and collard)	Onions	Corn	Brussels sprouts
Mushrooms	Garlic	Sweet potatoes!	
Cabbage	Romaine lettuce	Lima beans	
Spinach	Red peppers		

Meat

| Chicken | Turkey | Beef-Ground Chuck |
| Pork ribs | Steak (rib eye) | Lamb |

Fish & Seafood

| Salmon! | Orange Roughy | Lobster |
| Sardines | Tuna | |

Nuts

| Pistachio! | Cashew | Macadamia |
| Brazil | Pecan | |

Beans

Kidney	Pinto
Lentils!	Navy
White	Black beans

Grains

| Quinoa | Couscous | Oatmeal |

Sweeteners

Raw Honey (100% pure, unheated, unfiltered)   Sucanat (organically grown, dehydrated cane juice)   Stevia

Favorite Seasonings

| Grill Creations Smokey Mesquite | | Rosemary | Sage |
| Lawry's Garlic Salt | Sea Salt | Basil | |

Drinks (non pasteurized, non filtered)

Water!   Strawberry smoothie   Ginger Tea!

Freshly juiced/squeezed oranges/lemons/limes/pomellos/grapefruit

Freshly juiced apples

Dressings

Regarding dressings I haven't explored the various natural ones to date, **but I do pour about 25% of the salad dressing bottle size with Bragg's Apple Cider Vinegar**. I do have a recipe for my homemade Rosemary Garlic Vinaigrette in the Menu Sample (favorite recipe) section if you'd like to give it a try!

Oils

Canola, Extra Virgin Olive Oil, Coconut Oil and Ghee

Appendix D
MY MENU SAMPLE

General Breakfast

Any three (plus) fruits *or* homemade smoothie *or* oatmeal with crumbled walnuts and banana (honey or Sucanat is optional) is my usual breakfast. I might also start off with eggs and baked salmon patties, or eggs and bacon (not cured and no nitrates/nitrites) or *banana muffins (homemade) and eggs, which I enjoy at times. Yet, I highly appreciate fruit due to its extremely quick, easy way of being broken down by the body, particularly after fasting throughout the previous evening and night. I also enjoy having a bowl of fruit cereal (see in recipe section). In addition, I'll have a "green drink supplement" every morning. I take Green Vibrance (or any other green drink from the health food store on sale) which has barley greens and other nutrients from the earth in powder form but you can also take it in capsules. I recommend that you purchase this product (or a good food based multi-vitamin from the health food store) for the next 10 weeks.

*If you'd like to have bread, crackers, or biscuits that consists of God given ingredients and is completely homemade then check out the Specific Carbohydrate Diet on the following Internet sites:
www.scdiet.org
www.pecanbread.com
Some of the recipes follow the Temple Care philosophy of using God's given food without processing (which changes its biochemical, nutritional properties).

I tend to have varying fruit combinations every week.
I also like to have squeezed juices some mornings. One favorite recipe is to squeeze 1 grapefruit, 2 oranges, ½ lemon and ½ pomello. Keep fruit refrigerated so when you squeeze them you'll have a cold drink.

Specific Breakfast Menus
(summer menu which which is lighter then my fall/winter menu)

Week of 5/23
Every morning but Tuesday and Thursday, I had a cup of my Green Vibrance, and a big bunch of cherries and seedless grapes. On Thursday, I had my Green Vibrance and two scrambled eggs and Ezekiel 4:9 Cinnamon Raison English Muffin. On Tuesday I drank a cup of Green Vibrance and had "Fruit (Strawberry) Cereal" in recipe section.

Week of 5/30
Almost every morning, I ate my favorite fruit combination which is one ripe banana, cherries and one juicy Danjou pear, and a cup of Green Vibrance. I truly enjoy eating fruit in the morning because I start the day off feeling light and know that I've been truly nourished by God created vitamins, minerals, enzymes, and antioxidants. Also, there's very little preparation--just wash the fruit (I use a fruit wash for the majority of the fruit I eat which you can get at most health food stores). On Friday and Saturday I had a bowl of Kashi Cereal with Rice Dream-Rice Drink.

241

Week of 6/6
Every morning but Wednesday, Thursday, and Saturday I had a cup of Green Vibrance and two big pieces of watermelon. Very often I also like to have a piece of Watermelon as a dessert after dinner if I'm still a little hungry. On Wednesday and Thursday, I had a cup of Green Vibrance and a luscious, fresh strawberry smoothie (I used about 10 strawberries, poured in about 1 ½ cups of Vanilla Rice Dream and 1-2 tablespoons of raw honey— delicious!). I didn't have breakfast on Saturday because I wasn't hungry and later had an early lunch. Take a look at the Universal Food Chart and explore various types of fruit God-given fruit. He has given us so much variety! Also, you may like the frozen bags of cut fruit like a mixed-fruit bag (or single fruit in a bag). If you do like frozen fruit, then the night before, fill up a small bowl with the fruit, cover it and let it thaw throughout the night so it's ready for you in the morning.

Usually, I'm feeling a strong, healthy hunger after a couple of hours because of the light and easily digestible fruit for breakfast. After not eating for approximately 10 hours (from the previous night's dinner to breakfast the next morning), fruit and/or liquids can be a gentle transition into eating heavier foods. ***YET, if fruit for breakfast is not for you then God has provided many, many other options that I'm sure will suit your palate!***
I tend to eat a lot of fruit during the summer time yet during the fall/winter, I tend to eat more oatmeal, eggs, homemade potatoes and onions and/or bacon (from health food store) along with occasional fruit.

Lunch

I tend to have various types of salads every week, including ones with meat. Also, I usually have various types of nuts on the side with one of my favorite dressings. This assures me of getting a decent vegetable intake for the day. Also, I'll use goat crumbled cheese which has no antibiotics or hormones and the process is less detrimental then some other cheeses.

Sometimes when I'm not in the mood for a salad, *I'll eat in moderation whatever else God has created*, again, when I'm hungry. For instance, sometimes I'll eat some of the leftovers from the night before (favorite: ribs and dinner salad).

Dinner

For dinner I tend have meat along with any vegetable *or* grain and I'm usually satisfied. Yet, I do find that for some men that doesn't quite satisfy their hunger so eating another helping of meat or vegetable is often satisfying. If you desire two "sides" with your meat than have them yet in smaller portions than if you had one full "side" dish, so that you can eat both yet stop when you are satisfied. Also, I occasionally replace a meat protein with a meatless protein dish.

If, after dinner (I don't typically eat after 7 pm), I feel hungry again (maybe I ate lightly at 5pm and feel hungry again before 7pm), then I'll have a snack. Often, my snack is a bowl of strawberry cereal (!), a piece of watermelon or a handful of pistachio or cashew nuts.

Appendix E
Recipes
(Ingredients will be underlined)

Spinach-Kiwi Salad

Cut approximately 20 medium to large <u>strawberries</u> into quarters and 4 <u>kiwis</u> into halved slices. Mix with a large bag of fresh <u>baby</u> (or chopped) <u>spinach</u>. To make dressing mix ½ cup <u>Bragg's Apple Cider Vinegar</u>, ¼ cup <u>canola oil</u> (can use olive oil yet get light, extra virgin), 5 freshly minced <u>garlic cloves</u>, 1-2 packets of <u>Stevia</u> (to taste), 1 tbsp of <u>poppy seeds</u> and <u>sesame seeds</u>. Place spinach mix and dressing in container that you can shake to mix the salad well. Let sit in refrigerator 15-20 minutes, shake well again, garnish top with the strawberry-kiwi from the bowl and serve.

Protein Salad

On bed of spinach (or any green lettuce), spread 1/3 can of canned <u>salmon,</u> and next sprinkle chopped onions (to your liking. Then gently pull apart or crumble fermented soy (miso, particularly great for women) over onions, sprinkle goat cheese (much less processed than most cow based cheeses which I don't encourage) and lastly, pour on your favorite salad dressing. The favors are incredible together!

Meatloaf and sweet potatoes

Mix <u>hamburger</u>, and 1 tube of <u>sage sausage</u> (with no nitrates/nitrites and other unknown chemicals at health food store) along with 1 chopped <u>green bell pepper,</u> 2 slices of finely torn pieces of Ezekiel Bread, 1 egg, ½ chopped <u>red onion</u>, ½-1 cup of <u>raisins</u>, lots of <u>black pepper</u>, 2 tbsp of <u>Tones Rosemary and Garlic Seasoning and 2 tbsp of Grilled Creations Smokey Mesquite Seasoning</u>). Make sure you remove raisins from being on top of loaf before you bake because they will quickly burn.
Wash and wrap each <u>sweet potato</u> in foil and place on cookie sheet and bake. Potatoes are done when it begins to become candied and ooze out the sides of the foil.

Avocado Onion Sandwich

Take 1 or 2 slices of <u>Cinnamon Raisin Ezekiel 4:9 Bread</u> (non-flour only whole sprouts) and spread with mayonnaise. Slice avocado in half and store ½ in refrigerator. Slice the half avocado you have out and distribute slices on bread. Place red onion slices over avocado and sprinkle with garlic salt. It's delicious! You can throw some alfalfa sprouts on your sandwich also.

Banana Smoothie

1 <u>banana</u> (the more ripe the banana is the sweeter the smoothie is!)
1 cup <u>vanilla rice milk</u> or oat milk (Rice Dream)
¾ tablespoon of raw, <u>non pasteurized honey or tablespoon of Sucanat sugar (optional)</u>
1 tablespoon <u>vanilla flavoring</u>
Mix the above ingredients in a blender!
You can alter the recipe by using strawberries (use 6-8) alone or with bananas.

Fruit (Strawberry) Cereal

6-8 <u>strawberries</u> cut into slices
½-1 whole <u>banana</u> sliced in bit sized pieces
1 handful of <u>blueberries</u> and or 1 <u>Kiwi</u> or cherries (delicious added options!)
Vanilla Rice Dream Drink, or Oat Milk
Raw, unpasterized <u>honey or Sucanat Sugar or Stevia (zero calories)</u>

Place fruit into bowl and cover with milk and mix honey (to taste) or Stevia into dish. For me this is one of the best healthy desserts I've ever had! Now I call this fruit cereal because you can use ANY fruit you like. For instance, I sometimes enjoy just 3-4 sliced/cut kiwis, a banana, some Stevia and Hemp milk!

Overnight Oatmeal
Pour ¾ cup of whole <u>oatmeal</u> into bowl and fill bowl with <u>water</u> until oatmeal covered. Place covering over oatmeal and let sit over night. In the morning use as much <u>honey</u> as you'd like. And it is optional to include <u>banana slices</u> and/or <u>walnut</u> pieces.

Broccoli Salad
Chop the following ingredients:
4 cups fresh <u>broccoli</u>
1 cup <u>grape tomatoes</u>
½ cup <u>onions</u>
Mix above ingredients with 4 freshly minced <u>garlic cloves</u>, ½ <u>apple cup cider vinegar</u>, ½ cup <u>raisins</u>, and 1-2 Tbsp <u>Vidalia Onion Dressing</u> or favorite salad dressing. Place in bowl with tight lid and shake. Let salad sit upside down for 30 minutes and right side up 30 minutes. Great to eat the next day after broccoli has softened a bit. Toss once more before eating.
If you have leftovers, throw in ¼ cup of pecan nuts, toss again, refrigerate and have as a great lunch the next day!

Healthy Mush
Mix ¼ cup <u>sweet peas</u>, ¼ cup chopped <u>cucumber</u>, ¼ cup <u>walnuts or pecans</u>, ¼ cup chopped <u>avocado</u>, ¼ cup <u>sweet corn</u>, ¼ <u>onions</u>, ¼ <u>grape tomatoes</u> with <u>Sweet Garlic Vinaigrette</u> (included in this section) to taste and place inside a fresh <u>bell pepper</u> that has been cleaned out. This makes a great lunch.

Salmon Bake
Mix 2 cans of <u>salmon</u>, 2 <u>eggs</u>, 5 freshly minced <u>garlic</u> cloves, 1 Tbsp <u>salmon/fish seasoning</u>, 1 Tbsp of <u>Tones Rosemary Garlic Seasoning</u>, 2 medium sized potatoes, mashed, 2 Tbsp <u>salt</u> and 1 small, chopped <u>onion</u>. Pat mixture into non-stick muffin pan and let salmon cakes bake until tops are lightly browned and patties are firm yet moist inside. Let sit for 5 minutes and serve. Another tasty option is to just pan fry patties, in canola or olive oil in skillet.

Salmon and Sweet Potato
Frozen Atlantic <u>Salmon</u> from Sam's Club is excellent! Lightly pan fry the Salmon in olive <u>oil or butter</u> and sprinkled with your favorite seasoning (I use <u>Grilled Creations Smokey Mesquite, Tones Rosemary Garlic Seasoning or Lawry's Garlic Salt</u>). On medium heat pan fry 3-5 minutes on each side.
 I wrap my <u>sweet potato</u> in foil, placing a foiled pan under it and cook until it's oozing with a candied like substance.

Salmon Salad
If you have left over <u>salmon</u> from dinner, it's excellent for lunch the next day! Just flake it open and throw on a bed of <u>spinach</u> or a mixed green salad with <u>Vidalia Onion dressing (can get at Sam's Club)</u>!

Split-cado

Split pea flakes (from health food store), season to taste or 1 can of split pea soup. Chop ½ large avocado into bit sized pieces and place in soup bowl. Pour split pea soup over avocado and sprinkle with pepper. To add more zest, freshly mince 1 garlic clove or a few thinly sliced pieces of red onion and mix into soup.

Chicken and Mushrooms

Lightly pan-fry a skinless/boneless chicken breast (in olive oil) seasoned with Grilled Creations Smokey Mesquite and lightly sautéed fresh mushrooms in olive oil with garlic salt.

Steak and Potato Mash

Lightly pan fry a Ribeye steak (rubbed with freshly minced garlic and a bit of garlic salt) in olive oil in between low to medium heat. Cook approximately 10 minutes on each side, depending on how well done you want it.

Boil a potato along with potato skin (one per serving) until soft. Then mash along with three or four chopped green onions and one freshly minced garlic clove. Transfer to a skillet lightly coated with about 1 tablespoon of butter. Cover while on medium heat and stir periodically and salt to taste. You can do the same thing with red potatoes which due to the skin color looks very appetizing!

Meatballs and Mushrooms

Meatballs (pre-packed/cooked--Sam's has great ones!)

Place an appropriate serving size of meatballs on a baking pan (again you don't have to eat it all). Drizzle favorite barbeque sauce over meatballs, then place a nice layer of red onions (1/2 medium sized) over your meat. Lastly, place a thick layer of mushrooms over everything and lightly sprinkle with garlic salt. Cover dish with foil and bake for 15-20 minutes.

Enjoy with your favorite steamed vegetable.

Spicy Navy Beans

Boil two cups navy beans in slow cooker with 6 cups of water for approximately 45 minutes. Drain off water and refill with water covering beans about 1 inch over the top of beans. Slow cook over night. Next day, to taste, use sea salt, pepper, Tones Rosemary Garlic Seasoning (2 tablespoon for mild and 3 tablespoons for moderate-hot). Mince 3 fresh garlic cloves and dice1 onion and mix into beans. Slow cook for another few hours. An option is to fry some bacon from the health food store, crumble and throw (along with the oil) into the beans.   This is a wonderful side dish with baked chicken (or any of your favorite meat).

Spinach Berry (This is a tasty lunch!)

Spinach
Freshly minced garlic (one clove per one serving)
Ken's Steak House Raspberry Walnut Vinaigrette
½ handful of raisins
½ handful of crushed walnuts
Mix above ingredients well.
Serve with a side of cashew or pistachio nuts (one handful or more).

"Spicy Spinach Salad

This is another delicious spinach salad that is much heartier than the Spinach Berry Salad. Lightly pan fry in olive oil one chicken breast and season to taste. Cut chicken into cubes. Toss spinach, chicken, ½ handful of bacon bits, ½ handful of raisins, chopped onions and 1 tablespoon of Creations Smokey Mesquite Seasoning with Vidalia Onion Salad Dressing.

Garlicky Cole Slaw

Pre-shredded cabbage

Vidalia Onion Salad Dressing (mixed with Bragg's Apple Cider Vinegar)

Freshly minced garlic (1 clove per one serving)

Small handful of chopped red onions for color and added nutrients

Dash of garlic salt

Place ingredients in a large plastic bowl with lid. Stir ingredients and shake periodically before served.

This recipe is a great side dish OR a main lunch dish along with a serving of your favorite nuts (I enjoy this recipe with pistachio nuts).

Cabbage Salad

Mix pre-shredded cabbage with one chopped boiled egg, two freshly minced garlic cloves, one handful of thawed frozen sweet peas, ½ handful of homemade bacon bits (get bacon from health food store) and your favorite salad dressing.

Spaghetti Sauce

Cook one tube of sage sausage (get sausage from health food store and mix with 1 Tbsp of sage) and mix with 3 freshly minced garlic cloves and pinch of salt. Drain and mix into your favorite spaghetti sauce along with one tbsp of black pepper and 2-3 tablespoons of Tones Rosemary Garlic Seasoning.

Cook on medium heat, covered, for about 15 minutes and simmer on low for 10 minutes stirring periodically. When done pour on top of a baked potato, brown rice, or couscous and top with raisins.

California Blend

A tasty side dish consists of mixing 1 ½ cup California Blend frozen vegetables, sweet frozen corn (if not included in California Blend), ½ cubed avocado, ½ cup red onions, ½ cup cut grape tomatoes, 1 clove minced garlic with ranch dressing (to taste). Best after it has been refrigerated.

Edamame Salad

Another side dish includes mixing 1 cup frozen edamame soybeans, 1 chopped boiled egg, 2 cloves freshly minced garlic, sprinkle of raisins and a couple of teaspoons of an Italian vinaigrette. Best after it has been refrigerated and delicious with pan fried salmon.

Cashew Tuna

Mix one can of tuna (in water and drain) with ½ chopped cashew nuts, ¼ cup raisins, ¼ cup chopped sweet onion and a couple of teaspoons of a spicy Italian vinaigrette. Best after it has been refrigerated. Place mixture on a bed of chopped spinach or romaine lettuce.

Hawaiian Cashew Chicken

Cut boneless chicken breast into cubes and lightly pan fry in olive oil. Next mix slices of red bell peppers, 1 cup freshly chopped pineapple, red onion, 2 cloves of freshly minced garlic, ½ cup chopped cashew nuts, salt, and pepper.   Option- favorite sweet and sour sauce to taste. Place mixture on fluffy quinoa.

Barbeque Ribs

Heavily rub beef (or pork ribs) with a rib/chicken rub, and sprinkle with salt and pepper. Place in covered roasting pan with ½ inch water in bottom of pan. Place in oven over night (8-10 hours) on 200 degrees. For last 30 minutes pour out most of the excess fat and water, sprinkle with garlic salt and put favorite BQ sauce over ribs and place back in oven. If you'd like, cut up onions, bell peppers and mince garlic, then mix with sauce and pour over ribs for the last 30 minutes of cooking. You can also broil your ribs the last few minutes to get the tops looking more browned and glazed.

Sweet Garlic Dressing

Mix 1 cup Bragg's Apple Cider Vinegar, ½ cup canola or olive oil, 5 freshly minced garlic cloves and 2 packets of Stevia Plus. You can also add 1 Tbsp. of any seasoning you like, for instance, I often add Tones Rosemary Garlic Seasoning.

This is a homemade, all natural dressing I like to eat with many of my salads (particularly the ones with chicken or salmon in them). Then mix into green salad lettuce and chopped chicken/salmon.

When it comes to eating, I'd rather eat at home than eat out on a regular basis. First, eating out is an expense I'd rather not pay for. Second, I usually like to know the hands and hygiene of the individual preparing my food and the environment in which it will be cooked. Yet, for those of you who eat out often, the food selections are endless, and you can request healthier preparation (i.e. fresh salad greens; grilled chicken; steamed broccoli or turnip, mustard, or collard greens). I usually go out to dinner around twice a month and last week I had the most tender BQ ribs I've ever tasted with lightly steamed asparagus and a couple of bites of a baked potato! I ate moderately and enjoyed every bite!

These are just some of my favorites yet the combinations are endless. There's no need to shun the food that God has created for us. All of His created foods have nutrients that are perfectly designed for our bodies and we need not label some of them as *bad*.

Fruit and Vegetable Juice Fast

The key is to use the fasting experience as an opportunity to tap into God's Power through prayer, supplication (don't feel bad if you have to look this word up…I had to do it myself) and requesting (Philippians 4:6) for what ever your Temple Care need is! Also remember what I said on Day 6;

> "The Matthew Henry Commentary states that Matthew 6:1-18 speaks of alms, prayer and fasting. It is suggested that fasting be addressed last because it is not really considered a duty or requirement for us today. Yet (this is big!), it can be used as a 'means to dispose us for other duties. I thought this comment was profound, in that we can use the flesh-denying, spiritual tool of fasting to motivate or make us willing to engage in the duties which God does ask of us (i.e. to be temperate and not gluttonous!).

<u>Juice Fast Option #1</u>

-Hopefully you will pray the day before your fast, to seek God's strength and guidance to be able to control your flesh throughout your entire day of fasting. You may also want to continue praying to God on and throughout your fast day.

-Start the morning off by drinking 1 cup warm-hot prune juice and immediately follow with 1 cup warm-hot water. This is to help cleanse your colon and you should notice results from ½ to 3 hours. Another option is to use a product such as "DetoxiFiber" throughout the entire program everyday. It's a "Garden of Life" product and can be found at many health food stores. Also, it's excellent for individuals who experience "irregularity". A natural home enema (using clean water and a probiotic) is also very effective and over a period of time can completely heal a long standing problem of constipation. Dr. Natasha Campbell-McBride in "Gut and Psychology Syndrome" gives detailed instructions on how to heal the gut and use enemas properly to eliminate constipation.

-Drink vegetable juice every 2-3 hours (or more often if need be but no less than 2-3 hours). Drink 8 cups or more of water throughout the day between drinking juice.

-The juice recipes primarily consist of vegetables rather than fruit to help prevent to much natural sugars to be introduced into your system.

-Also, make sure you sip and swirl the juice around in your mouth before swallowing to activate your enzymes to begin breaking down the juice in your mouth.

-I also recommend taking a food based multi-vitamin or some form of "green drink" (can be found at health food stores) particularly if you feel your energy wane on your fast day (make sure you have rested the night before and if you are weak due to illness do not fast until you feel better). **As noted earlier, do not engage in exercise on your day of juice fasting and do not fast while you are pregnant or nursing.**

1

Circle the day you commit to setting aside as your spiritual fast day
Sunday Monday Tuesday Wednesday Thursday Friday Saturday

<u>Juice Fast Option #2</u>

-Hopefully you will pray the day before each of your 3 day dinner fasts, to seek God's strength and guidance to be able to control your flesh throughout your dinner fasts. I'm finding that some people are more willing to sacrifice 3 dinners a week (any evening out of the 7 that you'd like) more so than an entire day of fasting. You may also want to continue praying to God on and throughout your fast day.

-Drink plenty of water and if you'd like, one cup of the juices I speak about in the sections "Store-bought juice or Homemade juice options". Also use a product such as "DetoxiFiber" throughout the entire program everyday.

-The juice recipes primarily consist of vegetables rather than fruit to help prevent to much natural sugars to be introduced into your system.

-Also, make sure you sip and swirl the juice around in your mouth before swallowing to activate your enzymes to begin breaking down the juice in your mouth.

2

Circle the three days of dinners you will set aside for fasting.
Sunday Monday Tuesday Wednesday Thursday Friday Saturday

Homemade Juice Recipes
(Just push food through juicing machine)

1. **10 long carrots (preferably organic) & ¼ green cabbage**

2. **10 carrots, 2 sweet potatoes & 8 celery stalks**

3. **10 tomatoes (lightly cooked in ½ teaspoon of olive oil brings out more of its health benefits)**

4. **3 cucumbers, 3 garlic cloves, 1/4 head of cabbage & 5 carrots**

5. **5 beets, 8 carrots & 1 handful of spinach (and/or apple)**

6. **4 apples (take out stem and seeds) and 10 carrots**

7. **1/2 head of cabbage, 2 garlic cloves, 2 red pepper, 3 celery stalks, 3 cucumbers**

-Do not include the carrot top/leaves or seeds in an apple due to some reports of toxic chemicals in them.
-Although it is not a vegetable juice, I sometimes enjoy drinking homemade Ginger Tea (replacing vegetable juice) whenever I choose (and the Holy Spirit leads) me to fast. To make Ginger Tea you will need fresh ginger (size of your palm), local honey and Stevia. Chop the ginger into thin slices and place in a 6-1/2 quart pot with water (fill a little over ¾

of the pot with water). Turn on stove between low and simmer, with a lid on the pot for about 10 hours. Turn heat down if water is evaporating quickly. After 10 hours, pour about 4-5 tablespoons of honey into the ginger tea and 3-5 packets of Stevia (use to your preference). You can drink the tea warm (I usually do during the winter) or for cold tea, place in the refrigerator over night (I usually do this during the summer). You can also squeeze fresh lemon and/or lime juice into your tea!

Store-bought juice options

1. Tomato Juice from any health food store (it is typically low in sodium and has no preservatives). If a more natural tomato juice is unavailable then try V-8 100% Vegetable Juice (regular or low sodium) which you can purchase at any grocery store.

(Also you can make your own homemade Tomato Juice! There are many simple, inexpensive recipes online.)

-Depending on your taste preference 2 tablespoons of Bragg's Apple Cider Vinegar would be an additional health aid to any one of the recipes above.

Juice Fast Alternative

-Juice fasting _always_ gets easier so don't give up! *Yet, for those who need a milder transition to having juices all day, try eating throughout the day light homemade vegetable soups (w/o meat, potatoes, beans and grains). Although without meat, make sure that you make a homemade meat stock and then add vegetables. Boil whole chicken (or parts with joints, bones and add salt and garlic) for 10 minutes and simmer for approximately 3 hours. Separate meat from stock and add vegetables to stock and cook until tender.

3
Circle the day you commit to set aside for your vegetable soup fast
Sunday Monday Tuesday Wednesday Thursday Friday Saturday

References

Adam Clarke's Commentary (1996). Electronic Database by Biblesoft.

Barnes' Notes (1997). Electronic Database by Biblesoft.

Butcher, J.N., Mineka, S., and Hooley, J.M. (2004). Abnormal Psychology (12th ed.). Pearson Education, Inc.

Campbell-McBride, Natasha (2009). Gut and Psychology Syndrome. Halstan Printing Group, Amersham, Buckinghamshire.

Gottschall Elaine (1996). Breading the vicious cycle. Intestianl health through diet. The Kirkton Press.

International Standard Bible Encyclopedia (1996). Electronic Database Biblesoft.

Jamieson, Fausset, and Brown Commentary (1997). Electronic Database by Biblesoft.

Leupold, H.C. (1942). Exposition of Genesis (Vol. 1). Grand Rapids, Michigan: Baker Book House.

Lewis, C.S. (1952). Mere Christianity. HarperCollins Publishers,Inc.

Matthew Henry's Commentary on the Whole Bible: New Modern Edition (1991). Electronic Database by Biblesoft.

Meinz, David (2002). What Does the Bible Teach About Clean and Unclean Meats? Cincinnati:United Church of God.

Miller, Jule L. and Stevens, Texas H. (1992). Visualized Bible Study Series: An Objective Survey of the Bible and Church History. Houston: Gospel Services, Inc.

National Heart, Blood and Lung Institue.com, U.S. Department of Health and Human Services (2009).

Nelson's Illustrated Bible Dictionary (1986). Electronic Database by Biblesoft.

New International Version Life Application Study Bible (2005). Illinois:Tyndale House Publishers Inc.

Roach, Anthony (2003). God's Love Bank. God's Love Bank Enterprises Publishers.

Santrock, John W. (2004). Child Development (10th ed.). Boston: McGraw Hill.

The New Unger's Bible Dictionary (1988). Electronic Database by Biblesoft.

The Pulpit Commentary (1988-2006). Electronic Database by Biblesoft.

Vines Expository Dictionary (1996). Nashville: Thomas Nelson Inc.

Wardlow, Gordon (2003). Contemporary Nutrition (5th ed.). Boston: McGraw Hill.

Webster's 21st Century Dictionary (1995).   Nashville: Thomas Nelson Publishers.

Wycliffe Bible Commentary (1962). Electronic Database by Biblesoft.

Temple Care Order Form

A Holistic 10-week Program Daily Addressing One's Spiritual, Psychological and Nutritional Needs for Weight Loss, Weight Maintenance and Nutritional Health

*For speaking engagements and workshops contact Sonja Chisolm, Ph.D. at 361-244-8312 or email me at Schisolmphd@aol.com

Temple Care 10-Week Program

Week One---------Spiritual Tools
Week Two---------God's Created Image--You!
Week Three-------God's Word on Gluttony
Week Four-------God's Word on Temperance
Week Five-------God's Created Food Source for Mankind
Week Six--------God's Purpose for Food
Week Seven-----God's Intended Perspective on His Created Food
Week Eight-----God's Word on Thanksgiving
Week Nine------God's Word on Temptation
Week Ten-------Temple Care Review

----

*For purchasing a workbook complete the form below.

Print Name: _____

Date: _____ Address:_____

City _____ State_____ Zip code _____

E-mail Address: _____

_____

_____

QUANTITY	ITEM	PRICE	TOTAL
_____	Temple Care	$15.00 per workbook	_____

Shipping and Handling Fee   1 book--------------$3

2 books-------------$4

3 books -----------$5

4 books -----------$6

5 books -----------$7

Plus S & H   _____

2-4 week delivery)

Final Cost=

PAYMENT OPTIONS   MAILING ADDRESS

SEND CHECK OR MONEY ORDER TO: Sonja Chisolm

(Pay to Sonja Chisolm)   5205 Helsley Court

Summerfield, North Carolina

27358

PROGRAM FEEDBACK FORM

I would greatly value your comments and input regarding this program. Please feel free to provide me feedback in the space below and I will make sure to attend to your concerns. Also, words of encouragement are equally valued if you so choose! God Bless You!

_____
_____
_____
_____
_____
_____
_____
_____
_____
_____
_____
_____
_____
_____
_____
_____
_____
_____
_____
_____
_____
_____
_____
_____
_____
_____
_____
_____

THANK YOU!

Send to: Sonja Chisolm
       5205 Helsley Court
       Summerfield, North Carolina
       27358